Lecture Notes in Computer Science 4090

Commenced Publication in 1973
Founding and Former Series Editors:
Gerhard Goos, Juris Hartmanis, and Jan van Leeuwen

Stefano Spaccapietra   Karl Aberer
Philippe Cudré-Mauroux (Eds.)

Journal on Data Semantics VI

Special Issue on Emergent Semantics

 Springer

Volume Editors

Stefano Spaccapietra
École Polytechnique Fédérale de Lausanne, EPFL
IC LBD, Station 14
1015 Lausanne, Switzerland
E-mail: stefano.spaccapietra@epfl.ch

Karl Aberer
Philippe Cudré-Mauroux
École Polytechnique Fédérale de Lausanne, EPFL
I and C, LSIR, Station 14
1015 Lausanne, Switzerland
E-mail: {karl.aberer, philippe.cudre-mauroux}@epfl.ch

Library of Congress Control Number: 2006929224

CR Subject Classification (1998): H.2, H.3, I.2, H.4, C.2

LNCS Sublibrary: SL 3 – Information Systems and Application, incl. Internet/Web and HCI

ISSN   1861-2032
ISBN-10   3-540-36712-8 Springer Berlin Heidelberg New York
ISBN-13   978-3-540-36712-3 Springer Berlin Heidelberg New York

Springer is a part of Springer Science+Business Media

springer.com

© Springer-Verlag Berlin Heidelberg 2006
Printed in Germany

Typesetting: Camera-ready by author, data conversion by Scientific Publishing Services, Chennai, India
Printed on acid-free paper   SPIN: 11803034   06/3142   5 4 3 2 1 0

The LNCS Journal on Data Semantics

Computerized information handling has changed its focus from centralized data management systems to decentralized data exchange facilities. Modern distribution channels, such as high-speed Internet networks and wireless communication infrastructure, provide reliable technical support for data distribution and data access, materializing the new, popular idea that data may be available to anybody, anywhere, anytime. However, providing huge amounts of data on request often turns into a counterproductive service, making the data useless because of poor relevance or inappropriate level of detail. Semantic knowledge is the essential missing piece that allows the delivery of information that matches user requirements. Semantic agreement, in particular, is essential to meaningful data exchange.

Semantic issues have long been open issues in data and knowledge management. However, the boom in semantically poor technologies, such as the Web and XML, has boosted renewed interest in semantics. Conferences on the Semantic Web, for instance, attract crowds of participants, while ontologies on their own have become a hot and popular topic in the database and artificial intelligence communities.

Springer's LNCS *Journal on Data Semantics* (JoDS) aims at providing a highly visible dissemination channel for most remarkable work that in one way or another addresses research and development on issues related to the semantics of data. The target domain ranges from theories supporting the formal definition of semantic content to innovative domain-specific application of semantic knowledge. This publication channel should be of highest interest to researchers and advanced practitioners working on the Semantic Web, interoperability, mobile information services, data warehousing, knowledge representation and reasoning, conceptual database modeling, ontologies, and artificial intelligence.

Topics of relevance to this journal include:

- Semantic interoperability, semantic mediators
- Ontologies
- Ontology, schema and data integration, reconciliation and alignment
- Multiple representations, alternative representations
- Knowledge representation and reasoning
- Conceptualization and representation
- Multi-model and multi-paradigm approaches
- Mappings, transformations, reverse engineering
- Metadata
- Conceptual data modeling
- Integrity description and handling
- Evolution and change
- Web semantics and semi-structured data
- Semantic caching

- Data warehousing and semantic data mining
- Spatial, temporal, multimedia and multimodal semantics
- Semantics in data visualization
- Semantic services for mobile users
- Supporting tools
- Applications of semantic-driven approaches

These topics are to be understood as specifically related to semantic issues. Contributions submitted to the journal and dealing with semantics of data will be considered even if they are not within the topics in the list.

While the physical appearance of the journal issues looks like the books from the well-known Springer LNCS series, the mode of operation is that of a journal. Contributions can be freely submitted by authors and are reviewed by the Editorial Board. Contributions may also be invited, and nevertheless carefully reviewed, as in the case for issues that contain extended versions of best papers from major conferences addressing data semantics issues. Special issues, focusing on a specific topic, are coordinated by guest editors once the proposal for a special issue is accepted by the Editorial Board. Finally, it is also possible that a journal issue be devoted to a single text. The journal published its first volume in 2003 (LNCS 2800), its second volume at the beginning of 2005 (LNCS 3360), and its third volume in Summer 2005 (LNCS 3534). Volumes I, II and V are special issues composed of selected extended versions of best conference papers. Volume III is a special issue on Semantic-Based Geographical Information Systems, coordinated by guest editor Esteban Zimányi. The fourth volume is the first "normal" volume, composed of spontaneous submissions on any of the topics of interest to the journal. This volume is a special issue on Emergent Semantics. The Editorial Board comprises one Editor-in-Chief (with overall responsibility) and several members. The Editor-in-Chief has a four-year mandate to run the journal. Members of the board have a three-year mandate. Mandates are renewable. More members may be added to the board as appropriate. We are happy to welcome you to our readership and authorship, and hope we will share this privileged contact for a long time.

Stefano Spaccapietra
Editor-in-Chief
http://lbdwww.epfl.ch/e/Springer/

JoDS Volume VI – Guest Editorial

As Semantic Web technologies are attracting increasing attention, both from the academic and industrial worlds, more and more voices are raising concerns about the monolithic design principles of the original Semantic Web. Both foundational (e.g., RDF/S) and more recent recommendations (e.g., OWL) were heavily influenced by expert-systems and description logics, and in the view of many suffer from their intrinsic complexity (e.g., open-world semantics) and lack of scalability. As a reaction, some are currently suggesting much simpler formats based on XML like *microformats*, while others are promoting social tagging mechanisms such as those in place on Flickr[1], del.icio.us[2] or Google Co-op[3]. After a series of fruitful interactions within the IFIP Working Group 2.6. on Databases[4], we decided to promote a middle way, where end-user (imperfect) information is encoded using Semantic Web standards, but where its organization is delegated to decentralized, self-organizing processes. We refer to this paradigm using the term *emergent semantics*.

This special issue on *emergent semantics* starts with an invited paper entitled "Viewpoints on Emergent Semantics" summarizing some of the discussions held within the IFIP W.G. 2.6. and outlining *emergent semantics* principles and some of their applications. The issue continues with eight peer-reviewed papers (out of the original 19 submissions we received) authored by some of the foremost experts in domains related to the *emergent semantics* paradigm. The first three papers tackle the problem of encoding or relating imperfect information in logical frameworks. In "f-SWRL: A Fuzzy Extension of SWRL," Jeff Z. Pan *et al.* explore how to represent imprecise knowledge in SWRL, a highly expressive language derived from a combination of OWL and Horn rules. In "Intensional Semantics for P2P Data Integration," Zoran Majkić proposes a logical framework based on intensional logic to model weakly coupled information sources in decentralized (Peer-to-Peer) settings. In "Integrating and Exchanging XML Data using Ontologies," Huiyong Xiao and Isabel F. Cruz deal with the problem of integrating local and heterogeneous XML data sources using an RDF schema.

The last five papers concentrate on processes for organizing (imperfect) knowledge in automated ways. In "Managing Uncertainty in Schema Matching with Top-K Schema Mappings," Avigdor Gal extends current practice in schema matching by generating and examining K schema mappings simultaneously to identify useful mappings automatically. In "Semantic Data Management in Peer-to-Peer E-Commerce Applications," Yosi Ben-Asher and Shlomo Berkovsky propose to organize data objects in a multi-layered hypercube topology based on an underspecified and customizable ontology. In "Interoperability through Emergent Semantics. A semiotic Dynamics Approach," Luc Steels and Peter Hanappe

---

[1] http://www.flickr.com/

[2] http://del.icio.us/

[3] http://www.google.com/coop

[4] http://wise.vub.ac.be/ifipwg26/

advocate the use of mechanisms from natural language to foster semantic inter-operability in an emergent and adaptive way. In "Emergent Semantics from Folksonomies: A Quantitative Study," Lei Zhang *et al.* show how global seman-tics can be statically inferred from dynamic collections of user-defined tags (i.e., *folksonomies*). In "Emergent Semantics in Knowledge Sifter: An Evolutionary Search Agent based on Semantic Web Services," Larry Kerschberg *et al.* propose an agent-based framework to discover emergent concepts and user preferences in content retrieval systems using collaborative filtering.

Lastly, we would like to express our utmost gratitude to the reviewers, who invested much of their time in careful analysis and evaluation of the submissions:

Harith Alani, University of Southampton, UK
Budak Arpinar, University of Georgia, USA
Joe Bigus, IBM T.J. Watson Research Center, USA
Boualem Benatallah, University of New South Wales, Australia
Klemens Böhm, University of Karlsruhe, Germany
Paolo Bouquet, University of Trento, Italy
Adriana Budura, EPFL, Switzerland
Hans Chalupsky, University of Southern California, USA
Philipp Cimiano, University of Karlsruhe, Germany
Anwitaman Datta, EPFL, Switzerland
Tharam Dillon, University of Technology Sydney, Australia
David W. Embley, Brigham Young University, USA
Cristina Feier, Digital Enterprise Research Institute (DERI), Ireland
Frederico Fonseca, Pennsylvania State University, USA
Doug Foxvog, Digital Enterprise Research Institute (DERI), Ireland
Enrico Franconi, Free University of Bozen-Bolzano, Italy
Sarunas Girdzijauskas, EPFL, Switzerland
Mohand-Saïd Hacid, University Claude Bernard Lyon, France
Yannis Kalfoglou, University of Southampton, UK
Vipul Kashyap, Partners HealthCare System, USA
Malte Kiesel, DFKI, Germany
Maurizio Lenzerini, University of Rome "La Sapienza," Italy
Tim van Pelt, EPFL, Switzerland
Brigitte Safar, University of Paris Sud, France
Monica Scannapieco, University of Rome "La Sapienza," Italy
Roman Schmidt, EPFL, Switzerland
Christoph Schmitz, University of Kassel, Germany
Michael Sheng, Australian National University, Australia
Amandeep S. Sidhu, University of Technology Sydney, Australia
Gleb Skobeltsyn, EPFL, Switzerland
Sergio Tessaris, Free University of Bozen-Bolzano, Italy
Guy De Tré, Ghent University, Belgium

Karl Aberer and Philippe Cudré-Mauroux
Guest Editors

JoDS Editorial Board

Table of Contents

Emergent Semantics

Viewpoints on Emergent Semantics

Philippe Cudré-Mauroux[1,*], Karl Aberer[1] (*editors*),
Alia I. Abdelmoty[2], Tiziana Catarci[3], Ernesto Damiani[4],
Arantxa Illaramendi[5], Mustafa Jarrar[6], Robert Meersman[6],
Erich J. Neuhold[7], Christine Parent[1], Kai-Uwe Sattler[8],
Monica Scannapieco[3], Stefano Spaccapietra[1],
Peter Spyns[6], and Guy De Tré[9]

[1] EPFL, Switzerland
Tel.: +41-21-693 6787
philippe.cudre-mauroux@epfl.ch
[2] Cardiff University, UK
[3] University of Rome La Sapienza, Italy
[4] University of Milan, Italy
[5] University of the Basque Country, Spain
[6] Vrije Universiteit Brussel, Belgium
[7] Fraunhofer IPSI, Germany
[8] Technical University Ilmenau, Germany
[9] Ghent University, Belgium

Abstract. We introduce a novel view on how to deal with the problems of semantic interoperability in distributed systems. This view is based on the concept of emergent semantics, which sees both the representation of semantics and the discovery of the proper interpretation of symbols as the result of a self-organizing process performed by distributed agents exchanging symbols and having utilities dependent on the proper interpretation of the symbols. This is a complex systems perspective on the problem of dealing with semantics. We highlight some of the distinctive features of our vision and point out preliminary examples of its application.

1 Introduction

In this paper, we introduce a novel view on how to deal with the problems of semantic interoperability in distributed information systems. This view is based on the concept of emergent semantics, which sees both the representation of semantics and the discovery of the proper interpretation of symbols as the result of a self-organizing process performed by distributed agents exchanging symbols and having utilities dependent on the proper interpretation of the symbols. This is a complex systems perspective on the problem of dealing with semantics.

We first introduce a step by step reasoning underlying the concept of emergent semantics in Section 2. In the subsequent chapters, our goal is to identify current works that manifest the ideas of emergent semantics more concretely, within

---

* Corresponding author.

S. Spaccapietra et al. (Eds.): Journal on Data Semantics VI, LNCS 4090, pp. 1–27, 2006.

the scope of today's research in areas such as distributed database systems, the Semantic Web, peer-to-peer computing or agent-based systems. Also, we identify when possible potential starting points for future applications of the concept.

This paper results from extensive discussions that have been taking place within the IFIP WG 2.6. on databases over the last two years. Initial ideas resulting from these discussions have been published in earlier invited publications [3,5]. With this article, we intend to move the discussion one step further by connecting the general concept to concrete ongoing research efforts and existing technologies.

2   The Notion of Emergent Semantics

2.1   The Notion of Semantics

Despite its wide usage in many contexts, the notion of semantics lacks a precise definition. As a least common denominator, we can characterize semantics as a relationship or mapping established between a syntactic structure and some domain. The syntactic structure is a set of symbols that can be combined following specific rules. The possible domains these symbols are related through semantics can vary widely.

Observation 1: The semantics of a syntactic structure is a relationship between a syntactic structure and some domain.

In mathematical logic, a semantic interpretation for a formal language is specified by defining mappings from the syntactic constructs of the language to an appropriate mathematical model. Denotational semantics applies this idea to programming languages. Natural language semantics classically concerns a triadic structure comprising a *symbol* (how some idea is expressed), an *idea* (what is abstracted from reality) and a *referent* (the particular object in reality) [64].

2.2   Semantics in Information Systems

Programs, database schemas, models, ontologies are unconscious artifacts and have no capacity (yet?) to refer to reality. However, software agents have various mechanisms at their disposal for establishing relationships between internal and local symbols and external meaning.

In many cases, humans are responsible for providing software agents with their initial semantics. In the simplest case, natural language vocabulary is used for the local symbols while the associated relationship with the corresponding explanation or definition of the notion concerned is very often left implicit. The hidden assumption is that meaning exchange is achieved through human cognition [80]. This can lead to communication errors as natural language is not free of ambiguity. In addition, it might happen that in a local community of practice symbols acquire an additional meaning depending on the context, which is not propagated as the exact definition is not explicitly provided.

In the setting where humans provide semantics, relationships among symbols, such as constraints in relational databases are means to express semantics. Again, the assumption is that meaning exchange is achieved through human cognition, e.g., during requirement analyses and testing, suffering some of the same problems as with the use of natural language symbols.

In order to rectify some of the problems related to the implicit representation of semantics relying on human cognition, some have proposed the approach of using an explicit reference system for relating sets of symbols in a software system. Ontologies serve this purpose: an ontology vocabulary consists in principle of formal, explicit but partial definitions of the intended meaning for a domain of discourse [34,35]. In addition, formal constraints (e.g., on the mandatoriness or cardinality of relationships between concepts) are added to reduce the fuzziness of the informal definitions. Specific formal languages (e.g., OWL) allow to define complex notions and support inferencing capabilities (generative capacity).

Observation 2: Explicitly represented semantics of a syntactic structure in an information system consists of a relationship between this syntactic structure and some generally agreed-upon syntactic structure. Thus, the semantics is represented itself by a syntactic structure.

2.3   Semantics in Distributed Systems

In a distributed environment of information agents such as in the Semantic Web or peer-to-peer systems, the aim is to have the agents interoperate irrespective of the source of their initial semantics. To that aim, an agent has to map its vocabulary (carrying the meaning as initially defined in its *base* ontology) to the vocabulary of other agents with which it wants to interoperate. In this way, a relationship of the agents' symbols to the domain consisting of other agents' symbols is established. This relationship may be considered as another form of semantics, independent of the initial semantics of the symbols.

Assuming that autonomous software agents have acquired their semantics through relationships to other agents and that agents interact without human intervention, the original *human assigned* semantics would loose its relevance; from an agent's perspective, *new* semantics would then result from the relationships to its environment. We view this as a novel way of providing semantics to symbols of autonomous agents relative to the symbols of other agents they are interacting with. Typically, this type of semantic representation is distributed such that no agent holds a complete representation of a generally agreed-upon semantics.

Observation 3: Explicitly represented semantics of an agent in a system of distributed agents can be represented through the (distributed) ensemble of relationships to other agents' syntactic structures.

2.4   Processes Creating Semantics

With the classical notion of semantics in information systems, the process of generating semantic interpretations, e.g., the generation of ontologies which reflect shared semantics, is somewhat left outside the operation of the information systems proper. The process is assumed to rely on social interactions among humans, possibly supported in their collaborative effort by some computational and communicational tools.

Viewing semantics of information agents as a relationship to other agents allows us to internalize the discovery process of those relationships to their operation. We abandon the idea of a preexisting outside agency for forming semantic agreements, but see those as a result of the interaction of autonomous, self-interested agents. This is in line with the concept of expressing semantics through internal relationships in a distributed system. By this approach, we aim at consolidating the local semantics of autonomous information agents (respectively information systems) into a global semantics that results from a continuous interaction of the agents. The structures emerging from these continuous interactions provide meaning to the local symbols. We consider semantics constructed incrementally in this way as *emergent semantics*.

From a global perspective, considering a society of autonomous agents as one system, we observe that the agents form a complex, self-referential, dynamic system. It is well-accepted and known from many examples that such systems result (often) in global states, which cannot be properly characterized at the level of local components. This phenomenon is frequently characterized by the notion of *self-organization*. Thus, emergent semantics is not only a local phenomenon, where agents obtain interpretations locally through adaptive interactions with other agents, but also a global phenomenon where a society of agents agree on a common, global state as a representation of the current *semantic agreement* among the agents. This view of semantics as the emergence of a distributed structure from a dynamic process – or more specifically as an equilibrium state of such a process – is in-line with the generally accepted definitions of emergence and emergent structures in the complex systems literature.

Observation 4: Emergent semantics refers to distributed, emergent structures for representing semantics in a distributed information system and results from a dynamic process.

2.5   Assumptions for Enabling Emergent Semantics

The possibility to realize such an interaction process among autonomous and self-interested agents relies on a set of assumptions, each of which is quite natural in the context of distributed and autonomously operating software. First, the agents have to be able to relate their local symbols to each other. This is nothing else than the requirement of being able to communicate at a syntactic level. Then, the agents have to be able to measure the quality of the outcome of an interaction with another agent. Usually, such quality measures are encoded representations of utility measures of (human) users of the software agents. Finally, the agents have to be capable of adapting their relationships to other agents as a reaction to the measurable outcomes of earlier interactions. This corresponds to providing a certain level of autonomy to the agents in order to adapt their behavior, including their relationships to other agents, in response to earlier actions.

Observation 5: Emergent semantics is likely to occur in distributed information systems since the underlying assumptions are frequently and naturally satisfied.

2.6   Introducing Pragmatics

The careful reader will have noticed that by requiring the capability to qualitatively measure the outcomes of actions, we have introduced at this point a further dimension into the discussion, the dimension of *pragmatics*. Without pragmatics, it would be impossible to guide the process of constructing semantics during interactions with other agents. We are thus adopting a semiotic approach, jointly considering the dimensions of syntax, semantics and pragmatics. Syntax is required for agents to interact with their environment, namely other agents, semantics is required to formally describe the intended meaning of vocabularies, and in this context pragmatics provides the decision mechanisms to guide future actions based on the current interpretation of the agents state.

Observation 6: Pragmatics realized through self-interested agents that can measure the quality of the semantic interpretation of their syntactic structures in terms of their utility is an inherent prerequisite for emergent semantics.

In the following, we discuss some of the consequences we can derive from introducing the general concept of emergent semantics. These concern functional properties of emergent semantics, the potential of emergent semantics to better address hard problems of semantic interoperability, and questions related to applicability and acceptance of emergent semantics systems.

Semantic Interoperability in Information Systems. Relating information systems created independently has a long history in computer science. Section 3 illustrates how techniques drawn from distributed databases and peer data management systems can be relevant in an emergent semantics scenario. Section 4 revisits classical ontology-based systems in a similar context.

Uncertainty. Dealing with semantics and pragmatics implies the ability to quantify or measure properties of an agent's state in order to support decision making. In the case of emergent semantics, these measures are related to the proper interpretation of the agent's semantic structure. The better we understand the meaning of symbols and the more we remove uncertainty from their interpretation, the more beneficial the use of the symbols will be. Emergent semantics is based on incrementally reducing the uncertainty of symbols through exchanging information with other agents. In many cases, it will therefore be necessary to have the ability to represent uncertainty about symbols. Therefore, formalisms for representing uncertain data are an essential ingredient for emergent semantics systems.

We discuss in Section 5 which formal approaches exist for this purpose, and to what extent they are already in use in existing systems taking an emergent semantics approach.

Social Dimension. Emergent semantics systems are inherently social systems consisting of self-interested agents. Many issues relevant in artificial or natural social systems are relevant in emergent semantics systems. For example, the problem of privacy, i.e., protecting one's own information from others, leads to the inherent problem of having conflicting goals. By not revealing information, an agent can obtain an advantage in decision making whereas by revealing information it might improve the interpretation of other symbols and thus increase its utility. Also, information and the trustworthiness of agents play a role for assessing the extent to which information received from other agents is relevant for improving semantic interpretations, that is to reducing the uncertainty on the semantics of symbols.

We discuss in Section 6 current approaches in these two areas and in which ways they relate to emergent semantics.

Applicability of Emergent Semantics. The observation that emergent semantics results from a self-organizing process has some interesting consequences on the stability of emergent semantics structures. It is well-known that self-referential dynamic systems may exhibit stable states. Even if the state space of a dynamic systems is continuous, the space of stable states is discrete (Eigenstates) and stable states can be reached from many different initial states. Thus, the structure of the dynamic system implies specific states, corresponding to emergent semantics structures that we can interpret as the socially stable mutual interpretations of local symbols of autonomous agents.

This opens interesting perspectives and promises to address some of the inherently hard problems of classical ways of providing semantics in information systems. It is well known that ontologies are inherently unstable and ontology evolution is a constant challenge. Here, emergent semantics provides a natural solution as its definition is based on a process of finding stable agreements; constant evolution is part of the model and stable states, provided they exist, are autonomously detected. On the more speculative side, we see a further potential for emergent semantics. On one hand, the syntactic structure of ontologies (and other logic-based languages) is identical for local agents and for global semantic agreements. On the other hand, the available state space for processes generating emergent semantics structures might be more complexly structured and holds the potential to express semantics in a non-standard, more expressive way.

In Section 7 we outline some application areas where we expect the emergent semantics concept to be most applicable or where we can already find steps leading to solutions based on ideas related to emergent semantics.

3 Semantics in Distributed Database Systems

Observation 3 expresses semantics as a distributed ensemble of relationships to syntactic structures. Today, many distributed information systems can be characterized in a similar way, due to the existence of many interrelated data sources accessible over the Internet. Examples of such systems are among others information integration systems, data sharing and exchange applications, catalogs in e-business, and data annotation systems for scientific data. At a very abstract level, we can see all these systems as distributed systems of interconnected nodes where nodes represent data sources.

The most well-known example of this class of systems is the mediator-wrapper architecture [85]: a mediator defining the global schema and providing facilities for answering queries on this schema is linked to all data sources which are encapsulated by wrappers. A more advanced case is a Peer Data Management System (PDMS) where the peers (nodes) represent data sources providing query answering functionalities [4,38]. Here, each peer is linked to some *neighbor* peers. The difference to the first case is that the PDMS approach does not require a dedicated centralized mediator node – instead, each peer can both ask and reformulate queries.

In both cases, the links between nodes are *semantic* links representing mappings. A *mapping* explains the meaning of an element (schema element or data value) of a given node A in terms of concepts or elements of node B, which we assume have a known meaning (at least from B's point of view). Though mappings are primary used for query rewriting on heterogeneous schemas, they can also be seen as a way to capture semantics. Basically, we can distinguish two different ways of representing mappings:

Direct mapping: a schema element of node A is mapped onto one or more elements of B. Usually, these mappings are expressed as view definitions. Here, different approaches exist [50]. In the global-as-view (GAV) approach, the integrating schema is defined as a view on the local schema. In contrast, in the local-as-view (LAV) approach, the local schemas are expressed on the global schema defined by the integration node. The combination of both solutions, the GLAV approach, combines the expressive power and allows a more flexible mapping definition. For all these kinds of views, appropriate rewriting techniques exist, e.g., query unfolding for GAV or the bucket algorithm and the MiniCon algorithm for LAV [37].

Indirect mapping: here, a common conceptualization $\mathcal{C}$, i.e., a taxonomy or an ontology, is shared by all nodes. The meaning of the elements of each node is defined in terms of concepts from $\mathcal{C}$, e.g., by annotating (linking) the elements with the concepts [78]. Based on these links one can either infer direct mappings between the nodes or simply asking queries on the conceptual level. This approach is conceptually related to the lexical approach described in Section 4.

As observed above (Observation 4), emergent semantics refers to a dynamic process. Distributed data management applications as introduced above are not static: new nodes are added or deleted and mappings have to be adjusted due to schema changes. Thus, the system evolves in a a distributed dynamic process and new semantic structures are created implicitly or explicitly. So, the question arises if and how we can feedback this new knowledge into the system. The most obvious approach is repeating the initial steps of creating mappings by hand or using schema matching techniques. A more interesting approach, closer to emergent semantics concerns, is to do this incrementally and in a (semi)automatic way. For this purpose, we distinguish in the following three kinds of system dynamics and discuss their recent developments.

3.1 Link Improvement

Mappings used for query reformulation and result translation are often not exact due to several reasons, e.g., because some concepts are not supported by a source or because of wrong decisions during mapping design. Such inaccuracies result in information loss during query answering, i.e., incomplete results or irrelevant data. This might occur both at schema level (missing attributes) as well as at data level (missing data). In order to improve a mapping we have first to assess the mapping quality. For this purpose, several quality criteria can be used, e.g., extensional and intensional completeness and relevance. The quality indicators are not only useful to choose the best source for a given query but also to try to adapt the mapping.

A first approach for determining information loss was proposed by Mena et al. [57] in the context of a ontological mediator. In this work, information loss is defined for the intensional level as the terminological difference between a query and its translation. A difference exists if concepts which are referenced in the query are not subsumed by concepts used in the translated query. At the extensional level, the Information Retrieval measures *precision* and *recall* are used and are computed based on the size of the extensions of the queried concepts. A related approach is presented in [6]. Here, several similarity measures for queries and their translations are introduced. At the intensional level, *syntactic* similarity deals with attributes used in a query, which are lost after transformation. Whereas this measure ignores the semantics of attributes, *semantic* similarity measures take this into account using two mechanisms. First, cycles in the network and therefore in the mappings are exploited to detect implicit semantic agreements. The second mechanism is based on an analysis of the query results and therefore addresses the extensional level. Another measure is described in [7] which analyzes to which extent functional dependencies or other integrity constraints are preserved after translation.

Based on mapping quality measures, we can decide if an improvement is necessary. Basically, we could simply create a new mapping and asses its quality. This ranking of candidate mappings is an important step in schema matching and the search techniques used in these approaches can be applied directly (see also Section 5). An alternative solution is an incremental adaptation. Several approaches have been proposed for this problem, e.g., [82]. However, they are primary intended for schema evolution. Hence, the adaption process is triggered by predefined schema evolution primitives.

3.2 Deriving New Links

Very often in an environment with direct mappings, one needs to follow several links, thus to compose series of mappings, in order to query a distant database. The problem of *mapping composition* can be described as follows: given two mappings $M_{A \rightarrow B}$ and $M_{B \rightarrow C}$ for three data sources A, B, C, the goal is to derive a new but equivalent mapping $M_{A \rightarrow C}$, i.e., a mapping that produces for all queries the same answers as the mappings $M_{A \rightarrow B}$ and $M_{B \rightarrow C}$. A first approach addressing this problem was described by Madhavan and Halevy [55]. This algorithm is based on so-called query rewrite graphs (QRG) encoding the mapping formulas in the composition. In [87] another composition approach is proposed, which addresses mapping adaptations when schemas evolve. The idea is to to consider schema evolution itself as a mapping and – instead of performing a list of incremental adaptations for each schema change – to derive a composition of mappings which allows to obtain the adapted mapping through query rewriting.

Mapping composition addresses mainly the problem of deriving a shortcut for a sequence of mappings. However, if several alternative paths exist, there are still two questions: *(i)* which pair of nodes should be linked directly and *(ii)* which path among a set of candidates should be chosen? The latter can be treated as the shortest path problem in graphs where the weights of edges correspond to the quality of the represented mapping. The first question is related to the case of adding a new node. Here, we have to decide to which member node a link should be established. Under the assumption that mapping quality is the primary measure to be taken into account, this can be seen as a subproblem off clustering where we try to create direct links between nodes which are semantically close. Hence, standard (hierarchical) clustering algorithms (e.g., [11]) or dedicated decentralized approaches, e.g., as proposed in [71], can be applied.

3.3   Adding New Nodes

Adding a new data source to the system might introduce new concepts as long as they can be related to existing elements. Thus, the main task is to define a mapping between the new node and a node already participating in the system. This requires two steps: first to select an appropriate participant and second to match the schemas of the two nodes in order to derive a mapping. The first step can be supported by semantic clustering approaches described above, or by graph-theoretic heuristics assessing the connectivity of the semantic network (percolation theory) [25]. For the second step, several matching algorithms have been proposed in the literature (see [74] for a comprehensive survey). Finally, the new mapping can be further refined as already discussed.

4   Semantic Interoperability Through Linguistic Resources in Ontological Systems

4.1   On Usability Perspectives

Ontologies can be seen as *semantic axiomatizations*, that is, formal descriptions accounting for the intended meaning of a vocabulary [36]. As noted in Section 2, however, these descriptions are usually neither complete nor unequivocal [66]. Same semantics can be axiomatized in different ways, which usually reflect different *usability perspectives*, such as granularity, scope boundaries, representation primitives and constructs (i.e., epistemology), purpose/application/context, reasoning or computational scenarios. In other words, local semantic axiomatizations are substantially influenced by usability perspectives and application requirements at hand. In the problem solving research community, such an issue is called the *interaction problem*. Bylander and Chandrasekaran argued in [21] that "representing knowledge for the purpose of solving some problem is strongly affected by the nature of the problem and the inference strategy to be applied to the problem".

As undisputed and standard ontologies are only available for a few, specific domains today, this argument leads to a fundamental challenge in ontological systems: establishing formal semantic interoperability among different *local* semantic axiomatizations fails mostly due to the diversity of usability perspectives, although all axiomatizations might intuitively agree at the domain/knowledge level (See [63] for the definition of *knowledge level*). In other words, in most cases semantic interoperability might not be achieved between two agents because their semantics are formalized in different ways, rather than because these systems do not agree on the factual/intuitive meaning in reality (also called *ontological semantics*).

Some advocate the use of *ontology alignments* (see [40] for a recent survey) to tackle this problem. Ontology alignments usually consist of formal descriptions accounting for the relationships between heterogeneous ontologies. Analogously to the *Peer Data Management Systems* paradigm described in the preceding section, these alignments create semantically interoperable networks by linking pairs of related ontologies directly or indirectly. In the following, we propose a different, complementary approach to overcome semantic heterogeneity based on linguistic resources.

4.2   An Attachment Law for Emergent Semantics

One may wonder whether ontological semantics exists, and/or whether the intuitive meaning of vocabularies can be found, even informally. Intuitive definitions and agreements about the intended meaning of vocabularies are implicit assumptions shared among human cognitive agents. Informal definitions and agreements can be found in linguistic resources (e.g., dictionaries, lexicons, glossaries, lexical databases, etc.) [41]. A linguistic resource renders the intended meaning of a linguistic term – in a gloss – as it is commonly agreed. Such agreements are not rigorous, of course, but are *commonly accepted* meanings. For example, when we use the English word "book", we actually refer to the set of implicit rules that are common to English-speaking people for distinguishing "books" from other objects. Such implicit rules (i.e., meaning) are learnt from the repeated use of word-forms and their referents in the English literature. Usually, lexicographers and lexicon developers investigate the repeated use of a word-form (e.g., based on a comprehensive corpus) to determine its underlying concept(s).

Linking or rooting the vocabulary used in local axiomatizations with concepts found in linguistic resources can help achieving *basic* semantic interoperability between different axiomatizations. For example, by using (euro) WordNet synsets [33] as a shared vocabulary space, autonomous semantic axiomatizations will be able to interoperate at least freely from language ambiguity and multilingualism.

Using linguistic resources as shared vocabulary spaces could be seen as an attachment law of emergent semantic networks; or, it could be advised in case of failures or uncertain semantic interoperations.

Linguistic resources can thus be seen as common, basic elements guiding the distributed semantic agreement process in heterogeneous ontological systems. Notice that for this purpose, not all linguistic resources can be adopted and reused; the basic (or maybe the only) requirement for a linguistic resource to be used as such is that it should provide (1) a discrimination of word meaning(s) (2) in a machine-referable manner. Resources like WordNet provide a machine-readable conceptual system for English words. Lexical resources that only list vocabularies and their similarities or that mix meaning descriptions with morphological issues are irrelevant to our purposes. Semantic or linguistic relationships between word forms (such as hyponymy, meronymy, and synonymy) could be significant but not essential in this regard. Our basic target is to enable emergent semantics networks to communalize a large asset of common word senses (i.e., concepts), independently of usability perspectives.

4.3 Axiomatization Perspectives in Two Existing Approaches

Dogma is an ontology engineering approach (see [42,43]) that allows knowledge to be modeled and represented in a double-articulation manner (domain axiomatization versus application axiomatizations). Dogma uses the notion of *ontology base* as a controlled vocabulary space shared between application axiomatizations. Such axiomatizations are called applications ontological commitments to the ontology base. The ontology base is intended to capture domain vocabularies, i.e., lexical rendering of domain concepts, similar to the knowledge level of a linguistic resource. In this way, Dogma enables different application axiomatizations to coexist and interoperate regardless of the diversity of their usability perspectives.

Similarly, MADS (see [16,68,69]) supports multiple perceptions of the same real world approach, allowing each application/task to perceive and represent real world facts according to its usability perspectives and requirements. This multi-perception approach is motivated by the fact that each application/task perceives and represents the *factual meaning* of a vocabulary according to its usability perspectives and requirements at hand. In other words, applications perceptions are (in most cases) different views of the same semantics. In this approach, a multi-perception and multi-representation database model allows designers to describe all the perceptions in the same database, and users to access either a peculiar perception or several perceptions in the same query. The multi-perception approach has been applied successfully in geographical information systems, where different axiomatizations of the same maps are seen as multiple perceptions of the same semantics.

5 Imperfect Information in Emergent Semantics

5.1 Representing Imperfection

Emergent semantics processes need ways of representing and assessing imperfection in order to dynamically refine semantic agreements. Imperfection may be in the form of imprecision, vagueness, uncertainty, incompleteness, inconsistency, *etc.* Traditional database models and data management systems are not equipped to cope effectively with information imperfection. However, emergent semantics systems can benefit from several richer, more flexible database models better equipped to handle imperfections, both at the modeling (design time) level and at the querying (run-time) level. At design time, traditional database models (e.g., the relational model) are enriched with an ability to quantitatively or qualitatively specify imperfection, using tools such as probability theory, Dempster-Shafer theory, fuzzy logic, surprisal, and entropy. At run-time, flexible querying is introduced, defining preferences inside queries [17]. This can be done at two levels, namely intra-query and inter-query. Intra-query preferences allow to express that some values are more adequate than others, whereas inter-query preferences are used to associate different levels of importance with query conditions.

Over the years, several categorical classifications of the different types and sources of imperfect information have been presented. In accordance with the classifications of Bosc and Prade [18], Motro [60], and Parsons [70], imperfect information can be categorized as follows:

Uncertain information: information for which it is not possible to determine whether it is true or false.

Imprecise information: information which is not as specific as it should be.

Vague information: information that include elements (e.g., predicates or quantifiers) that are inherently vague (in the common day-to-day sense of the word cf. [60]).

Inconsistent information: information which contains two or more assertions that cannot hold at the same time.

Incomplete information: information for which some data are missing.

Data management approaches dealing with *uncertainty* include the possibilistic approaches and the probabilistic approaches. With possibilistic approaches, possibility theory [89] is used, where a possibility distribution is used to model the value of an attribute that is known to be uncertain. Each possible value for the attribute is assigned a membership grade that is interpreted as the degree of uncertainty [72]. Furthermore, possibility and necessity measures are attached to each tuple in the result set of a query to express the possibility and necessity of the result to be an answer to a query. Probabilistic approaches are based on probability theory, where each result in the result set of a query is extended with a probability, representing the probability of it belonging to the set [86]. Both approaches have their advantages and disadvantages. Probabilities represent the relative occurrence of an event and therefore provide more information than possibilities. Possibilities, however, are easier to apply because they are not restricted by a stringent normalization condition of probability theory.

Imprecision of data is mostly modeled with fuzzy set theory [88] and its related possibility theory [89]. Fuzzy set theory is a generalization of regular set theory in which it is assumed that there might be elements that only partially belong to a set. Therefore, a so-called membership grade, denoting the extent to which the element belongs to the fuzzy set, is associated with each element of the universe. Two main approaches can be distinguished when modeling imprecision. First, similarity relations are used to model the extent to which the elements of an attribute domain may be interchanged [20]. Second, possibility distributions [72] are used, having the benefit of being suitable to cope with uncertainty (see above) and *vagueness*.

The treatment of *incomplete* information in databases has been widely addressed in research. A survey that gives an overview of the field is presented in [28]. The most commonly adopted technique is to model missing data with a pseudo-description, called *null*, denoting missing information. A more recent approach, based on possibility theory, [81] provides an explicit distinction between the cases of unknown data and inapplicable data.

5.2   Assessing Imperfection in Emergent Semantics Systems

Pragmatics realized through self-interested agents that can measure the degree of imperfection of semantic interpretations is an inherent prerequisite for emergent semantics (Observation 6). Modeling imperfection, however, is insufficient when it comes to measuring it. Measuring imperfection often involves an iterative process, in which initial assumptions are strengthened or discarded, and initial measures of imperfection are being refined. Such an iterative process may involve bringing together and relating information from several sources. Alternatively, one may attempt accessing a user with well-defined questions that eventually will minimize imperfection. In approaches based on possibility theory, refinement can be done by composing all available fuzzy sets related to the same imperfect data. Hereby, the intersection operators for fuzzy sets (t-norms) can be used as composition operators [89].

Recently, specific approaches emerged for assessing and dealing with imperfection in schema or ontology mappings. OMEN [59] is a probabilistic ontology mapping tool based on Bayesian Networks. Pan et. al [67] introduced ontology mapping based on a probabilistic framework developed for modeling uncertainty on the Semantic Web. Haase et al. [32] surveyed different approaches to handling inconsistency in description logics based ontologies. Corpus-Based Schema Matching [54] shows how a corpus of schemas and mappings can be used to augment the evidence about the schemas being matched. Probabilistic Message Passing [26] creates a probabilistic network to assess mapping qualities and route queries in a peer data management system. In [11], the statistical method Latent Class Analysis (LCA) is used to compute uncertainties of class memberships in an integrated database. The estimation of the completeness criteria in integrated sources is discussed in [62].

Finally, several papers appearing in this special issue deals with the problem of handling imperfect information in semantic applications. In the paper titled "Managing Uncertainty in Schema Matching with Top-K Schema Mappings", uncertainty is refined by a comparison of K schema mappings, each with its own uncertainty measure (modeled as a fuzzy relation over the two schemata). The process yields an improved schema mapping, with higher precision. In

"Intensional Semantics for P2P Data Integration", a new logical framework based on intensional logic is proposed to take into account the incomplete and locally inconsistent information on the Semantic Web. In "f-SWRL: A Fuzzy Extension of SWRL", finally, Pan et al. propose f-SWRL, a highly expressive language for the Semantic Web supporting fuzzy assertions and fuzzy rules.

6   Introduction on Social Aspects of Trust and Privacy

Emergent semantics systems are inherently social systems consisting of self-interested agents. However, while in social networks there is some form of trust among individuals belonging to the same social network, in emergent semantics systems individual peers may have serious concerns about the extent to which they may be unknowingly sharing private or personal information due to a possible inappropriate usage of these information by other peers.

This section mainly deals with the problems of sharing structures or data to enable semantic emergence, when privacy constraints are taken into account and specific agents play the role of trusted-parties whose structures are preferred in the emergence process. Data publishing and exchange are dynamic processes which are required in order for semantics to emerge: whereas private data need to be exchanged, specific protocols should be devised. Trustworthiness it related to the way local agents can build local semantics by selecting some (trustworthy) structures.

6.1   Data Privacy in Data Publishing and Data Exchange

Preserving privacy of information owned by each peer/agent is a major challenge of the emergent semantics paradigm. Peers joining a semantic community have to disclose information in order to bootstrap the agreement process and accept propositions [65]. Nevertheless, peers require privacy guarantees on data they make available to the community, such as the protection of the identities of individuals and entities. A peer can choose different forms for sharing data within the semantic community:

Data Publishing: the peer can publish its own data so that they are available to the whole community.
Data Exchange: the peer can choose to conduct data exchanges with some peers of the community. This means that data querying capabilities must be ensured, and, therefore appropriate data integration strategies (see Section 3) must be adopted in order for the peers to communicate with each other.

In the following, we summarize the current strategies and techniques relevant to privacy preservation in emergent semantics systems.

In data publishing, a major problem is to assess the risk of privacy violation, once properly disclosed data are published. Typically, anonimyzation does not mean zero privacy risk. Therefore, more sophisticated techniques need to be applied for properly dealing with privacy assurance. Among the techniques proposed in the literature, two major classes can be distinguished, namely: perturbation-based techniques and suppression-based techniques. The former techniques have been deeply investigated in the context of statistical databases [9] and privacy preserving data mining [83]. We focus instead on some recent proposals for suppression-based methods, namely for methods that either suppress single data items in order for privacy to be preserved, or alter elementary data, e.g., by means of attribute domain generalization. K-anonimity [77] is a technique that given a relation T, ensures that each record of T can be indistinctly matched to at least k individuals. It is enforced by considering a subset of T's attributes, called quasi-identifiers, and forcing the values that T's records have on quasi-identifiers to appear with at least k occurrences. A recent technique [49] considers the quantitative evaluation of the privacy risk in case anonymized data are released. In this work, a database is modeled as a sequence of transactions, and the frequency of an item x in the database is the fraction of transactions that contain that item. An hypothetical attacker can have access to similar data and use them in order to breach the privacy of disclosed data. The knowledge of the attacker is modeled as a belief function that represents the guess that the attacker can make on the actual frequencies of items in the database. In [58], the authors provide an analysis of the query-view security problem. Given n views, the problem is to check if the views disclose any information about a given secret query. The query-view security problem is characterized by means of the notion of critical tuple for a query Q, that considers a tuple t critical for Q if there are some instances of the database for which dropping t makes a difference. In [58], the authors demonstrate that a query Q is insecure w.r.t. a set of views if and only if they share some common critical tuples.

In data exchange, proposed techniques investigate how to perform query processing by revealing to the involved parties only a controlled, a-priori defined set of data. More specifically, $S1$ and $S2$ being two data peers, and given a query Q involving data at both peers, privacy preserving query answering ensures that only the result of Q will be learnt by $S1$ and $S2$, without revealing any additional information to either party.

Some of most interesting results in our context regard secure set intersection protocols [61]. Secure set intersection protocols deal with performing intersection between two lists with each party only learning the result of the intersection. In an emergent semantics system, this may be used by two agents to discover which elements they have in common. A work that specifically deals with privacy preserving query answering is Agrawal's work [10] relying on commutative encryption. In [30], aggregation operations are added to the intersection and equijoin operations proposed by Agrawal, and computational costs due to encryption/decription are reduced. In [52], several extension to Agrawal's protocol are proposed, and the notion of secure data ownership certificate is provided, with purpose of attesting the proper ownership of data in a database.

Privacy preservation in both data publishing and data exchanges is a new area that presents several interesting research challenges including: approximate operations, e.g., secure approximate joins and secure record linkage; symmetric protocols that would be useful for emergent semantics contexts, in which there is no distinction between sender and receiver in data exchanges; schema-level privacy management, in which the rewriting of queries should be performed by taking into account privacy requirements also on schema information.

6.2   Learning Metadata Trustworthiness

On the global Internet, information interchange within distributed communities is mostly self-organizing: as community members interact, useful information is published and exchanged more frequently, soon becoming widespread. Community members often use metadata for creating and spreading their opinions about content, quality, type, creation, and even spatial geo-location of the information items they share. Research has widely acknowledged that sharing metadata within communities makes information discovery easier and may reduce data redundancy; but it is also important to remember that shared metadata are subject to constant scrutiny and debate in the social interaction between community members. Even apparently innocuous assertions on class subsumption (e.g., "*Contemporary Music is a subset of Classical Music*") or instance classification (e.g., "*Mussorgski's "Pictures at-an-Exibition" suite belongs to Contemporary Music*") may turn out to be debatable or plainly wrong according to the prevailing usability perspectives (see Section 4) in the community. In the following, we describe how explicit representation of trust metadata can be a source of emergent semantics. Our discussion is based on a recent research approach [23], which exploits user feedback for adapting metadata to the specific contexts and belief systems where communities operate. The overall effect of a community-wide trust management mechanism can be twofold:

Knowledge Quality Improvement obtained by keeping the community's overall body of knowledge under a continuous evolutionary pressure.

Knowledge Enrichment achieved by generating a layer of metadata expressing the evolution of users' views on each other's assertions. This procedural knowledge can later be queried to monitor the community's collective behavior, and even used to restructure the original metadata.

Trust management in decentralized (P2P) networks was first addressed by Aberer [8]. A complete survey of trust and reputation management systems can be found in [14]. More recently, the research focus shifted to secure algorithms for reputation management in P2P environments, like the P2PRep algorithm described in [27]. Unfortunately, the terminology used in the field is not always consistent [14]; for the sake of clarity, we shall use the term *trust* to denote a user p's willingness to rely for some practical purpose on a metadata assertion a stated by another user q (denoted as $T_a(p, q)$). The term *reputation* will be used to quantitatively express p's judgment about q's trustworthiness, denoted by $R(p, q)$ and based on the latest assertion and/or on all metadata q has produced. Indeed, one might be tempted to identify trust and reputation concepts, e.g., by writing $R(p, q) = min_a\{T_a(p, q)\}$. However, in a community-based knowledge sharing scenarios, trust (on an assertion) and reputation (of its source) do not always coincide. In real-world communities, reputation is only one among the many factors determining mutual trust; at the very least, any model of trust and reputation should take into account *reputation aging*, e.g., by writing $T_a(p,q,t) = R(p,q,t_0)e^{-\beta(t-t_0)}$, for $t > t_0$.

Based on users' behavior, it is possible to generate and publish specific *trust assertions*. For the sake of simplicity, we consider simple assertions of the form $T_a(p,q) = \alpha$, expressing the level of trust α of a peer p in the assertion a put forward by peer q. These assertions are community-specific and provide an interesting example of emergent semantics. For instance, suppose that an assertion a put forward by a user q states that a resource r, a .mp3 file, belongs to the class of CountrySongs. If after downloading r, user p stores it into a local directory named CountryMusic, a *trust assertion* $T_a(p,q) = \alpha$ can be automatically generated. Defining the semantics of *trust values* like α in terms of *belief* in assertion a, in terms of a's *relevance* to their purposes, is in itself an open research problem, especially in a non-anonymous scenario. Another open issue is defining the appropriate *trust algebra* for combining trust assertions in order to create a *Web of trust* (an important although preliminary step toward a solution was made in [75]). Here, we simply assume $\alpha \in [0,1]$. Trust assertions form an independent, evolving metadata layer that can be stored at a central server or at distributed peers. Emergent semantics hidden within the trust metadata layer can be exploited to compute *trusted views* over the original metadata assertions, e.g., by disregarding assertions whose community-wide trust level is below a given threshold.

In this process, individual trust degrees have to be aggregated (in the simplest case, by user and/or by resource). Some approaches [22] use Fuzzy Cognitive Maps (FCM) to model the relevance of the trust inputs before their aggregation, while the REGRET system [76] was an early attempt to use fuzzy concepts for analyzing the impact on trust of social networks in electronic marketplaces. Multi-criteria compensative aggregators like the *Ordered Weighted Average* (OWA) and the *Weighted Ordered Weighted Average* (WOWA)[31] are computationally very efficient and appear to be well suited to the synthesis of peer opinions in decentralized networks [13]. Hybrid approaches including approximate reasoning [79], where aggregated trust assertions are used as inputs to an inference system, look more promising inasmuch they provide a high-level symbolic representation of trust computation as an inference process, potentially supporting full human understanding of trust degree levels.

7   Emergent Semantics Applications

Through the years, organizations and enterprises have developed data and information exchange systems that are now vital for their daily operations. Currently deployed solutions, however, are now facing a major challenge. On today's global information infrastructure, data semantics is more and more context and time-dependent, and cannot be fixed once and for all at design time. Perhaps more importantly, identifying emerging relationships among previously unrelated information items (e.g., during data exchange) may dramatically change their business value. In this Section, we explore several applications trying to address this challenge.

7.1   Communication of Agent-Based Data Systems

A recent trend has been developed toward enhancing the functionality of data systems by appropriate data agents. A step forward in this scenario consists in offering a real interoperation possibility among agents coming from independently developed data systems, by making minor adaptations on them. By real interoperation, we mean an interoperation based on the semantics of the communications (communication among agents is in general based on the interchange of messages) which takes the matter far beyond the syntactic functionality provided by exchange standards such as the widely spread XML [19] or, more specifically, EDI standards [1] in the area of electronic commerce.

There are two ways in which agent-based data systems can interoperate among themselves. First, through messages that are interchanged among the agents of both systems, and second, using Web Services provided by each data system. We consider here the first way, where agents typically have to be aware in advance of the structure, language and semantics of the messages in order to deal with them. In the following, we sketch an approach based on emergent semantics to relax those constraints, enabling communication (total or partial) for agents coming from different and independently developed systems.

In our opinion, real data systems interoperation will be possible only if there exists some agreement on the classes of messages used by the agents and the possibility of constructing new kinds of messages by composition or restriction of already known classes. Furthermore, the interpretation of a message should be made on the fly and adapted to the context where it appears. In that scenario, we advocate for a proposal that favors the interoperation among agentized data systems by allowing to send/receive suitable messages to/from agents of another system without requiring the establishment of a common communication pattern in advance. Our proposal (see [15] for details) is used as a basis for automating the detection and resolution of conflicts that arise when dealing with messages interchanged by agents from different systems.

In particular, we have developed a formal ontology we call *CommOnt* (Communication acts Ontology), which is a key element in the proposal and acts as an implicitly shared lexical resource (see Section 4). Agents commit to that ontology if their *observable* actions are consistent with the definitions in the ontology. The main part of CommOnt is constituted by terms related to the messages interchanged by agents representing different data systems. If a data system can deal with a particular class M of messages, then it can also deal with any message of a subclass of M in the CommOnt ontology. We claim that the CommOnt ontology provides interoperability support due to the recognition of communication acts from one language as instances of communication acts in another language. Sometimes, the *translation* will be incomplete, but correctly modeled partial interoperability is a starting point for the emergent agreement process (see Sections 3 and 5), and is most of the time more preferable to the *not understood* answer given nowadays.

7.2 Self-organizing Hierarchical Structures in Trust-Based Architectures

Current knowledge management systems classify resources of interest within hierarchical structures. In this context, customization and evolution of categories is a major issue, inasmuch there is no unique access structure that suits every community. Traditionally, the approach to this problem involved human attention, valorizing the contribution of each community member in the knowledge creation activity with his daily work [51,84]. As human attention is today considered as one of the scarcest resources, we propose below an approach based on emergent semantics principles to derive hierarchical structures and create customized categories semi-automatically.

We designed an architecture to be deployed in association with existing systems proposed by industrial research groups for *bottom-up* construction of categories. Specific examples of existing systems include the intelligent personal hierarchy for information iPHI proposed by BT Exact [56] as well as the KIWI knowledge sharing platform [24], later integrated within the Verity knowledge organizer tool by IBM[73]. The idea behind iPHI is to auto-configure access to multiple sources of information based on customized categories and fuzzy matching of meta-data structure as well as content. Support for emerging trust enables our architecture to validates existing hierarchies according to the views (*usability perspectives*) of the user community and to discover new categories.

Generally speaking, we introduce a *Trust Layer* including a centralized *Metadata Publication Center* that acts as a Napster-style index, collecting and displaying metadata assertions, possibly in different formats and coming from different sources. Metadata are indexed by the Publication Center and anonymous users interact with them, providing an implicit or explicit evaluation of metadata trustworthiness. Periodically, trust-based evaluations are forwarded by the Publication Center to a *Trust Manager* module, in the form of signed assertions built using the well-known technique of *reification*. This choice allows our system to interact with heterogeneous formats, including Semantic-Web style metadata and XML-based metadata like iPHI. In turn, our Trust Manager is composed of two functional sub-modules: the *Trust Evaluator* examines metadata and evaluates their reliability while the *Trust Aggregator* aggregates all inputs coming from the (possibly multiple) trust evaluators. This Trust Layer can manage a large amount of assertions produced by heterogeneous sources, and allows the emergence of metadata complying with specific community views.

7.3 Semantics for the Geospatial Web

Numerous efforts are currently active toward the development of the *Geospatial Semantic Web* (GSW). The GSW, based on a sound spatial data infrastructure

(SDI), aims to enable the discovery, access and utilization of dynamic, global geographic data sets, web resources and services and to allow for their coherent combination and management. Standardized spatial ontologies are at the heart of the GSW and are proposed as means of handling problems of semantic interoperability resulting from the ad-hoc use of geographic data and spatial methods. Specification of such ontologies is the focus of the recently announced Open Geospatial Consortium (OGC) Geospatial Semantic Web Interoperability Experiment [53]. The intention is to develop means of expressing spatial queries in a semantic manner (i.e., with an ontology) and to provide web services to fulfill these queries. An architecture of ontologies is proposed [47], including a base ontology, for capturing the spatial models underlying the geographic information, a geospatial service ontology and domain ontologies. Also, place-name ontologies have been shown to play a central role in supporting the development of a spatially-aware search engines, allowing for geographic information retrieval on the web [44].

The question of which semantics to encode in such ontologies is an active research question [2,29,48]. There are inherent complexities associated with modeling information in the geographic domain, firstly related to the nature of the phenomena themselves, for example, with regards to handling multiple representations and levels of generalization or accommodating levels of error in the geometric locations, and secondly due to the variations in the ways we interpret and use the data (*usability perspectives*), e.g., national, cultural and institutional differences in the description of the data. The problem is non-trivial, as much of the useful semantics of the data are implicit in their inherent spatial structure. In particular, the multiple types of spatial relationships that exist between the geographic phenomena are not normally explicitly derived or coded. In what follows, some examples are given that employ emergent semantics methods for discovering and self-organizing geospatial data.

Automatic extraction of metadata from geographic data sets has been described in [39,46]. However, existing metadata standards facilitate the encoding of only limited semantics of the data, related for example, to the date of creation, geo-referencing system used, total extent, etc. A large amount of useful semantics is implicit and can be interpreted only by the identification of *relationships* between features, and characteristics of features such as their density, distribution, etc. For example, the area designating a city centre on a map can be identified by studying the types of buildings and roads, and their structure and density. Similar studies can distinguish between small towns and large cities, etc. Spatial data mining techniques are proposed in [39] to allow for the automatic extraction of such semantics. One can envision that such a process of semantic discovery and enrichment of metadata to be continuous and dynamic reflecting data updates and evolving geo-ontologies.

Folksonomies have been proposed by Keating and Montoya [45] as a complementary method for metadata enrichment in geoportals. Data mining is used to identify the interesting metadata from the collection of tags, annotations and comments provided by users. New semantics in the form of new concepts or classification hierarchies or relationships may emerge as a result of this process which can then be reflected back in the underlying ontologies. Geo-semantics discovery of the impreciseness in geographic place names has been demonstrated in the works of Arampatzis et al. [12]. Many place names that are commonly employed within web document and in search queries are vague. For example, terms such as "Midwest" in the US and "Midlands" in the UK have no formal geometric boundary and may be interpreted differently by different people. The method proposed involved soliciting information about the spatial extent of the imprecise region by identifying places that are contained inside it. The assumption is that place names that co-occur in the same web document are related. Hence, web documents are geo-parsed to detect related places, and techniques for isolating places which are likely to be part of the target region are then employed. Boundaries of the contained *crisp* places are derived from the geo-ontology and the new delineated boundary of the imprecise region is added to the geo-ontology. The process is dynamic, as iterative refinement of the boundary of the region may be envisaged when new web resources are found.

7.4   PicShark: Recontextualizing Structured Metadata in a Distributed Photo-Sharing Application

Metadata have long been recognized as an efficient way to help manage data and are today widely used by operating systems, personal information managers or media libraries. The general idea is simple: adding a set of keywords or series of attributes in order to facilitate information categorization and retrieval. What is new is the recent focus on formats that let end-users freely define custom metadata schemas befitting their annotation needs.

More and more applications take advantage of structured metadata to organize large amount of information such as picture collections. The problem we want to tackle lies in the fact that *none* of these applications allows to meaningfully share structured metadata to enable global search capabilities in large scale distributed settings. Exploiting structured metadata in distributed environments is intrinsically difficult, given that the metadata have to be extracted from their original context and integrated, i.e., *recontextualized*, into the distributed infrastructure. In the end, we are confronted with two fundamental hurdles preventing photos annotated with local metadata from being shared:

Local Semantics: The classes and instances introduced by end-users to annotate their photos locally might not make sense on a larger scale, and have to be related to their counterparts in the distributed infrastructure.

Metadata scarceness: Realistically, a (potentially large) fraction of shared photos will not be annotated by the user, leaving some (most) of the related assertions incomplete. This lack of annotation hampers any system relying on annotations to retrieve instances.

PicShark is a distributed, peer-to-peer system taking advantage of structured metadata to meaningfully share annotated pictures in very large scale decentralized environments. It provides a solution to both of the aforementioned problems in a self-organizing context where information entropy (in terms of missing metadata and ontological heterogeneity) is gradually alleviated through user interaction. PicShark indexes photos, low-level features extracted from the photos, metadata and schemas in a distributed index structure. The system then tries to find correspondences between pictures, metadata and schemas in order to relate instances and schemas (through mappings, see Section 3), and to *propagate* metadata from one photo to other related photos. Queries are forwarded dynamically using Semantic Gossiping [7], and schema mappings self-organize through Probabilistic Message Massing [26]. The overall system can be seen as a decentralized emergent semantics application, where computationally expensive operations are confined to the edge of the network and global processes rely on a distributed hash table to ensure graceful scalability.

8   Conclusions

With the rapid emergence of social applications on the Web, self-organization principles have once again proven their practicability and scalability: through Technorati Ranking, Flickr Interestingness or del.icio.us recommendations, an ever-increasing portion of the Web self-organizes around end-users semantic input. The Semantic Web, with its rich heritage in logic, has so far little benefitted from this trend. In this paper, we advocate a more decentralized, user-driven and imperfect (in terms of soundness and completeness) Web of semantics that self-organizes dynamically. We tried to highlight some of the distinctive features of our vision as well as point out existing examples of its application.

One of the important remaining issues we did not tackle in this paper is the necessary human trust that has to be given to the resulting emergent semantics structure. Interpretations of precise formal structures, when they are concerned with real world models, remain incomplete and ambiguous. The very rich and varying experience of human beings allows many interpretations of formal models and as a consequence acceptance of such models is usually only achieved after extensive human experimentation and interpretation. Companies like Google or eBay already have to face similar problems today, but this issue gets even more sensitive in an emergent semantics scenario where data organization, data description and data manipulation all depend on semi-automatically generated, self-organizing structures.

Acknowledgment

We would like to thank Avigdor Gal for his insightful comments and suggestions about this work.

References

1. United nations directories for electronic data interchange for administration, commerce and transport. http://www.unece.org/trade/untdid/.
2. A. I. Abdelmoty, P.D. Smart, C.B. Jones, G. Fu, and D. Finch. A critical evaluation of ontology languages for geographic information retrieval on the internet. *Journal of Visual Languages and Computing*, 16(4):331–358, 2005.
3. K. Aberer, T. Catarci, P. Cudré-Mauroux, T. Dillon, S. Grimm, M. Hacid, A. Illarramendi, M. Jarrar, V. Kashyap, M. Mecella, E. Mena, E. J. Neuhold, A. M. Ouksel, T. Risse, M. Scannapieco, F. Saltor, L. de Santis, S. Spaccapietra, S. Staab, R. Studer, and O. De Troyer. Emergent Semantics Systems. In *International Conference on Semantics of a Networked World (ICSNW)*, 2004.
4. K. Aberer and P. Cudré-Mauroux. Semantic Overlay Networks. In *International Conference on Very Large Databases (VLDB)*, 2005.
5. K. Aberer, P. Cudré-Mauroux, and A. M. Ouksel (Eds.). Emergent Semantics Principles and Issues. In *International Conference on Database Systems for Advanced Applications (DASFAA)*, 2004.
6. K. Aberer, P. Cudré-Mauroux, and M. Hauswirth. Start making sense: The Chatty Web approach for global semantic agreements. *Journal of Web Semantics*, 1(1):89–114, 2003.
7. K. Aberer, P. Cudré-Mauroux, and M. Hauswirth. The chatty web: emergent semantics through gossiping. In *WWW 2003*, pages 197–206, 2003.
8. K. Aberer and Z. Despotovic. Managing trust in a p2p information systems. In *Intl. Conf. on Information and Knowledge Management (CIKM)*, 2001.
9. N.R. Adam and J.C. Wortmann. Security control methods for statistical databases: A comparative study. *ACM Computing Surveys*, 21(4), 1989.
10. R. Agrawal, A. Evfimievski, and R.Srikant. A formal analysis of information disclosure in data exchange. In *Proc. of SIGMOD*, 2003.
11. E. Altareva and S. Conrad. Statistical Analysis as Methodological Framework for Data(base) Integration. In *ER 2003*, pages 17–30, 2003.
12. A. Arampatzis, M. Kreveld, C.B. Jones, S. Vaid, P. Clough, H. Joho, M. Sanderson, M. Benkert, and A. Wolff. Web-based delineation of imprecise regions. In *SIGIR Workshop on Geographic Information Retrieval*, 2004.
13. R. Aringhieri, E. Damiani, S. De Capitani Di Vimercati, S. Paraboschi, and P. Samarati. Fuzzy techniques for trust and reputation management in anonymous peer-to-peer systems. *Journal of the American Society for Information, Science and Technology*, 1(1), 2006.
14. J. Audun, I. Roslan, and C.A. Boyd. Survey of trust and reputation systems for online service provision. *Decision Support Systems*, To appear.
15. M. I. Bagüés, J. Bermúdez, A. Illarramendi, A. Tablado, and A. Goñi. Semantic interoperation among data systems at a communication level. *Journal on Data Semantics V*, 2006.
16. S. Balley, C. Parent, and S. Spaccapietra. Modeling geographic data with multiple representations. *International Journal of Geographic Information Systems*, 18(4):329–354, 2004.
17. P. Bosc, D. Kraft, and F. Petry. Fuzzy sets in database and information systems: status and opportunities. *Fuzzy Sets and Systems*, 153(3):418–426, 2005.
18. P. Bosc and H. Prade. An introduction to fuzzy set and possibility theory based approaches to the treatment of uncertainty and imprecision in database management systems. In *Workshop on Uncertainty Management in Information Systems: From Needs to Solutions*, Catalina, California, 1993.

19. T. Bray, J.Paoli, C.M. Sperberg-McQueen, E. Maler, and F. Yergeau. Extensible markup language (xml) 1.0. http://www.w3.org/TR/2004/REC-xml-20040204.
20. B.P. Buckles and F. Petry. Generalised database and information systems. In J.C. Bezdek, editor, *Analysis of fuzzy Information*. CRC Press, 1987.
21. T. Bylander and B. Chandrasekaran. Generic tasks in knowledge-based reasoning: The right level of abstraction for knowledge acquisition. *Knowledge Acquisition for Knowledge Based Systems*, 1, 1988.
22. C. Castelfranchi, R. Falcone, and G. Pezzulo. Trust in information sources as a source for trust: a fuzzy approach. In *International Joint Conference on Autonomous Agents and Multiagent systems (AAMAS)*, 2003.
23. P. Ceravolo, E. Damiani, and M. Viviani. *Soft Computing for Information Retrieval on the Web*, chapter Adding a Trust Layer to Semantic Web Metadata. Elsevier, 2006.
24. A. Corallo, E. Damiani, and G. Elia. An ontology-based knowledge management system enabling regional innovation. In *Eurasia-ICT Workshop on E-Learning Platforms Technologies*, 2002.
25. P. Cudré-Mauroux and K. Aberer. A Necessary Condition For Semantic Interoperability in the Large. In *Ontologies, DataBases, and Applications of Semantics for Large Scale Information Systems (ODBASE)*, 2004.
26. P. Cudré-Mauroux, K. Aberer, and A. Feher. Probabilistic Message Passing in Peer Data Management Systems. In *International Conference on Data Engineering (ICDE)*, 2006.
27. E. Damiani, S. De Capitani di Vimercati, S. Paraboschi, and P. Samarati. Managing and sharing servents' reputations in p2p systems. *IEEE Trans. Knowl. Data Eng.*, 15(4):840–853, 2003.
28. C.E. Dyreson. A bibliography on uncertainty management in information systems. In A. Motro and P. Smets, editors, *Uncertainty Management in Information Systems: From Needs to Solutions*. Kluwer Academic Publishers, Boston, MA, 1997.
29. M. Egenhofer. Towards the semantic geospatial web. In *Proceedings of ACM-GIS*, pages 1–4, 2002.
30. F. Emekci, D. Agrawal, A. El Abbadi, and A. Gulbeden. Privacy preserving query processing using third parties. In *Proc. ICDE*, 2006.
31. J. Fodor, J. L. Marichal, and M. Roubens. Characterization of the ordered weighted averaging operators. *IEEE Trans. on Fuzzy Systems*, 3(2):236–240, 1995.
32. A Framework for Handling Inconsistency in Changing Ontologies. P. Haase and F. van Harmelen and Z. Huang and H. Stuckenschmidt and Y. Sure. In *International Semantic Web Conference (ISWC)*, 2005.
33. M. George, R. Beckwithand C. Fellbaum, C. Gross, and K. Miller. Introduction to wordnet: an on-line lexical database. *International Journal of Lexicography*, 3(4):235–244, 1990.
34. T. R. Gruber. A Translation Approach to Portable Ontology Specifications. *Knowledge Acquisition*, 6(2):199–221, 1993.
35. N. Guarino. Formal ontologies and information systems. In Nicola Guarino, editor, *Proceedings of FOIS '98*, pages 3 – 15. IOS Press, 1998.
36. N. Guarino. Formal ontology in information systems. In *Proceedings of FOIS*, pages 3–15, 1998.
37. A. Y. Halevy. Answering queries using views: A survey. *VLDB Journal*, 10(4):270–294, 2001.
38. A. Y. Halevy, Z. G. Ives, J. Madhavan, P. Mork, D. Suciu, and I. Tatarinov. The Piazza Peer Data Management System. *IEEE Trans. Knowl. Data Eng.*, 16(7):787–798, 2004.

39. F. Heinzle and M. Sester. Derivation of implicit information from spatial data sets with data mining. In *20th Congress of the International Society for Photogrammetry and Remote Sensing (ISPRS)*, 2004.

40. J. Euzenat et al. State of the art on current alignment techniques. In *KnowledgeWeb Deliverable 2.2.3, http://knowledgeweb.semanticweb.org.*

41. M. Jarrar. Towards the notion of gloss, and the adoption of linguistic recourses in formal ontology engineering. In *Global Wordnet Conference (GWC)*, 2006.

42. M. Jarrar, J. Demey, and R. Meersman. On using conceptual data modeling for ontology engineering. *Journal on Data Semantics (Special issue on Best papers from the ER, ODBASE, and COOPIS 2002 Conferences)*, LNCS 2519:185–207, 2002.

43. M. Jarrar and R. Meersman. Formal ontology engineering in the dogma approach. In *International Conference on Ontologies, Databases and Applications of Semantics (ODBase)*, pages 1238–1254, 2002.

44. C.B. Jones, A. Abdelmoty, D. Finch, G. Fu, and S. Vaid. The spirit spatial search engine: Architecture, ontologies and spatial indexing. In *Geographic Information Science: Third International Conference, (GIScience'04)*, volume LNCS 3234, pages 125–139, 2004.

45. T. Keating and A Montoya. Folksonomy extends geospatial taxonomy. *Directions Magazine*, 2005.

46. E. Klien and M. Lutz. The role of spatial relations in automating the semantic annotation of geodata. In *COSIT*, pages 133–148, 2005.

47. D. Kolas, J. Hebeler, and M. Dean. Geospatial semantic web: Architecture of ontologies. In *GeoSpatial Semantics: First International Conference*, volume LNCS 3799, pages 183–194, 2005.

48. W. Kuhn. Geospatial semantics: Why, of what and how. *Journal on Data Semantics III*, LNCS 3534:1–24, 2005.

49. L.V.S. Lakshmanan, R.T. Ng, and G. Ramesh. To do or not to do: the dilemma of disclosing anonymized data. In *Proc. of SIGMOD*, 2005.

50. M. Lenzerini. Data Integration: A Theoretical Perspective. In *PODS 2002*, pages 233–246, 2002.

51. E. Lesser and K. Everest. Using communities of practice to manage intellectual capital. *Ivey Business Journal*, pages 37–41, March/April 2000.

52. Y. Li, J. D. Tygar, and J.M. Hellerstein. Private matching. Intel Research, IRB-TR-04-005, 2004.

53. J. Lieberman, T. Pehle, and M. Dean. Semantic evolution of geospatial web services. In *W3C Workshop on Frameworks for Semantics in Web Services*, 2005.

54. J. Madhavan, Ph. A. Bernstein, A. Doan, and A. Y. Halevy. Corpus-based Schema Matching. In *International Conference on Data Engineering (ICDE)*, 2005.

55. J. Madhavan and A. Y. Halevy. Composing Mappings Among Data Sources. In *VLDB 2003*, pages 572–583, 2003.

56. T. P. Martin and B. Azvine. Acquisition of soft taxonomies for intelligent personal hierarchies and the soft semantic web. *BT Technology Journal*, 21(4):113–122, 2003.

57. E. Mena, V. Kashyap, A. Illarramendi, and A. P. Sheth. Imprecise Answers in Distributed Environments: Estimation of Information Loss for Multi-Ontology Based Query Processing. *Int. J. Cooperative Inf. Syst.*, 9(4):403–425, 2000.

58. G. Miklau and D. Suciu. A formal analysis of information disclosure in data exchange. In *Proc. of SIGMOD*, 2004.

59. P. Mitra, N. F. Noy, and A. R. Jaiswal. OMEN: A Probabilistic Ontology Mapping Tool. In *International Semantic Web Conference (ISWC)*, 2005.

60. A. Motro. Management of uncertainty in database systems. In W. Kim, editor, *Modern Database Systems, The object model, interoperability and beyond.* Addison-Wesley, Reading, Massachusetts, 1995.
61. M. Naor and B. Pinkas. Oblivious transfer and polynomial evaluation. In *Proc. of the 31th ACM Symposium on Theory of Computing*, 1999.
62. F. Naumann, C. Freytag, and U. Leser. Completeness of integrated information sources. *Inf. Syst.*, 29(7):583–615, 2004.
63. A. Newell. The knowledge level. *Artificial Intelligence*, 18(1), 1982.
64. C.K. Ogden and I.A. Richards. *The Meaning of Meaning: A Study of the Influence of Language upon Thought and of the Science of Symbolism.* Routledge & Kegan Paul Ltd., London, 10 edition, 1923.
65. A. M. Ouksel. *A Framework for a Scalable Agent Architecture of Cooperating Heterogeneous Knowledge Sources.* Springer Verlag, 1999.
66. A. M. Ouksel and I. Ahmed. Ontologies are not the panacea in data integration: A flexible coordinator for context construction. *Journal of Distributed and Parallel Databases*, 7,1, 1999.
67. R. Pan, Z. Ding, Y. Yu, and Y. Peng. A Bayesian Network Approach to Ontology Mapping. In *International Semantic Web Conference (ISWC)*, 2005.
68. C. Parent, S. Spaccapietra, and E. Zimanyi. *Conceptual Design for Traditional and Spatio-Temporal Applications – The MADS Approach.* Springer, 2005.
69. C. Parent, S. Spaccapietra, and E. Zimanyi. The murmur project: Modeling and querying multi-representation spatio-temporal databases. *Information Systems*, 2005.
70. S. Parsons. Current approaches to handling imperfect information in data and knowledge bases. *IEEE Transactions on Knowledge and Data Engineering*, 8(3):353–372, 1996.
71. Y. Petrakis and E. Pitoura. On Constructing Small Worlds in Unstructured Peer-to-Peer Systems. In *EDBT Workshops 2004*, pages 415–424, 2004.
72. H. Prade and C. Testemale. Generalizing database relational algebra for the treatment of incomplete or uncertain information and vague queries. *Information Sciences*, 34:115–143, 1984.
73. P. Raghavan. Structured and unstructured search in enterprises: Verity. *IEEE Data Engineering Bulletin*, 4(6), 2001.
74. E. Rahm and P. A. Bernstein. A survey of approaches to automatic schema matching. *VLDB Journal*, 10(4):334–350, 2001.
75. M. Richardson, R. Agrawal, and P. Domingos. Trust management for the semantic web. In *Proceedings of the Second International Semantic Web Conference (ISWC 03)*, 2003.
76. J. Sabater and C. Sierra. Reputation and social network analysis in multi-agent systems. In *International Joint Conference on Autonomous Agents and Multiagent systems (AAMAS)*, 2002.
77. P. Samarati and L. Sweeney. Generalizing data to provide anonymity when disclosing information. In *Proc. of PODS*, 1998.
78. K.-U. Sattler, I. Geist, and E. Schallehn. Concept-based querying in mediator systems. *VLDB Journal*, 14(1):97–111, 2005.
79. S. Schmidt, R. Steele, T. S. Dillon, and E. Chang. Building a fuzzy trust network in unsupervised multi-agent environments. In *OTM Workshops*, 2005.
80. P. Spyns and J. De Bo. Ontologies: a revamped cross-disciplinary buzzword or a truly promising interdisciplinary research topic? *Linguistica Antverpiensia - NS*, (3):279 – 292, 2004.

81. G. De Trè, R. De Caluwe, and H. Prade. The ansi/x3/sparc dbms framework: Report of the study group on data base management system. *Information Systems*, 3, 1978.
82. Y. Velegrakis, R. J. Miller, and L. Popa. Mapping Adaptation under Evolving Schemas. In *VLDB 2003*, pages 584–595, 2003.
83. V. Verykios, E.Bertino, I.N. Fovino, L.P. Provenza, Y. Saygin, and A.K. Elmagarmi. State of the art on privacy preserving data mining. *Sigmod Record*, 33(1), 2004.
84. E. Wenger. Communities of practice: The key to knowledge strategy. *Knowledge Directions*, 6(4):48–64, 1999.
85. G. Wiederhold. Mediators in the Architecture of Future Information Systems. *IEEE Computer*, 25(3):38–49, 1992.
86. S.K.M. Wong, Y. Xiang, and X. Nie. Representation of bayesian networks as relational databases. In *International Conference on Information Processing and Management of Uncertainty*, pages 159–165, Paris, France, 1994.
87. C. Yu and L. Popa. Semantic Adaptation of Schema Mappings when Schemas Evolve. In *proc. of VLDB 2005*, pages 1006–1017, 2005.
88. L.A. Zadeh. Fuzzy sets. *Information and Control*, 8:338–353, 1965.
89. L.A. Zadeh. Fuzzy sets as a basis for a theory of possibility. *Fuzzy Sets and Systems*, 1:3–28, 1978.

f-SWRL: A Fuzzy Extension of SWRL*

Jeff Z. Pan[1], Giorgos Stoilos[2], Giorgos Stamou[2], Vassilis Tzouvaras[2],
and Ian Horrocks[3]

[1] Department of Computing Science, University of Aberdeen,
Aberdeen AB24 3UE, UK
[2] Department of Electrical and Computer Engineering, National Technical University
of Athens, Zographou 15780, Greece
[3] School of Computer Science, The University of Manchester,
Manchester, M13 9PL, UK

Abstract. Although the combination of OWL and Horn rules results
in the creation of a highly expressive language, i.e. SWRL, there are
still many occasions where this language fails to accurately represent
knowledge of our world. In particular, SWRL fails at representing vague
and imprecise knowledge and information. Such type of information is
apparent in many applications like multimedia processing and retrieval,
information fusion, etc. In this paper, we propose f-SWRL, a fuzzy extension to SWRL to include fuzzy assertions (such as 'Mary is tall in the
degree of 0.9') and fuzzy rules (such as 'being healthy is more important
than being rich to determine if one is happy').

1 Introduction

According to widely known proposals for a Semantic Web architecture, Description Logics (DLs)-based ontologies will play a key role in the Semantic
Web [Pan04]. This has led to considerable efforts to developing a suitable ontology language, culminating in the design of the OWL Web Ontology Language [BvHH+04b], which is now a W3C recommendation. Although OWL adds
considerable expressive power with respect to languages such as RDF, it does
have expressive limitations, particularly with respect to what can be said about
properties. E.g., there is no composition constructor, so it is impossible to capture relationships between a composite property and another (possibly composite) property. One way to address this problem would be to extend OWL
with some form of "rules language" [HPS04]. One such proposed extension is
SWRL (Semantic Web Rule Language) [HPSB+04], which is a Horn clause rules
extension to OWL DL[1] that overcomes many of these limitations.

---

* This is a revised and extended version of a paper with the same title that was published in the International Conference on Artificial Neural Networks (ICANN 2005).
This work is supported by the FP6 Network of Excellence EU project Knowledge
Web (IST-2004-507842).
[1] OWL DL is a key sub-language of OWL.

S. Spaccapietra et al. (Eds.): Journal on Data Semantics VI, LNCS 4090, pp. 28–46, 2006.

Even though the combination of OWL and Horn rules results in the creation of a highly expressive language, there are still many occasions where this language fails to accurately represent knowledge of our world. In particular these languages fail at representing vague and imprecise knowledge and information [Kif05]. Such type of information is very useful in many applications like multimedia processing and retrieval [SST+05, BvHH+04a], information fusion [Mat05], and many more. Experience has shown that in many cases dealing with such type of information would yield more efficient and realistic applications [AL05, ZYZ+05]. Furthermore, in many applications, like ontology alignment and modularization, the interconnection of disparate and distributed ontologies and modules is hardly ever a true or false situation, but rather a matter of a confidence or relatedness degree.

In order to capture imprecision in rules, we propose a fuzzy extension of SWRL, called f-SWRL. In f-SWRL, fuzzy individual axioms can include a specification of the "degree" (a truth value between 0 and 1) of confidence with which one can assert that an individual (resp. pair of individuals) is an instance of a given class (resp. property); and atoms in f-SWRL rules can include a "weight" (a truth value between 0 and 1) that represents the "importance" of the atom in a rule. For example, the following fuzzy rule asserts that being healthy is more important than being rich to determine if one is happy:

$$\mathsf{Rich}(?p) * 0.5 \wedge \mathsf{Healthy}(?p) * 0.9 \rightarrow \mathsf{Happy}(?p),$$

where Rich, Healthy and Happy are classes, and 0.5 and 0.9 are the weights for the atoms Rich(?p) and Healthy(?p), respectively. Additionally, observe that the classes Rich, Healthy and Happy are best represented by fuzzy classes, since the degree to which someone is Rich is both subjective and non-crisp.

In this paper, we will present the formal syntax and semantics of f-SWRL. In particular, we specify a set of key constraints of the desired semantics of f-SWRL. These constraints provides a unified framework for model theoretic semantics of f-SWRL based on fuzzy and weight operations. We will provide several examples illustrate the features of f-SWRL. To the best of our knowledge, this is the first effort on fuzzy extensions of the SWRL language.

2 Preliminaries

2.1 OWL

OWL is a standard (W3C recommendation) for expressing ontologies in the Semantic Web. The OWL language facilitates greater machine understandability of Web resources than that supported by RDFS by providing additional constructors for building class and property descriptions (vocabulary) and new axioms (constraints), along with a formal semantics. The OWL recommendation actually consists of three languages of increasing expressive power: OWL Lite, OWL DL and OWL Full. *OWL Lite* and *OWL DL* are, like DAML+OIL,

Table 1. OWL Class and Property Descriptions

Abstract Syntax	DL Syntax	Semantics
Class(A)	A	$A^{\mathcal{I}} \subseteq \Delta^{\mathcal{I}}$
Class(owl:Thing)	$\top$	$\top^{\mathcal{I}} = \Delta^{\mathcal{I}}$
Class(owl:Nothing)	$\bot$	$\bot^{\mathcal{I}} = \emptyset$
intersectionOf($C_1, C_2, \dots$)	$C_1 \sqcap C_2$	$(C_1 \sqcap C_2)^{\mathcal{I}} = C_1^{\mathcal{I}} \cap C_2^{\mathcal{I}}$
unionOf($C_1, C_2, \dots$)	$C_1 \sqcup C_2$	$(C_1 \sqcup C_2)^{\mathcal{I}} = C_1^{\mathcal{I}} \cup C_2^{\mathcal{I}}$
complementOf(C)	$\neg C$	$(\neg C)^{\mathcal{I}} = \Delta^{\mathcal{I}} \setminus C^{\mathcal{I}}$
oneOf($o_1, o_2, \dots$)	$\{o_1\} \sqcup \{o_2\}$	$(\{o_1\} \sqcup \{o_2\})^{\mathcal{I}} = \{o_1^{\mathcal{I}}, o_2^{\mathcal{I}}\}$
restriction(R someValuesFrom(C))	$\exists R.C$	$(\exists R.C)^{\mathcal{I}} = \{x \mid \exists y.\langle x, y \rangle \in R^{\mathcal{I}} \wedge y \in C^{\mathcal{I}}\}$
restriction(R allValuesFrom(C))	$\forall R.C$	$(\forall R.C)^{\mathcal{I}} = \{x \mid \forall y.\langle x, y \rangle \in R^{\mathcal{I}} \rightarrow y \in C^{\mathcal{I}}\}$
restriction(R hasValue(o))	$\exists R.\{o\}$	$(\exists R.\{o\})^{\mathcal{I}} = \{x \mid \langle x, o^{\mathcal{I}} \rangle \in R^{\mathcal{I}}\}$
restriction(R minCardinality(m))	$\geqslant mR$	$(\geqslant mR)^{\mathcal{I}} = \{x \mid \sharp\{y.\langle x, y \rangle \in R^{\mathcal{I}}\} \geq m\}$
restriction(R maxCardinality(m))	$\leqslant mR$	$(\leqslant mR)^{\mathcal{I}} = \{x \mid \sharp\{y.\langle x, y \rangle \in R^{\mathcal{I}}\} \leq m\}$
restriction(T someValuesFrom(u))	$\exists T.u$	$(\exists T.u)^{\mathcal{I}} = \{x \mid \exists t.\langle x, t \rangle \in T^{\mathcal{I}} \wedge t \in u^{\mathbf{D}}\}$
restriction(T allValuesFrom(u))	$\forall T.u$	$(\forall T.u)^{\mathcal{I}} = \{x \mid \exists t.\langle x, t \rangle \in T^{\mathcal{I}} \rightarrow t \in u^{\mathbf{D}}\}$
restriction(T hasValue(w))	$\exists T.\{w\}$	$(\exists T.\{w\})^{\mathcal{I}} = \{x \mid \langle x, w^{\mathbf{D}} \rangle \in T^{\mathcal{I}}\}$
restriction(T minCardinality(m))	$\geqslant mT$	$(\geqslant mT)^{\mathcal{I}} = \{x \mid \sharp\{t \mid \langle x, t \rangle \in T^{\mathcal{I}}\} \geq m\}$
restriction(T maxCardinality(m))	$\leqslant mT$	$(\leqslant mT)^{\mathcal{I}} = \{x \mid \sharp\{t \mid \langle x, t \rangle \in T^{\mathcal{I}}\} \leq m\}$
ObjectProperty(S)	S	$S^{\mathcal{I}} \subseteq \Delta^{\mathcal{I}} \times \Delta^{\mathcal{I}}$
ObjectProperty(S' inverseOf(S))	S^-	$(S^-)^{\mathcal{I}} \subseteq \Delta^{\mathcal{I}} \times \Delta^{\mathcal{I}}$
DatatypeProperty(T)	T	$T^{\mathcal{I}} \subseteq \Delta^{\mathcal{I}} \times \Delta_{\mathbf{D}}$

basically very expressive Description Logics (DLs); they are almost[2] equivalent to the $\mathcal{SHIF}(\mathbf{D^+})$ and $\mathcal{SHOIN}(\mathbf{D^+})$ DLs. *OWL Full* provides the same set of constructors as OWL DL, but allows them to be used in an unconstrained way (in the style of RDF). It is easy to show that OWL Full is undecidable, because it does not impose restrictions on the use of transitive properties [HST99]; therefore, when we mention OWL in this paper, we usually mean OWL DL.

Let $\mathbf{C}$, $\mathbf{R_I}$, $\mathbf{R_D}$ and $\mathbf{I}$ be the sets of URIrefs that can be used to denote classes, *individual-valued* properties, *data-valued* properties and individuals respectively. An OWL DL *interpretation* is a tuple $\mathcal{I} = (\Delta^{\mathcal{I}}, \Delta_{\mathbf{D}}, \cdot^{\mathcal{I}})$ where the individual domain $\Delta^{\mathcal{I}}$ is a nonempty set of individuals, the datatype domain $\Delta_{\mathbf{D}}$ is a nonempty set of data values, $\cdot^{\mathcal{I}}$ is an individual interpretation function that maps

- each individual name $a \in \mathbf{I}$ to an element $a^{\mathcal{I}} \in \Delta^{\mathcal{I}}$,
- each class name $\mathsf{CN} \in \mathbf{C}$ to a subset $\mathsf{CN}^{\mathcal{I}} \subseteq \Delta^{\mathcal{I}}$,
- each *individual-valued* property name $RN \in \mathbf{R_I}$ to a binary relation $RN^{\mathcal{I}} \subseteq \Delta^{\mathcal{I}} \times \Delta^{\mathcal{I}}$ and
- each *data-valued* property name $TN \in \mathbf{R_D}$ to a binary relation $TN^{\mathcal{I}} \subseteq \Delta^{\mathcal{I}} \times \Delta_{\mathbf{D}}$.

Let $RN \in \mathbf{R_I}$ an *individual-valued* property URIref, R an *individual-valued* property, $TN \in \mathbf{R_D}$ a *data-valued* property URIref and T a *data-valued* property. Valid OWL DL *individual-valued* properties are defined by the DL syntax: $R ::= RN \mid R^-$; valid OWL DL *data-valued* properties are defined by the DL

---

[2] They also provide annotation properties, which Description Logics do not.

syntax: $T ::= TN$. Let $\mathsf{CN} \in \mathbf{C}$ be a class name, C, D class descriptions, $o \in \mathbf{I}$ an individual, u an OWL datatype range and $m \in \mathbb{N}$ an integer. Valid OWL DL class descriptions are defined by the DL syntax:

$$C ::= \top \mid \bot \mid \mathsf{CN} \mid \neg C \mid C \sqcap D \mid C \sqcup D \mid \{o\}$$
$$\exists R.C \mid \forall R.C \mid \geqslant mR, \mid \leqslant mR$$
$$\exists T.u \mid \forall T.u \mid \geqslant mT, \mid \leqslant mT$$

The individual interpretation function can be extended to give semantics to class and property descriptions shown in Tables 2, where $\mathsf{A} \in \mathbf{C}$ is a class URIref, $C, C_1, \ldots, C_n$ are class descriptions, $S \in \mathbf{R_I}$ is an *individual-valued* property URIref, R is an *individual-valued* property description and $o, o_1, o_2 \in \mathbf{I}$ are individual URIrefs, u is a data range, $T \in \mathbf{R_D}$ is a *data-valued* property and $\sharp$ denotes cardinality.

An OWL DL ontology can be seen as a DL knowledge base [HPSvH03], which consists of a set of *axioms*, including class axioms, property axioms and individual axioms.[3] A DL knowledge base consists of a TBox, an RBox and an ABox. A *TBox* is a finite set of class inclusion axioms of the form $C \sqsubseteq D$, where C, D are $\mathcal{L}$-classes. An interpretation $\mathcal{I}$ satisfies $C \sqsubseteq D$ if $C^{\mathcal{I}} \subseteq D^{\mathcal{I}}$. An *RBox* is a finite set of role axioms, such as role inclusion axioms $(R \sqsubseteq S)$, functional role axioms $(\mathsf{Func}(R))$ and transitive role axioms $(\mathsf{Trans}(R))$; the kinds of role axioms that can appear in an RBox depend on the expressiveness of $\mathcal{L}$. An interpretation $\mathcal{I}$ satisfies $R \sqsubseteq S$ if $R^{\mathcal{I}} \subseteq S^{\mathcal{I}}$; $\mathcal{I}$ satisfies $\mathsf{Func}(R)$ if, for all $x \in \Delta^{\mathcal{I}}$, $\sharp\{y \in \Delta^{\mathcal{I}} \mid \langle x, y \rangle \in R^{\mathcal{I}}\} \leq 1$ ($\sharp$ denotes cardinality); $\mathcal{I}$ satisfies $\mathsf{Trans}(R)$ if, for all $x, y, z \in \Delta^{\mathcal{I}}$, $\{\langle x, y \rangle, \langle y, z \rangle\} \subseteq R^{\mathcal{I}} \rightarrow \langle x, z \rangle \in R^{\mathcal{I}}$. An *ABox* is a finite set of individual axioms of the form $a : C$, called *class assertions*, or $\langle a, b \rangle : R$, called *role assertions*. An interpretation $\mathcal{I}$ satisfies $a : C$ if $a^{\mathcal{I}} \in C^{\mathcal{I}}$, and it satisfies $\langle a, b \rangle : R$ if $\langle a^{\mathcal{I}}, b^{\mathcal{I}} \rangle \in R^{\mathcal{I}}$. An interpretation $\mathcal{I}$ satisfies a knowledge base Σ if it satisfies all the axioms in Σ. Σ is *satisfiable* (*unsatisfiable*) iff there exists (does not exist) such an interpretation $\mathcal{I}$ that satisfies Σ. Let C, D be $\mathcal{L}$-classes, C is *satisfiable* w.r.t. Σ iff there exist an interpretation $\mathcal{I}$ of Σ s.t. $C^{\mathcal{I}} \neq \emptyset$; C subsumes D w.r.t. Σ iff for every interpretation $\mathcal{I}$ of Σ we have $C^{\mathcal{I}} \subseteq D^{\mathcal{I}}$.

2.2 SWRL

SWRL is proposed by the Joint US/EU ad hoc Agent Markup Language Committee.[4] It extends *OWL DL* by introducing *rule axioms*, or simply *rules*, which have the form:

antecedent $\rightarrow$ consequent,

where both antecedent and consequent are conjunctions of atoms written $a_1 \wedge \ldots \wedge a_n$. Atoms in rules can be of the form $C(\mathrm{x})$, $P(\mathrm{x,y})$, $Q(\mathrm{x,z})$, sameAs(x,y), differentFrom(x,y) or builtIn($pred, z_1, \ldots, z_n$), where C is an OWL DL description, P is an OWL DL *individual-valued* property, Q is an OWL DL *data-valued*

---

[3] Individual axioms are called *facts* in OWL.

[4] See http://www.daml.org/committee/ for the members of the Joint Committee.

property, *pred* is a datatype predicate URIref, x,y are either *individual-valued* variables or OWL individuals, and z, $z_1, \ldots, z_n$ are either *data-valued* variables or OWL data literals. An OWL data literal is either a typed literal or a plain literal; see [BvHH+04b, PH05] for details. Variables are indicated using the standard convention of prefixing them with a question mark (e.g., $?x$). For example, the following rule asserts that one's parents' brothers are one's uncles:

$$parent(?x, ?p) \wedge brother(?p, ?u) \rightarrow uncle(?x, ?u), \tag{1}$$

where *parent, brother* and *uncle* are all *individual-valued* properties.

In SWRL, URI references (URIrefs) are used to identify ontology elements such as classes, *individual-valued* properties and *data-valued* properties. A *URI reference* (or URIref) is a URI, together with an optional fragment identifier at the end. Uniform Resource Identifiers (URIs) are short strings that identify Web resources [Gro01]. The reader is referred to [HPSB+04] for full details of the model-theoretic semantics and abstract syntax of SWRL.

2.3 Fuzzy Sets

While in classical set theory any element belongs or not to a set, in fuzzy set theory [Zad65] this is a matter of degree. More formally, let X be a collection of elements (the universe of discourse) with cardinality m, i.e $X = \{x_1, x_2, \ldots, x_m\}$. A fuzzy subset A of X, is defined by a membership function $\mu_A(x)$, or simply $A(x)$, $x \in X$. This membership function assigns any $x \in X$ to a rational number between 0 and 1 that represents the degree in which this element belongs to X. The *support, Supp(A)*, of A is the crisp set $Supp(A) = \{x \in X \mid A(x) \neq 0\}$.

Using the above idea, the most important operations defined on crisp sets and relations (complement, union, intersection) are extended in order to cover fuzzy sets and fuzzy relations. These operations are now being performed by mathematical functions over the unit interval. More precisely, the complement $\neg A$ of a fuzzy set A is given by $(\neg A)(x) = c(A(x))$ for any $x \in X$, where the function $c : [0, 1] \rightarrow [0, 1]$ is called a fuzzy complement (or simply c-norm), which should satisfy the *boundary conditions*, $c(0) = 1$ and $c(1) = 0$, and be *monotonic decreasing*, i.e. for $a \leq b$, $c(a) \geq c(b)$. Examples of c-norms include the Lukasiewicz negation $c(a) = 1 - a$, which additionally is *continuous* and *involutive*, i.e., for each $a \in [0, 1]$, $c(c(a)) = a$ holds. The intersection of two fuzzy sets A and B is given by $(A \cap B)(x) = t[A(x), B(x)]$, where the function $t : [0, 1]^2 \rightarrow [0, 1]$ is called a triangular norm (t-norm) that should satisfy *boundary condition*, i.e. $t(a, 1) = a$, be *monotonic increasing*, *commutative*, i.e. $t(a, b) = t(b, a)$, and *associative*, i.e., $t(a, t(b, c)) = t(t(a, b), c)$. Examples of t-norms include the Gödel t-norm $t(a, b) = min(a, b)$, which additionally is *idempotent*, i.e. $min(a, a) = a$. The union of two fuzzy sets A and B is given by $(A \cup B)(x) = u[A(x), B(x)]$, where the function $u : [0, 1]^2 \rightarrow [0, 1]$ is called a triangular conorm (or simply s-norm, or u-norm), which should satisfy *boundary condition*, i.e. $u(a, 0) = a$, be *monotonic increasing*, *commutative* and *associative*. Examples of u-norms include the Gödel u-norm $u(a, b) = max(a, b)$, which additionally is *idempotent*.

A binary fuzzy relation R over two countable crisp sets X and Y is a function $R : X \times Y \to [0, 1]$. The composition of two fuzzy relation $R_1 : X \times Y \to [0, 1]$ and $R_2 : Y \times Z \to [0, 1]$ is given by $[R_1 \circ^t R_2] = \sup_{y \in Y} t[R_1(x, y), R_2(y, z)]$. Such a type of composition is referred to as sup-t composition.

Another important operation in fuzzy logics is the *fuzzy implication*, which gives a truth value to the predicate $A \Rightarrow B$. A fuzzy implication is a function ω of the form $\omega : [0, 1]^2 \to [0, 1]$, which is *monotonic decreasing (increasing)* on the first (second) argument. In fuzzy logics, we are usually interested in two kinds of fuzzy implications, i.e.,

- S-implication: $\omega_{u,c}(a, b) = u(c(a), b)$,
- R-implication: $\omega_t(a, b) = \sup\{x \in [0, 1] \mid t(a, x) \leq b\}$,

where a, b are the truth values for A and B, respectively.

We now recall some properties of the above two fuzzy operations that we are going to use in the investigation of the properties of the f-SWRL language.

Lemma 1. *[KY95] For any $a, b, c \in [0, 1]$, t a t-norm, ω_t the respective R-implication and ω an R or an S-implication, the following properties are satisfied:*

1. $t(a, b) \leq c$ iff $\omega_t(a, c) \geq b$,
2. $\omega_t(a, b) = 1$ iff $a \leq b$,
3. $\omega(0, b) = 1$, (dominance of falsity)
4. $\omega(1, b) = b$ (neutrality of truth)

The last two properties follow easily from the definitions of the fuzzy implications and the boundary conditions of t-norms and u-norms.

The reader is referred to [KY95, Haj98] for details of fuzzy logics and their applications.

3   A Motivating Use Case

In this section, we discuss a motivating use case from a casting company, which has a knowledge base that consists of person-models. Advertisement companies are using this knowledge base to look for models to be used in advertisements or other activities. Each entry in the knowledge base contains a photo of the model, personal information and some body and face characteristics. The casting company has created a user interface for inserting the information of the models as instances of a predefined ontology. It also provides a query engine to search for models with specific characteristics. A user can query the knowledge base providing high-level information about the models (such as the name, the height, the type of the hair etc.).

Now we suppose that we have only information about the following two models in the knowledge base:

- Mary has height 172cm and has weight 50kg.
- Susan has height 180cm and has weight 61kg.

If an advertisement company requires a *thin* female model. Since thinness can be regarded as a function of both the weight as well as the height of a person, one can define thinness as follows.

— One is *thin* iff one is both tall and light.
— One is *tall* iff one's height is larger than 175cm.
— One is *light* iff one's weight is less than 60kg.

Under such definitions, it is obvious that there are no thin female models in the knowledge base. Susan is over 175cm tall but is not under 60kg, while Mary is under 60kg but not over 175cm. Although Mary fails to satisfy the height requirement for only 3cm, which in fact is a rather small value, she satisfies the weight condition; in fact, she is 10kg lighter than the required weight. In fact, the advertisement company might classify her as a thin model if it regards weight a more important factor than height in terms of thinness.

The above problems can be solved if we use a fuzzy knowledge representation, instead of a crisp knowledge representation. In particular, we can define tall and light in a fuzzy way, i.e., by using degrees of confidence. For instance, based on the above data of the two models as well as the policy of the advertisement company, we can have the following fuzzy assertions.

— Mary is tall with a degree no less than 0.65.
— Mary is light with a degree no less than 0.9.
— Susan is tall with a degree no less than 0.8.
— Susan is light with a degree no less than 0.6.

Note that the above membership degrees of the individuals Mary and Susan to the fuzzy classes "tall" and "light" have resulted by providing a *fuzzy partition* [KY95] of the space of the possible values that ones height and weight can obtain. For example, the fuzzy partitions in our example can be depicted in Fig. 1.

In addition to the fuzzy assertion, we can also deduce "one is thin" in a fuzzy way. For instance, we can introduce the following fuzzy rule about thinness: One is thin if one is tall (with importance factor 0.7) and light (with importance factor 0.8).

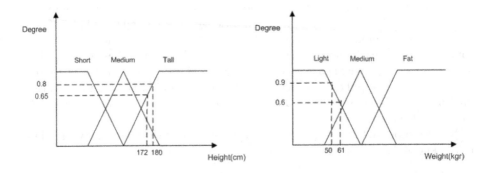

Fig. 1. The fuzzy partition of Height and Weight

After introducing the syntax and semantics of f-SWRL, we will revisit this use case in Section 4.

4   f-SWRL

Fuzzy rules are of the form antecedent → consequent, where atoms in both the antecedent and consequent can have weights (i.e., importance factors), i.e., numbers between 0 and 1. More specifically, atoms can be of the forms C(x)*w, P(x,y)*w, Q(x,z)*w, sameAs(x,y)*w, differentFrom(x,y)*w or builtIn(pred,$z_1, \ldots, z_n$), where $w \in [0, 1]$ is the weight of an atom, and omitting a weight is equivalent to specifying a value of 1. For instance, the following fuzzy rule axiom, inspired from the field of emotional analysis, asserts that if a man has his eyebrows raised enough and his mouth open then he is happy, and that the condition that he has his eyebrows raised is a bit more important than the condition that he has his mouth open.

$$\text{EyebrowsRaised}(?a) * 0.9 \wedge \text{MouthOpen}(?a) * 0.8 \rightarrow \text{Happy}(?a), \qquad (2)$$

In this example, EyebrowsRaised, MouthOpen and Happy are class URIrefs, ?a is a *individual-valued* variable, and 0.9 and 0.8 are the weights of the atoms Eyebrows- Raised(?a) and MouthOpen(?a), respectively.

In this paper, we only consider *atomic* fuzzy rules, i.e., rules with only one atom in the consequent. The weight of an atom in a consequent, therefore, can be seen as indicating the weight that is given to the rule axiom in determining the degree with which the consequent holds. Consider, for example, the following two fuzzy rules:

$$\text{parent}(?x, ?p) \wedge \text{Happy}(?p) \rightarrow \text{Happy}(?x) * 0.8 \qquad (3)$$

$$\text{brother}(?x, ?b) \wedge \text{Happy}(?b) \rightarrow \text{Happy}(?x) * 0.4, \qquad (4)$$

which share Happy(?x) in the consequent. Since $0.8 > 0.4$, more weight is given to rule (3) than to rule (4) when determining the degree to which an individual is Happy.

In what follows, we formally introduce the syntax and model-theoretic semantics of fuzzy SWRL.

4.1   Syntax

In this section, we present the syntax of fuzzy SWRL. To make the presentation simple and clear, we use DL syntax (see the following definition) instead of the XML, RDF or abstract syntax of SWRL.

Definition 1. *Let* a,b *be individual URIrefs,* l *a OWL data literal,* C, D *OWL class descriptions,* r, s *OWL individual-valued property descriptions,* r_1, r_2 *individual-valued property URIrefs,* s, s_1 *data-valued property URIrefs,* pred *a datatype predicate,* $w, w_1, \ldots, w_n \in [0, 1]$, $\vec{v}, \vec{v}_1, \ldots, \vec{v}_n$ *are (unary or binary)* *tuples of variables and/or individual URIrefs, $a_1(\vec{v_1}), \ldots, a_n(\vec{v_n})$ and $c(\vec{v})$ are of the forms $C(x)$, $r(x,y)$, $s(x,z)$, $sameAs(x,y)$, $differentFrom(x,y)$, $\overline{m}$ or builtIn(pred, $z_1, \ldots, z_n$), where x, y are* individual-valued *variables or individual URIrefs, $\overline{m}$ is a truth constant, which is a rational number between 0 and 1, and $z, z_1, \ldots, z_n$ are* data-valued *variables or OWL data literals.*

An f-SWRL ontology can have the following kinds of axioms:

- *class axioms: $C \sqsubseteq D$ (class inclusion axioms);*
- *property axioms: $r \sqsubseteq r_1$ (individual-valued property inclusion axioms),* $\mathsf{Func}(r_1)$ *(functional individual-valued property axioms),* $\mathsf{Trans}(r_2)$ *(transitive property axioms), $s \sqsubseteq s_1$ (data-valued property inclusion axioms),* $\mathsf{Func}(s_1)$ *(functional data-valued property axioms);*
- *individual axioms (facts): $(\mathsf{a} : C) \geq m$, $(\mathsf{a} : C) \leq m$ (fuzzy class assertions), $(\langle \mathsf{a,b} \rangle : r) \geq m$, $(\langle \mathsf{a,b} \rangle : r) \leq m$ (fuzzy individual-valued property assertions), $(\langle \mathsf{a,l} \rangle : r) \geq m$, $(\langle \mathsf{a,l} \rangle : r) \leq m$ (fuzzy data-valued property assertions), $\mathsf{a} = \mathsf{b}$ (individual equality axioms) and $\mathsf{a} \neq \mathsf{b}$ (individual inequality axioms);*
- *rule axioms: $a_1(\vec{v_1}) * w_1 \wedge \cdots \wedge a_n(\vec{v_n}) * w_n \rightarrow c(\vec{v}) * w$ (fuzzy rule axioms).*

Omitting a degree or a weight is equivalent to specifying the value of 1. $\Diamond$

According to the above definition, f-SWRL extends SWRL with fuzzy class assertions, fuzzy property assertions and fuzzy rule axioms. We have some remarks here. Firstly, in f-SWRL, there are two (i.e. $\geq$ and $\leq$) kinds of fuzzy assertions; as first pointed out in [HKS02], we can simulate the form of $(a : C) = m$ by considering two assertions of the form $(a : C) \geq m$ and $(a : C) \leq m$. Secondly, although f-SWRL supports degrees in fuzzy assertions, it does not support degrees in fuzzy class axioms and fuzzy property axioms because it is not very clear how to obtain degrees for them. Nevertheless, it is worth noting that fuzzy class axioms and fuzzy property axioms *have* fuzzy interpretations instead of crisp interpretations (see Section 4.3). Furthermore, we allow the use of truth constants $\overline{m}$ [Pav79, Haj98] in the consequence of a fuzzy rule axiom. This could enable us to simulate fuzzy assertions of the form $(a : C) \leq m$ with fuzzy rule axioms (see Section 4.3).

4.2   Constraints on Semantics

In order to make the semantics of f-SWRL more intuitive, in this section we briefly clarify the constraints of our desired semantics for f-SWRL. The proposed constraints provide a unified framework for giving model theoretic semantics for f-SWRL based on fuzzy intersections (t-norms), fuzzy union (u-norms), fuzzy negations (c-norms), fuzzy implications (ω-norms) and weight operations $g(w,d) : [0,1]^2 \rightarrow [0,1]$, i.e. how to handle the degree d of an atom (in antecedents) and its weight w.

Firstly, one of the most useful relationships which is used to manipulate expressions in propositional logic is the *modus ponen*, which states that $A \cap (A \Rightarrow B) \Rightarrow B$ (if A is true and A implies B, then B is also true). This suggests the following constraint on fuzzy implications.

Constraint 1. *The fuzzy implications used in the semantics of f-SWRL should satisfy the modus ponen:*

$$\omega(t(a, \omega(a, b)), b) = 1.$$

It is easy to verify that, e.g., the following two sets of fuzzy operations satisfy the above constraint:

- $\{t(a, b) = min(a, b), \omega_t(a, b) = \sup\{x \in [0, 1] \mid t(a, x) \leq b\}\}$,
- $\{t(a, b) = a \cdot b, \omega_t(a, b) = \sup\{x \in [0, 1] \mid t(a, x) \leq b\}\}$,

while the set of fuzzy operations $\{t(a, b) = min(a, b), u(a, b) = max(a, b), c(a) = 1 - a, \omega_{u,c}(a, b) = u(c(a), b)\}$ does not (e.g., when $a = 0.4, b = 0.5$). In short, R-implication satisfies Constraint 1, while S-implication does not.

Secondly, we require the weight operations $g(w, d)$ in antecedents satisfy the following properties.

Constraint 2. *The weight operations $g(w, d)$ used in the semantics of f-SWRL should satisfy the following properties:*

1. *monotone in d: if $d_1 < d_2$ then $g(w, d_1) < g(w, d_2)$,*
2. *$g(0, d) = 1, g(1, d) = d$.*

The intuition of Property 1 is immediate. Property 2 ensures that the weight 0 would not affect the result of fuzzy intersections in the antecedent, and that the full membership degree would participate in fuzzy intersections when the weight is 1.

It is easy to verify that, e.g., the following two weight operations satisfy the above constraint:

- $g(a, b) = \begin{cases} a \cdot b & \text{if } a \neq 0 \\ 1 & \text{if } a = 0 \end{cases}$,
- $g(a, b) = \omega_t(a, b)$,

while the weight operation $g(a, b) = min(a, b)$ does not (e.g. when $a = 0$).

Thirdly, in order to enable the use of weights in the head atoms as the weights of the rule axiom, we have the following constraint.

Constraint 3. *Given a fuzzy rule $A \rightarrow c * w$, where A is the antecedent of the rule and c is the consequent atom with weight w, the semantics of f-SWRL should satisfy the following property:*

$$\omega(A(\mathcal{I}), c(\mathcal{I})) \geq w,$$

where $A(\mathcal{I})$ and $c(\mathcal{I})$ are interpretations of A and c, respectively.

Intuitively speaking, the above constraint requires that the degree of fuzzy implication should be no less than the weight. This constraint is inspired by Theorem 5 from [DP01], which shows an important property of the weighted rules of the form $A \xrightarrow{\theta} C$, where θ is a weight of the rule.

Furthermore, individual axioms (or facts) are special forms of rule axioms in SWRL. This suggests yet another constraint on the semantics of f-SWRL.

Constraint 4. *The semantics of f-SWRL should ensure that fuzzy individual axioms (fuzzy facts) are special forms of fuzzy rule axioms.*

It is worth noting that we do not require fuzzy class (or property) axioms be special forms of fuzzy rule axioms. In some decidable sub-languages of SWRL, such as the DL-safe SWRL [MSS04], class (or property) axioms are not special forms of rule axioms.

4.3   Model-Theoretic Semantics

In this section, we give a model-theoretic semantics for fuzzy SWRL, based on the constraints specified in the precious section. Although many f-SWRL axioms share the same syntax as their counterparts in SWRL, such as class inclusion axioms, they have different semantics because we use fuzzy interpretations in the model-theoretic semantics of f-SWRL.

Before we provide a model-theoretic semantics for f-SWRL, we introduce the notions of datatype predicates and datatype predicate maps.

Definition 2. (Datatype Predicate) *A datatype predicate (or simply predicate) p is characterised by an arity $a(p)$, or a minimum arity $a_{min}(p)$ if p can have multiple arities, and a predicate extension (or simply extension) $E(p)$.* ◇

For example, $=^{int}$ is a datatype predicate with arity $a(=^{int}) = 2$ and extension $E(=^{int}) = \{\langle i_1, i_2 \rangle \in V(integer)^2 \mid i_1 = i_2\}$, where $V(integer)$ is the set of all integers. Datatypes can be regarded as *special* predicates with arity 1 and predicate extensions equal to their value spaces; e.g., the datatype *integer* can be seen as a predicate with arity $a(integer) = 1$ and predicate extension $E(integer) = V(integer)$.[5]

Definition 3. (Predicate Map) *We consider a predicate map $\mathbf{M}_p$ that is a partial mapping from predicate URI references to predicates.* ◇

Intuitively, datatype predicates (resp. datatype predicate URIrefs) in $\mathbf{M}_p$ are called built-in datatype predicates (resp. datatype predicate URIrefs) w.r.t. $\mathbf{M}_p$. Note that allowing the datatype predicate map to vary allows different implementations of f-SWRL to implement different datatype predicates.

Based on the constraints we specified in the previous section, we define the semantics of f-SWRL as follows.

Definition 4. *Let c, t, u be fuzzy negations, fuzzy intersections and fuzzy unions, g weight operations that satisfy Constraints 2. Due to Constraint 1, we choose the R-implication as the fuzzy implication. Given a datatype predicate map $\mathbf{M}_p$, a fuzzy interpretation is a triple $\mathcal{I} = \langle \Delta^{\mathcal{I}}, \Delta_{\mathbf{D}}, \cdot^{\mathcal{I}} \rangle$, where the abstract domain $\Delta^{\mathcal{I}}$ is a non-empty set, the datatype domain contains at least all the data values in the extensions of built-in datatype predicates in $\mathbf{M}_p$, and $\cdot^{\mathcal{I}}$ is a fuzzy interpretation function, which maps*

---

[5] See [Pan04] for detailed discussions on the relationship between datatypes and datatype predicates.

1. *individual URIref and* individual-valued *variables to elements of $\Delta^{\mathcal{I}}$,*
2. *a class description C to a membership function $C^{\mathcal{I}} : \Delta^{\mathcal{I}} \to [0,1]$,*
3. *an* individual-valued *property URIref r to a membership function $r^{\mathcal{I}} : \Delta^{\mathcal{I}} \times \Delta^{\mathcal{I}} \to [0,1]$,*
4. *an* data-valued *property URIref q to a membership function $q^{\mathcal{I}} : \Delta^{\mathcal{I}} \times \Delta_{\mathbf{D}} \to [0,1]$,*
5. *a truth constant $\overline{m}$ to itself: $\overline{m}^{\mathcal{I}} = m$,*
6. *a built-in datatype predicate URIref pred to its extension $pred^{\mathcal{I}} = E(\mathbf{M}_p(pred)) \in (\Delta_{\mathbf{D}})^n$, where $n = a(\mathbf{M}_p(pred))$, so that*

$$builtIn^{\mathcal{I}}(pred, z_1, \ldots, z_n) = \begin{cases} 1 & \text{if } \langle z_1^{\mathcal{I}}, \ldots, z_n^{\mathcal{I}} \rangle \in pred^{\mathcal{I}} \\ 0 & \text{otherwise,} \end{cases}$$

7. *the built-in property sameAs to a membership function*

$$sameAs^{\mathcal{I}}(x,y) = \begin{cases} 1 & \text{if } x^{\mathcal{I}} = y^{\mathcal{I}} \\ 0 & \text{otherwise,} \end{cases}$$

8. *the built-in property differentFrom to a membership function*

$$differentFrom^{\mathcal{I}}(x,y) = \begin{cases} 1 & \text{if } x^{\mathcal{I}} \neq y^{\mathcal{I}} \\ 0 & \text{otherwise.} \end{cases}$$

The fuzzy interpretation function can be extended to give semantics for fuzzy class descriptions listed in Table 2.

A fuzzy interpretation $\mathcal{I}$ satisfies a class inclusion axiom $C \sqsubseteq D$, written $\mathcal{I} \models C \sqsubseteq D$, if $\forall o \in \Delta^{\mathcal{I}}, C^{\mathcal{I}}(o) \leq D^{\mathcal{I}}(o)$.

A fuzzy interpretation $\mathcal{I}$ satisfies an individual-valued *property inclusion axiom $r \sqsubseteq r_1$, written $\mathcal{I} \models r \sqsubseteq r_1$, if $\forall o, q \in \Delta^{\mathcal{I}}, r^{\mathcal{I}}(o,q) \leq r_1^{\mathcal{I}}(o,q)$. $\mathcal{I}$ satisfies a functional individual-valued property axiom $\mathsf{Func}(r_1)$, written $\mathcal{I} \models \mathsf{Func}(r_1)$, if $\forall o \in \Delta^{\mathcal{I}}, \inf_{q_1,q_2 \in \Delta^{\mathcal{I}}} u(c(r_1^{\mathcal{I}}(o,q_1)), c(r_1^{\mathcal{I}}(o,q_2))) \geq 1$. $\mathcal{I}$ satisfies a transitive property axiom $\mathsf{Trans}(r_2)$, written $\mathcal{I} \models \mathsf{Trans}(r_2)$, if $\forall o, q \in \Delta^{\mathcal{I}}, r_2^{\mathcal{I}}(o,q) = \sup_{p \in \Delta^{\mathcal{I}}} t[r_2^{\mathcal{I}}(o,p), r_2^{\mathcal{I}}(p,q)]$, where t is a triangular norm. A fuzzy interpretation $\mathcal{I}$ satisfies a* data-valued *property inclusion axiom $s \sqsubseteq s_1$, written $\mathcal{I} \models s \sqsubseteq s_1$, if $\forall \langle o, l \rangle \in \Delta^{\mathcal{I}} \times \Delta_{\mathbf{D}}, s^{\mathcal{I}}(o,l) \leq s_1^{\mathcal{I}}(o,l)$. $\mathcal{I}$ satisfies a functional* data-valued *property axiom $\mathsf{Func}(s_1)$, written $\mathcal{I} \models \mathsf{Func}(s_1)$, if $\forall o \in \Delta^{\mathcal{I}}, \inf_{l_1,l_2 \in \Delta_{\mathbf{D}}} u(c(s_1^{\mathcal{I}}(o,l_1)), c(s_1^{\mathcal{I}}(o,l_2))) \geq 1$.*

A fuzzy interpretation $\mathcal{I}$ satisfies a fuzzy class assertion $(\mathsf{a} : C) \geq m$, written $\mathcal{I} \models (\mathsf{a} : C) \geq m$, if $C^{\mathcal{I}}(\mathsf{a}) \geq m$. $\mathcal{I}$ satisfies a fuzzy individual-valued property assertion $(\langle \mathsf{a}, \mathsf{b} \rangle : r) \geq m_2$, written $\mathcal{I} \models (\langle \mathsf{a}, \mathsf{b} \rangle : r) \geq m_2$, if $r^{\mathcal{I}}(\mathsf{a}, \mathsf{b}) \geq m_2$. $\mathcal{I}$ satisfies a fuzzy data-valued property assertion $(\langle \mathsf{a}, l \rangle : s) \geq m_3$, written $\mathcal{I} \models (\langle \mathsf{a}, l \rangle : s) \geq m_3$, if $s^{\mathcal{I}}(\mathsf{a}, l) \geq m_3$. The semantics of fuzzy assertions using $\leq$ are defined analogously. $\mathcal{I}$ satisfies an individual equality axiom $\mathsf{a} = \mathsf{b}$, written $\mathcal{I} \models \mathsf{a} = \mathsf{b}$, if $\mathsf{a}^{\mathcal{I}} = \mathsf{b}^{\mathcal{I}}$. $\mathcal{I}$ satisfies an individual inequality axiom $\mathsf{a} \neq \mathsf{b}$, written $\mathcal{I} \models \mathsf{a} \neq \mathsf{b}$, if $\mathsf{a}^{\mathcal{I}} \neq \mathsf{b}^{\mathcal{I}}$.

A fuzzy interpretation $\mathcal{I}$ satisfies a fuzzy rule axiom $a_1(\vec{v_1}) * w_1 \wedge \cdots \wedge a_n(\vec{v_n}) * w_n \to c(\vec{v}) * w$, written $\mathcal{I} \models a_1(\vec{v_1}) * w_1 \wedge \cdots \wedge a_n(\vec{v_n}) * w_n \to c(\vec{v}) * w$, if $t(g(w_1, a_1^{\mathcal{I}}(\vec{v_1}^{\mathcal{I}})), \ldots, g(w_n, a_n^{\mathcal{I}}(\vec{v_n}^{\mathcal{I}}))) \leq \omega_t(w, c^{\mathcal{I}}(\vec{v}^{\mathcal{I}}))$.   ◇

Table 2. Syntax and Semantics of Fuzzy Class and Property Descriptions

DL Syntax	Semantics
A	$A^{\mathcal{I}} : \Delta^{\mathcal{I}} \to [0,1]$
$\top$	$\top^{\mathcal{I}}(a) = 1$
$\bot$	$\bot^{\mathcal{I}}(a) = 0$
$C_1 \sqcap C_2$	$(C \sqcap D)^{\mathcal{I}}(a) = t(C^{\mathcal{I}}(a), D^{\mathcal{I}}(a))$
$C_1 \sqcup C_2$	$(C \sqcup D)^{\mathcal{I}}(a) = u(C^{\mathcal{I}}(a), D^{\mathcal{I}}(a))$
$\neg C$	$(\neg C)^{\mathcal{I}}(a) = c(C^{\mathcal{I}}(a))$
$\{o_1\} \sqcup \{o_2\}$	$(\{o_1\} \sqcup \{o_2\})^{I}(a) = 1$ if $a \in \{\, o_1^{I}, o_2^{I} \}$
	$(\{o_1\} \sqcup \{o_2\})^{I}(a) = 0$ otherwise
$\exists r.C$	$(\exists r.C)^{\mathcal{I}}(a) = \sup_{b \in \Delta^{\mathcal{I}}} t(r^{\mathcal{I}}(a,b), C^{\mathcal{I}}(b))$
$\forall r.C$	$(\forall r.C)^{\mathcal{I}}(a) = \inf_{b \in \Delta^{\mathcal{I}}} \omega_t(r^{\mathcal{I}}(a,b), C^{\mathcal{I}}(b))$
$\exists r.\{o\}$	$(\exists (r.\{o\})^{\mathcal{I}}(a) = \sup_{b \in \Delta^{\mathcal{I}}} t(r^{\mathcal{I}}(a,b), \{o\}^{\mathcal{I}}(b))$
$\geqslant mr$	$(\geqslant mr)^{\mathcal{I}}(a) = \sup_{b_1,\ldots,b_m \in \Delta^{\mathcal{I}}} t_{i=1}^{m} r^{\mathcal{I}}(a, b_i)$
$\leqslant mr$	$(\leqslant mr)^{\mathcal{I}}(a) = \inf_{b_1,\ldots,b_{m+1} \in \Delta^{\mathcal{I}}} u_{i=1}^{m+1} c(r^{\mathcal{I}}(a, b_i))$
$\exists s.d$	$(\exists s.d)^{\mathcal{I}}(a) = \sup_{y \in \Delta_{\mathbf{D}}} t(s^{\mathcal{I}}(a,y), y \in d^{\mathcal{I}})$
$\forall s.d$	$(\forall s.d)^{\mathcal{I}}(a) = \inf_{y \in \Delta_{\mathbf{D}}} \omega_t(s^{\mathcal{I}}(a,y), y \in d^{\mathcal{I}})$
$\geqslant ms$	$(\geqslant ms)^{\mathcal{I}}(a) = \sup_{y_1,\ldots,y_m \in \Delta_{\mathbf{D}}} t_{i=1}^{m} s^{\mathcal{I}}(a, y_i)$
$\leqslant ms$	$(\leqslant ms)^{\mathcal{I}}(a) = \inf_{y_1,\ldots,y_{m+1} \in \Delta_{\mathbf{D}}} u_{i=1}^{m+1} c(s^{\mathcal{I}}(a, y_i))$
R^-	$(R^-)^{\mathcal{I}}(a,b) = R^{\mathcal{I}}(b,a)$

There are some remarks on the above definition. Firstly, as we have seen in the previous section, only R-implication satisfies Constraint 1. Therefore, we implicitly use R-implication for fuzzy rule axioms (see below). In fact, given a fuzzy rule axiom $A \to C$, Definition 4 asserts that an fuzzy interpretation $\mathcal{I}$ satisfies $A \to C$ if $A(\mathcal{I}) \leq C(\mathcal{I})$, where $A(\mathcal{I})$ and $C(\mathcal{I})$ are interpretations of the antecedent A and conclusion C, respectively. By applying Property 2 of Lemma 1, it follows that $\omega_t(A(\mathcal{I}), C(\mathcal{I})) = 1$. One of the consequences of such semantics is the support of *chaining* of rules. Suppose that we have two fuzzy rule axioms $A_1 \to C_1, C_1 \to C_2$, if an fuzzy interpretation $\mathcal{I}$ satisfies both of them, i.e. $A_1(\mathcal{I}) \leq C_1(\mathcal{I})$ and $C_1(\mathcal{I}) \leq C_2(\mathcal{I})$, it follows $A_1(\mathcal{I}) \leq C_2(\mathcal{I})$. In other words, $\mathcal{I}$ also satisfies the fuzzy rule axiom $A_1 \to C_2$.

Secondly, there is more than one choice of semantics of fuzzy class descriptions. The one we presented in Table 2 is simply a relatively straightforward one out of many possible choices. For example, we decide to use R-implication in value restriction $(\forall r.C)$ and datatype value restriction $(\forall s.d)$ because we use R-implication in fuzzy rule axioms. The semantics of fuzzy number restrictions were first presented in [Str05]. They are derived by the fuzzy version of the First-Order formulae of classical number restrictions [Str05]. It is easy to see that the fuzzy interpretation of $(\geqslant 1r)$ is equivalent to that of $(\exists r.\top)$.

Furthermore, the semantics of fuzzy functional role axioms is equivalent to that of the fuzzy class inclusion axiom $\top \sqsubseteq \leqslant 1r$. Note that there are two ways to encode fuzzy disjointness axioms. For example, to assert that C is disjoint with D, one can encode it as the fuzzy class axiom $C \sqcap D \sqsubseteq \bot$ or $C \sqsubseteq \neg D$, which have different semantics. In this paper, we do not prejudge which approach is better and leave it to the users to choose, based on the modelling requirements in their applications.

Let us conclude this section by showing that f-SWRL satisfies all the constraints presented in Section 4.2.

Lemma 2. *Given a f-SWRL rule axiom $A \to c*w$, where A is the antecedent of the rule and c is the consequent atom with weight w, we have $\omega_t(A(\mathcal{I}), c(\mathcal{I})) \geq w$, where $A(\mathcal{I})$ and $c(\mathcal{I})$ are interpretations of A and c, respectively.*

Proof: According to the Definition 4, we have $A(\mathcal{I}) \leq \omega_t(w, c(\mathcal{I}))$. Due to Property 1 of Lemma 1, we have $t(w, A(\mathcal{I})) \leq c(\mathcal{I})$; i.e., $t(A(\mathcal{I}), w) \leq c(\mathcal{I})$. Due to Property 1 of Lemma 1 again, we have $\omega_t(A(\mathcal{I}), c(\mathcal{I})) \geq w$. □

Lemma 3. *In f-SWRL, fuzzy assertions are special forms of fuzzy rule axioms.*

Proof: $(a : C) \geq m$ can be simulated by $\top(a) \to C(a) * m$. According to Definition 4, we have $1 \leq \omega_t(m, C^{\mathcal{I}}(a))$. Due to Property 2 of Lemma 1, we have $C^{\mathcal{I}}(a) \geq m$, which is the interpretation of $(a : C) \geq m$.

$(a : C) \leq m$ can be simulated by $C(a) \to \overline{m}$, where $\overline{m}$ is a truth constant. According to Definition 4, we have $C^{\mathcal{I}}(a) \leq \omega_t(1, m)$. Due to Property 4 of Lemma 1, we have $C^{\mathcal{I}}(a) \leq m$, which is the interpretation of $(a : C) \leq m$.

Similarly, $(\langle a, b \rangle : r) \geq m$ can be simulated by $\top(a) \wedge \top(b) \to r(a, b) * m$, and $(\langle a, b \rangle : r) \leq m$ can be simulated by $r(a, b) \to \overline{m}$. □

Based on Definition 4, Lemma 2 and Lemma 3, we have the following theorem.

Theorem 1. *f-SWRL satisfies Constraints 1-4.*

5   Examples

In this section, we use some examples to further illustrate the semantics of f-SWRL. Firstly, let us revisit our motivating example presented in Section 3, so as to show that the use of different fuzzy and weight operations could lead to very different results.

Example 1. The corresponding f-SWRL knowledge base about models consists of the following fuzzy axioms:

- Mary is Tall with a degree no less than 0.65: $(\text{Mary} : \text{Tall}) \geq 0.65$.
- Mary is Light with a degree no less than 0.9: $(\text{Mary} : \text{Light}) \geq 0.9$.
- Susan is Tall with a degree no less than 0.8: $(\text{Susan} : \text{Tall}) \geq 0.8$.
- Susan is Light with a degree no less than 0.6: $(\text{Susan} : \text{Light}) \geq 0.6$.
- One is Thin if one is Tall (with importance factor 0.7) and Light (with importance factor 0.8):

$$\text{Tall}(?p) * 0.7 \wedge \text{Light}(?p) * 0.8 \to \text{Thin}(?p).$$

The interpretation of the above rule axiom is as follows.

$$t(g(0.7, \mathsf{Tall}^{\mathcal{I}}(?p^{\mathcal{I}})), g(0.8, \mathsf{Light}^{\mathcal{I}}(?p^{\mathcal{I}}))) \leq w_t(1, \mathsf{Thin}^{\mathcal{I}}(?p^{\mathcal{I}})).$$

In this example, we first use the following operations: $t(a, b) = min(a, b), w_t(a, b)$
$= \begin{cases} 1 & \text{if } a \leq b \\ b & \text{if } a > b \end{cases}, g(a, b) = \begin{cases} a \cdot b & \text{if } a \neq 0 \\ 1 & \text{if } a = 0 \end{cases}$. According to Definition 4, we have
$\mathsf{Thin}^{\mathcal{I}}(\mathsf{Mary}^{\mathcal{I}}) \geq min(0.7 \cdot 0.65, 0.8 \cdot 0.9) = min(0.455, 0.72) = 0.455$, while
$\mathsf{Thin}^{\mathcal{I}}(\mathsf{Susan}^{\mathcal{I}}) \geq min(0.7 \cdot 0.8, 0.8 \cdot 0.6) = min(0.56, 0.48) = 0.48$. As a result,
Susan seems to be thinner than Mary in this setting.

If we choose another set of operations, the conclusion, however, can be completely different.

For example, now we use the following operations: $t(a, b) = a \cdot b, w_t(a, b) =$
$\begin{cases} 1 & \text{if } a \leq b \\ b/a & \text{if } a > b \end{cases}, g(a, b) = w_t(a, b)$. According to Definition 4, we have
$\mathsf{Thin}^{\mathcal{I}}(\mathsf{Mary}^{\mathcal{I}}) \geq w_t(0.7, 0.65) \cdot w_t(0.8, 0.9) = 0.929 \cdot 1 = 0.929$, while
$\mathsf{Thin}^{\mathcal{I}}(\mathsf{Susan}^{\mathcal{I}}) \geq w_t(0.7, 0.8) \cdot w_t(0.8, 0.6) = 1 \cdot 0.75 = 0.75$. As a result, Mary
seems to be quite thinner than Susan in this setting. $\diamond$

The above example indicates that t-torm based weights give quite different meaning than w_t based weights.

Secondly, we revisit rules (3) and (4) discussed at the beginning of Section 4. Interestingly, this time the above two sets of operations lead to the agreeing result.

Example 2. Suppose we have an f-SWRL knowledge base as follows:

- Tom is Happy with a degree no less than 0.7: $(\mathsf{Tom} : \mathsf{Happy}) \geq 0.7$,
- Tom is a *parent* of Jane: $\langle \mathsf{Jane}, \mathsf{Tom} \rangle : parent$,
- Tom is a *brother* of Kate: $\langle \mathsf{Kate}, \mathsf{Tom} \rangle : brother$,
- if one's *parent* is Happy, then one is Happy (with importance factor 0.8):

$$\mathsf{parent}(?x, ?p) \wedge \mathsf{Happy}(?p) \rightarrow \mathsf{Happy}(?x) * 0.8,$$

- if one's *brother* is Happy, then one is Happy (with importance factor 0.4):

$$\mathsf{brother}(?x, ?b) \wedge \mathsf{Happy}(?b) \rightarrow \mathsf{Happy}(?x) * 0.4.$$

Let us use the two sets of operations in Example 1 with this knowledge base.

Firstly, we use the following operations: $t(a, b) = min(a, b), w_t(a, b) =$
$\begin{cases} 1 & \text{if } a \leq b \\ b & \text{if } a > b \end{cases}, g(a, b) = \begin{cases} a \cdot b & \text{if } a \neq 0 \\ 1 & \text{if } a = 0 \end{cases}$. According to Definition 4, we have
$w_t(0.8, \mathsf{Happy}^{\mathcal{I}}(\mathsf{Jane}^{\mathcal{I}})) \geq min(1 \cdot 1, 1 \cdot 0.7) = 0.7$. Due to Property 1 of Lemma
1, we have $\mathsf{Happy}^{\mathcal{I}}(\mathsf{Jane}^{\mathcal{I}}) \geq 0.7$. As for Kate, we have $w_t(0.4, \mathsf{Happy}^{\mathcal{I}}(\mathsf{Kate}^{\mathcal{I}})) \geq$
$min(1 \cdot 1, 1 \cdot 0.7) = 0.7$; hence, $\mathsf{Happy}^{\mathcal{I}}(\mathsf{Kate}^{\mathcal{I}}) \geq 0.4$. Hence, Jane seems to be
happier than Kate.

Now we use the following operations: $t(a, b) = a \cdot b, w_t(a, b) = \begin{cases} 1 & \text{if } a \leq b \\ b/a & \text{if } a > b \end{cases}$,
$g(a, b) = w_t(a, b)$. According to Definition 4, we have $w_t(0.8, \mathsf{Happy}^{\mathcal{I}}(\mathsf{Jane}^{\mathcal{I}})) \geq$

$\omega_t(1,1)\cdot\omega_t(1,0.7) = 0.7$; hence, $\mathsf{Happy}^{\mathcal{I}}(\mathsf{Jane}^{\mathcal{I}}) \geq t(0.8,0.7) = 0.56$. As for Kate, we have $\omega_t(0.4,\mathsf{Happy}^{\mathcal{I}}(\mathsf{Kate}^{\mathcal{I}})) \geq \omega_t(1,1) \cdot \omega_t(1,0.7) = 0.7$; hence, $\mathsf{Happy}^{\mathcal{I}}(\mathsf{Kate}^{\mathcal{I}}) \geq t(0.4,0.7) = 0.28$. Again, Jane seems to be happier than Kate. $\diamond$

So far we have only seen fuzzy assertions of the form $(a : C) \geq m$; in the next example, we will use fuzzy assertions of the form $(a : C) \leq m$.

Example 3. Suppose we have a slightly different f-SWRL knowledge base from that in the previous example.

- Jane is Happy with a degree no larger than 0.75: $(\mathsf{Jane} : \mathsf{Happy}) \leq 0.75$,
- Kate is Happy with a degree no larger than 0.85: $(\mathsf{Kate} : \mathsf{Happy}) \leq 0.85$,
- Tom is a *parent* of Jane: $\langle\mathsf{Jane}, \mathsf{Tom}\rangle : parent$,
- Tom is a *brother* of Kate: $\langle\mathsf{Kate}, \mathsf{Tom}\rangle : brother$,
- if one's *parent* is Happy, then one is Happy (with importance factor 0.8):

$$\mathsf{parent}(?x, ?p) \wedge \mathsf{Happy}(?p) \rightarrow \mathsf{Happy}(?x) * 0.8 \tag{5}$$

- if one's *brother* is Happy, then one is Happy (with importance factor 0.4):

$$\mathsf{brother}(?x, ?b) \wedge \mathsf{Happy}(?b) \rightarrow \mathsf{Happy}(?x) * 0.4, \tag{6}$$

Here we use the following operations: $t(a,b) = min(a,b)$, $\omega_t(a,b) = \begin{cases} 1 & \text{if } a \leq b \\ b & \text{if } a > b \end{cases}$, $g(a,b) = \begin{cases} a \cdot b & \text{if } a \neq 0 \\ 1 & \text{if } a = 0 \end{cases}$. From (5), we have $\mathsf{Happy}^{\mathcal{I}}(\mathsf{Tom}^{\mathcal{I}}) \leq \omega_t(0.8, \mathsf{Happy}^{\mathcal{I}}(\mathsf{Jane}^{\mathcal{I}})) \leq \omega_t(0.8, 0.75) = 0.75$. Hence, we have $\mathsf{Happy}^{\mathcal{I}}(\mathsf{Tom}^{\mathcal{I}}) \leq 0.75$. From (6), we have $\omega_t(0.4, \mathsf{Happy}^{\mathcal{I}}(\mathsf{Kate}^{\mathcal{I}})) \geq \mathsf{Happy}^{\mathcal{I}}(\mathsf{Tom}^{\mathcal{I}})$. Due to Property 1 of Lemma 1, we have $\mathsf{Happy}^{\mathcal{I}}(\mathsf{Kate}^{\mathcal{I}}) \geq min(0.4, \mathsf{Happy}^{\mathcal{I}}(\mathsf{Tom}^{\mathcal{I}}))$.

It is easy to verify that we have the same results if we use the other set of operations. $\diamond$

6   Discussion

In this paper, we have proposed f-SWRL, a fuzzy extension to SWRL to include fuzzy assertions and fuzzy rules. We have provided formal syntax and semantics for f-SWRL, shown how weights of atoms in consequences of fuzzy rule can be used as important factors of fuzzy rules, illustrated the features of f-SWRL with several examples.

The main strength of the proposal is the openness of the use of fuzzy and weight operations. As many theoretical and practical studies [Voj01] have pointed out, the choice of these operations is usually context dependent. Therefore, it is appropriate to simply specify some key constraints of the desired semantics of f-SWRL and to allow the use of any of these operations as long as they conform to the key constraints. Like in SWRL, in f-SWRL assertions are special forms of rules. Although class and property axioms are not associated with any degrees or important factors, they have fuzzy interpretations instead of crisp interpretations. We show that f-SWRL may be applied in many applications, such as multimedia processing and retrieval. To the best of our knowledge, this is the first effort on fuzzy extensions of SWRL.

Several ways of extending Description Logics using the theory of fuzzy logic have been proposed in the literature [Yen91, TM98, Str01, Str05, SST⁺05]. Furthermore, in [Str04] an approach to extend *Description Logic Programs* (DLPs) with uncertainty was provided, where DLP is extended with *negation as failure*. DLPs are different from SWRL in that rules in DLPs are programs instead of axioms; therefore, the semantics of rules in DLPs are based on Herbrand models instead of model theoretic semantics. [Voj01] presents an approach to fuzzy logic programs which is similar to ours. In that approach, interpretations of rules are based on Herbrand models, instead of model theoretic semantics. The main difference from our work is that weights are only for the whole rules, not for rule atoms. The semantics of weights, accordingly, are based on *fuzzy aggregation* functions, such as linear aggregation or weighted sum.

Our future work includes further investigation of logical properties and computational aspect of f-SWRL. Another interesting direction is to extend f-SWRL to support datatype groups [Pan04], which allows the use of customised datatypes and datatype predicates in ontologies.

References

[AL05]   S. Agarwal and S. Lamparter. smart- a semantic matchmaking portal for electronic markets. In *International WWW Conference Committee*, 2005.

[BvHH⁺04a]   Sean Bechhofer, Frank van Harmelen, James Hendler, Ian Horrocks, Deborah L. McGuinness, Peter F. Patel-Schneider, and Lynn Andrea Stein eds. OWL Web Ontology Language Reference, Feb 2004.

[BvHH⁺04b]   Sean Bechhofer, Frank van Harmelen, Jim Hendler, Ian Horrocks, Deborah L. McGuinness, Peter F. Patel-Schneider, Lynn Andrea Stein; Mike Dean, and Guus Schreiber (editors). OWL Web Ontology Language Reference. Technical report, W3C, February 10 2004. http://www.w3.org/TR/2004/REC-owl-ref-20040210/.

[DP01]   Carlos Viegas Damásio and Luís Moniz Pereira. Monotonic and residuated logic programs. In *Proceedings of the 6th European Conference on Symbolic and Quantitative Approaches to Reasoning with Uncertainty*, pages 748–759. Springer-Verlag, 2001.

[Gro01]   Joint W3C/IETF URI Planning Interest Group.   URIs, URLs, and URNs: Clarifications and Recommendations 1.0.   URL http://www.w3.org/TR/uri-clarification/, 2001. W3C Note.

[Haj98]   P. Hajek. *Metamathematics of fuzzy logic*. Kluwer, 1998.

[HKS02]   Steffen Hölldobler, Tran Dinh Khang, and Hans-Peter Störr. A fuzzy description logic with hedges as concept modifiers. In *Proceedings InTech/VJFuzzy'2002*, pages 25–34, 2002.

[HPS04]   Ian Horrocks and Peter F. Patel-Schneider. A Proposal for an OWL
             Rules Language. In *Proc. of the Thirteenth International World Wide
             Web Conference (WWW 2004)*, pages 723–731. ACM, 2004.
[HPSB⁺04]   Ian Horrocks, Peter F. Patel-Schneider, Harold Boley, Said Tabet, Ben-
             jamin Grosof, and Mike Dean. SWRL: A Semantic Web Rule Lan-
             guage — Combining OWL and RuleML. W3C Member Submission,
             http://www.w3.org/Submission/SWRL/, May 2004.
[HPSvH03]   Ian Horrocks, Peter F. Patel-Schneider, and Frank van Harmelen. From
             SHIQ and RDF to OWL: The making of a web ontology language.
             Journal of Web Semantics, 1(1):7–26, 2003.
[HST99]   I. Horrocks, U. Sattler, and S. Tobies. Practical Reasoning for Ex-
             pressive Description Logics. In H. Ganzinger, D. McAllester, and
             A. Voronkov, editors, *Proceedings of the 6th International Conference on
             Logic for Programming and Automated Reasoning (LPAR'99)*, number
             1705 in Lecture Notes in Artificial Intelligence, pages 161–180. Springer-
             Verlag, 1999.
[Kif05]   Michael Kifer. Requirements for an expressive rule language on the
             semantic web. W3C Workshop on Rule Languages for Interoperability,
             2005.
[KY95]   G. J. Klir and B. Yuan. *Fuzzy Sets and Fuzzy Logic: Theory and Appli-
             cations*. Prentice-Hall, 1995.
[Mat05]   C.J. Matheus. Using ontology-based rules for situation awareness and
             information fusion. W3C Work. on Rule Languages for Interoperability,
             2005.
[MSS04]   Boris Motik, Ulrike Sattler, and Rudi Studer. Query Answering for
             OWL-DL with Rules. In *Proceedings of the 3rd International Semantic
             Web Conference (ISWC 2004)*, 2004.
[Pan04]   Jeff Z. Pan. *Description Logics: Reasoning Support for the Semantic
             Web*. PhD thesis, School of Computer Science, The University of Manch-
             ester, Oxford Rd, Manchester M13 9PL, UK, Sept 2004.
[Pav79]   J. Pavelka. On fuzzy logic i, ii, iii. *Zeitschrift fur Math. Logik und
             Grundlagen der Math.*, 25:45–52, 119–134, 447–464, 1979.
[PH05]   Jeff Z. Pan and Ian Horrocks. OWL-Eu: Adding Customised Datatypes
             into OWL. In *Proc. of Second European Semantic Web Conference
             (ESWC 2005)*, 2005. To appear.
[SST⁺05]   G. Stoilos, G. Stamou, V. Tzouvaras, J.Z. Pan, and I. Horrocks. A fuzzy
             description logic for multimedia knowledge representation. Proc. of the
             International Workshop on Multimedia and the Semantic Web, 2005.
[Str01]   U. Straccia. Reasoning within fuzzy description logics. *Journal of Ar-
             tificial Intelligence Research*, 14:137–166, 2001.
[Str04]   U. Straccia. Uncertainty and description logic programs: A proposal for
             expressing rules and uncertainty on top of ontologies. Technical report,
             Pisa, Italy, 2004.
[Str05]   Umberto Straccia. Towards a fuzzy description logic for the semantic
             web (preliminary report). In *2nd European Semantic Web Conference
             (ESWC-05)*, Lecture Notes in Computer Science, Crete, 2005. Springer
             Verlag.
[TM98]   C. Tresp and R. Molitor. A description logic for vague knowledge. In *In
             proc of the 13th European Conf. on Artificial Intelligence (ECAI-98)*,
             1998.

[Voj01]   P. Vojtás. Fuzzy logic programming. *Fuzzy Sets and Systems*, 124:361–370, 2001.

[Yen91]   J. Yen. Generalising term subsumption languages to fuzzy logic. In *In Proc of the 12th Int. Joint Conf on Artificial Intelligence (IJCAI-91)*, pages 472–477, 1991.

[Zad65]   L. A. Zadeh. Fuzzy sets. *Information and Control*, 8:338–353, 1965.

[ZYZ⁺05]   L. Zhang, Y. Yu, J. Zhou, C. Lin, and Y. Yang. An enhanced model for searching in semantic portals. In *Int. WWW Conference Committee*, 2005.

Intensional Semantics for P2P Data Integration

Zoran Majkić

University of Maryland, College Park, USA
zoran@cs.umd.edu
http://www.cs.umd.edu/ ∼ zoran/

Abstract. One of the main issue in formalizing the Peer-To-Peer (P2P) database systems is the semantic characterization of P2P mappings. Each peer must be robust enough in order to take in account the incomplete and locally inconsistent information of its source databases, typical in Web applications. We consider a peer as a local epistemic logic system with its own belief, independent from other peers and their own beliefs. The traditional extensional semantics for mappings between peers destroys such epistemic independence of peers: the beliefs of other peers (also when change dynamically) are locally introduced into a given peer, so that its own belief depends directly and automatically from other peers. Moreover, the information that one peer provides to another peer may be inconsistent with the information known by the later. This motivates the need of a new, alternative semantic characterization of P2P mappings based not on the extension but on the *meaning* of concepts used in the mappings. We present a novel proposal, based on intensional logic, and show that it adequately models this weakly-coupled framework and supports decidable query answering.

1 Introduction

In this paper, we study the key challenge in building the Semantic Web, that is, the problem of definition of a semantics for P2P database mappings, and relative query-answering issues. Given the de-centralized nature of the development of the Semantic Web, there will be an explosion in the number of ontologies. Many of these ontologies (that is, peers) will describe similar domains, but using different terminologies, and others will have overlapping domains. To integrate data from disparate ontologies, we must know the *semantic correspondence* between their elements [1]. Recently are given a number of different architecture solutions [2,3,4,5,6,7,8].

Indeed, current P2P systems focus strictly on handling semantic-free, large-granularity requests for objects by identifier (typically a name), which both limits their utility and restricts the techniques that might be employed to distribute the data. These current sharing systems are largely limited to applications in which objects are large, opaque, and atomic, and whose content is well-described by their name. Moreover, they are limited to caching, prefetching, or pushing of content at the object level, and know nothing of overlap between objects.

These limitations arise because the P2P world is lacking in the areas of semantics, data transformation, and data relationships, yet these are some of the core strengths of the data management community. Queries, views, and integrity constraints can be used

S. Spaccapietra et al. (Eds.): Journal on Data Semantics VI, LNCS 4090, pp. 47–66, 2006.

to express relationships between existing objects. Let see some of these new approaches to the P2P integration.

One of these new architectures is the Piazza system [2]: data origins serve original content, peer nodes cooperate to store materialized views and answer queries, nodes are connected by bandwidth-constrained links and advertise their materialized views and belong to spheres of cooperation with which they share resources.In order to support dynamic data as well as dynamic workloads, Piazza must refresh materialized views when original data is updated. For scalability reasons, they have elected to use expiration times on data items, rather than a coherence protocol. This reduces network traffic but does not achieve the strong semantics of traditional databases.

The other, more semantic, approach is given in [3]. In that paper they introduce the Local Relational Model (LRM) as a data model specifically designed for P2P applications. LRM assumes that the set of all data in P2P network consists of local (relational) databases, each with a set of acquaintances, which define the P2P network topology. For each acquaintance link, domain relations define translation rules between data items, and coordination formulas define semantic dependencies between the two databases.

The LRM semantics is a variation of the semantic of distributed first-order logic, which itself is an extension of the Local Models Semantics, proposed in [4] . The coordination formulas that relate the contents of peer databases and define what it means for a coordination formula to be satisfied (with respect to a relational space) are used as *deductive rules* and define a global answer to a query with respect to a relational space. The intuition is to compute the union of all the answers of the peer databases, taking into account the information carried by domain relations. The Reiter [5] proves that any partional database can be uniquely represented by a generalized relation theory: they generalize this result by showing that a relational space is uniquely represented by a new kind of formal system called *multi-context system*, consisting of a set of generalized relational theories (one per database) and a set of coordination rules.

The Peer-to-Peer (P2P) database systems offer an alternative to traditional client-server systems for some application domains. A P2P system has no centralized schema and no central administration. Instead, each peer is an autonomous information system, and information integration is achieved by establishing P2P mappings among various peers. Queries are posed to one peer, and the role of query processing is to exploit both the data that are internal to the peer, and the mappings with other peers in the system.

An increasing amount of data is becoming available in the World-Wide Web, and the data is managed under an increasing diversity of data model and access mechanisms. Much of this data is semistructured. In what follows we will consider the reach ontology of peer databases, formally expressed as a global schema of a Data Integration system. A Data Integration System (DIS) [9] is a triple $\mathcal{I}_i = (\mathcal{G}_i, \mathcal{S}_i, \mathcal{M}_i)$, where $\mathcal{G}_i = (\mathcal{G}_{T_i}, \Sigma_{T_i})$ is a global schema (ontology),expressed in a language $\mathcal{L}_\mathcal{O}$ over an alphabet $\mathcal{A}_{\mathcal{G}_i}$, Σ_{T_i} are the integrity constraints, $\mathcal{S}_i$ is a source schema and $\mathcal{M}_i$ is a set of mappings between a global schema $\mathcal{G}_{T_i}$ and a source schema $\mathcal{S}_i$.

References: The article [10] is the first seminal work (referred also in [6]) which introduces an *autoepistemic semantics* for *decidable* peer's (conjunctive) query-answering (it is known that the first-logic semantics for a query answering is undecidable). What is needed here is:

- a mechanism that is able, given any two peer databases, to define mappings between them, without resorting to any unifying (global) conceptual structure.
- a completely decentralized network of database peers: each peer serves as entry points for search, offering its relational schema in order to formalize user queries.
- We do not assume the existence of a single, common set of constants for denoting the interpretation domain of all the peers. In real applications, this is a too strong assumption, as the various peers are obviously autonomous in choosing the mechanisms for denoting the domain elements.
- query answering is based on interactions which are strictly local and guided by locally defined mappings of a considered peer w.r.t. other peers in a network.
- we do not want to limit a-priori the topology of the mapping assertions between peers in the system. In particular, we do not impose acyclicity of assertions.
- we seek for a semantic characterization that leads to setting where query answering is decidable, and possibly, polynomially tractable (under arbitrary P2P interconnections, query answering under the first-order semantics is undecidable).

Consequently, we conceive a peer P_i as a software module, which encapsulates a DIS $\mathcal{I}_i$. The internal structure of a peer database is hidden to the user, encapsulated in the way that only its logical relational schema $\mathcal{G}_{T_i}$ can be seen by users, and is able to respond to the union of conjunctive queries by *known* answers (true in all models of a peer-database).

We consider a view definition $q_k(x_k)$ as a conjunctive query $head(q_k) \leftarrow body(q_k)$ where $body(q_k)$ is a sequence $b_1, b_2, ..., b_m$, where each b_j is an atom over a global relation name of a peer P_i. The *known* answer to this conjunctive query corresponds to true facts of the modal formula $K_i q_k(x_k)$ where K_i is the local modal epistemic operator of the epistemic logic of the peer P_i.

Comparative Analysis: The first introduction of an *autoepistemic semantics* for a peer-database, specified as encapsulation of a DIS, with a *decidable* query answering, and given in [10], is compared with other approaches in [6].

Such formal framework does not specify *if* and *how* the local epistemic knowledge of any peer is influenced by the epistemic knowledge of other peer. In fact we are able to individuate at least two extreme scenarios presented in the literature developed from the initial article [10] followed in the Lenzerini's approach for Data Integration Systems: *strongly-coupled* [11,7,12] and *weakly-coupled* [13,14,8] P2P database systems. The fundamental differences between the two approaches can be summarized as follows:

- The *strongly-coupled* semantics for peer mappings [11,7] is a direct extension of *extensionally based* database mappings between views of peers [15] used for a (strong) data integration systems: For any given peer its own knowledge is locally enlarged by extensional knowledge of other peers: any dynamic change of the knowledge of other peers is directly reflected into the local knowledge of this peer. As showed in [7], the added knowledge of other peers is seen as some kind of local 'source' database of data-integration system of a given peer. We can paraphrase this by taking two peers, 'Peter' and 'John' for example, and then *imperatively* assert that '*John must know all facts about the Italian art in the 15'th century known by Peter*' (also when 'Peter' in his life cycle changes this part of its own knowledge).

In this way, also when 'John' does not know anything by himself about Italian art, by such direct *extensional mapping* he will be able to answer to questions about Italian art in the 15'th century as 'Peter'. Really, the relational schema of a peer represents a global schema for the whole answering system able to provide complete answer to queries: the data-integration system of a peer is composed by proper source databases and 'source' databases transferred by other peers to this particular peer. So, we remain in the classical data-integration framework [9]. There is also the query-answering problem for a given peer: he is able to guarantee for the quality of known answers but not for the part of his answer composed by exported knowledge from other peers, so that later answers can not be epistemically considered certain as its own belief.

– The *weakly-coupled* semantics for peer mappings [13,14,8], where each peer is completely independent entity with its own epistemic state, which has not to be directly, externally, changed by the mutable knowledge of other independent peers, needs other approach to the mapping between their local knowledge based on the *meaning* of the mapped concepts.

First requirement is that the knowledge of other peers can not be directly transferred into the local knowledge of a given peer.

The second requirement is that, during the life time of a P2P system, any local change of knowledge must be independent of the beliefs that can have other peers: thus, we have not to constrain the *extension* of knowledge which may have different peers about the same type of real-world concept.

In the example above, 'John' can answer only for a part of knowledge that it really has about Italian art, and not for a knowledge that 'Peter' has. Thus, when somebody (call him 'query-agent') ask 'John' about the Italian art in the 15'th century, 'John' is able to respond only by the facts known by himself (i.e., *certain* answers), and eventually indicate to query-agent that for such question, probably, also 'Peter' is able to give some answer. Thus, it is the task of the *query-agent* to reformulate the request (w.r.t. the local language of 'Peter') to 'Peter' in order to obtain some other *possible* answers.

We can paraphrase this by the kind of *belief-sentence*-mapping '*John believes that also Peter knows something about Italian art in the 15'th century*'. Such belief-sentence has *referential* (i.e., extensional) *opacity*. In this case we do not specify that the knowledge of 'John' is included in the knowledge of 'Peter' (or viceversa) for the concept 'Italian art in the 15'th century', but only that this concept, c_J, for 'John' (expressed in a language of 'John') *implicitly corresponds* to the 'equivalent' concept, c_P, for 'Peter' (expressed in a language of 'Peter'). In [13,14] is presented the formal framework for weakly-coupled P2P systems based on the consideration of the incomplete and locally inconsistent information in Web, but it lacks of the *formal* semantics for the "equivalent" concepts contained in the local knowledge of different peers.

Formally, the mappings between any two different peer-databases, P_i, P_k, can be defined as follows: let $q_{P_i}(\mathbf{x})$ and $q_{P_k}(\mathbf{x})$ be a two views (conjunctive queries) over P_i and P_j respectively, with the same set of free variables $\mathbf{x}$. Then,

1. The *strong (extensional)* multi-modal mapping, introduced in [8], by a formula
   $K_i q_{P_i}(\mathbf{x}) \Rightarrow K_k q_{P_k}(\mathbf{x})$, where $' \Rightarrow '$ is the logic implication, used in a single S5 modality [6,7,12], and very recently adopted in K45 multi-modality [12].
2. The *weak (intensional)* mapping is defined by
   $K_i q_{P_i}(\mathbf{x}) \approx_{in} K_k q_{P_k}(\mathbf{x})$, where $' \approx'_{in}$ is the intensional equivalence [8,13,14,16], denoted also by $q_{P_i}(\mathbf{x}) \approx q_{P_k}(\mathbf{x})$.

What is the fundamental difference of these two approaches?

1. First of all in the first 'strong' mapping case, the instance database of any peer is *strictly dependent* of current (in a given instance of time) instance databases of other peers. That means that we can not encapsulate a peer as an independent ADT (Abstract Data Type) and see it as a block module of data during query-answering processing. More over we need a global logic for all peers in order to determine the exact extension of one peer database. Thus, also if we do not provide any 'global schema' of a P2P network, semantically we must assume it: the way in which it is used for conjunctive-query answering is explained in [7], where is used a recursive Datalog for this *whole P2P logic theory*, in order to process a given conjunctive-query over a single peer-database. This global P2P Datalog program returns with the union of conjunctive queries for each peer database in considered P2P network. Such, query-rewriting approach, based on a global P2P recursive Datalog logic theory, *avoids to materialize* the propagations of facts between peer databases, caused by material implications, $K_i q_{P_i}(\mathbf{x}) \Rightarrow K_k q_{P_k}(\mathbf{x})$, between peers: in Web applications such dynamic (and cyclic) transfer of ground facts between peer databases practically can not be accepted, because so high traffic of data in the internet would drastically slow-down the whole web system.

In the second approach we have not such problems: each logic theory of a single peer database is completely independent from all other peers, and can be encapsulated in a modular P2P structure as an ADT (as will be explained in what follows), so easily implemented in a greed computation framework. Moreover, each peer is free to change not only its data extension, but also its schema representation, without invalidating the P2P mapping system.

2. The second problem is that in the first 'strong' approach, the 'system' has to know the whole set of peer databases in the P2P network in any time, otherwise no one peer database can know which are other peers which maps the data toward himself: thus, must exist some centralized control. The addition of other peer databases must be explicitly communicated to this global system controller. This information is used by the query-answering agent (consequently, every query-agent *knows the global* P2P database schema, differently from the declared fact against any globalization) with above described recursive Datalog program which contains the whole logic theory of a P2P network. Otherwise, when any other peer, which was not considered in the actually P2P network, makes one mapping (by the material implication defined above) toward some existing peer database in a P2P network, if the 'system' (basic part of any query-answering agent) does not know for that, the query-answer is incomplete and can be also unsound (in the case when this new mapping introduces the mutually inconsistent information in the P2P network system).

In the second, weak approach, there is no any concept explicitly or implicitly assumed for a global P2P system. Differently from the first approach where the mappings between peers are part of the underlying 'system' (i.e., global logic theory of the whole P2P network system), the mappings based on intensional equivalences are local component of each peer: each peer define its belief set of the correspondent equivalent views of other peers, and query agent can use these mappings only when it access to a particular peer. When the user query is generated over a schema (ontology) of a given peer, the activated query-agent has no any global knowledge about the 'whole' P2P network system, but can only use the local mappings of the accessed peer to pass to other locally mapped peers.

3. The third problem is the *inconsistency   tolerance*. When we consider a peer database as a single Data Integration system with GLAV (Global/local as views) mappings between the data sources and the global (virtual) peer database schema, the problem with mutually-inconsistent information from different sources can be localized and resolved inside the local peer database (its logic theory defined by the Data Integration System), by a kind of 2-valued, for example in [17,18], or many-valued belief revision, for example 4-valued Belnap's bilattice based belief revision [19]. Such approach for the resolution of local inconsistency inside a particular peer database is valid, just because it is local to a peer, and there is a team of developers which are responsible for a correct implementation of this particular peer database. This handling of local inconsistency of a peer database is common for both approaches to mapping semantics between different peers. What is problematic in the first 'strong' approach is that also when each peer database is consistent by himself (by handling its proper local consistency), the externally mapped data from other peers into a particular peer database can generate the inconsistency (in peer databases with integrity constraints) of this particular peer. In the first approach such problem is addressed in [12] and have not an easy, also from a theoretical point of view, solution: in that approach it is only *partially* resolved by the very strong requirement to simply *eliminate* any external data coming from an other *single* peer, which is potentially inconsistent with the information of this peer. But such drastic approach, which lose a part of information (instead of considering the mutually inconsistent information as 'possible' versions of the same information) it does not resolve the problem: let us consider, for example, two different data which comes into the same peer from two different peers, and each of these data, taken singularly, is consistent with the local knowledge of a peer, but these two data are mutually inconsistent if taken together (for example, the destination peer has a key constraint for the attribute x of a relation Person(x,y) where x is name of a person and y is its age, and two external data which come from two different peers are $\{John, 40\}$ and $\{John, 41\}$).

In the weak mapping semantic instead, such problem do not exists, just because there is not any correlation between *extensions* of concepts in different peers, but only intensional mapping between them, based on belief sentences of each local peer. Differently from the 'strong' approach, where if we adopt the possibility of materialization of consequences of material implications between peers, an interrogated peer can completely respond to the user query, in the 'weak' approach it is not possible theoretically also: each peer who has the knowledge about the user query has to respond by himself only to the (appropriately rewritten for it) user query: thus we make an *epistemic difference* between the certain answers of the peer interrogated directly by the user, from the 'possible' answers obtained from all other peers. We do not eliminate any information which comes from different peers, but the user who receives all answers will take the appropriate for him actions to verify the part of information that he considers mutually inconsistent.

It is easy to understand that the complexity of the 'weak' approach, in a presence of mutually inconsistent P2P information, is less than the complexity of the First order multi-modal logic for the 'strong' semantic mapping.

Motivation: In this paper we adopt the second, weakly-coupled semantics for P2P mappings, with the following motivation: What we argue is the *full* epistemic independency of peer databases where there is no any forced transfer of a local knowledge of one peer to other peers, but only their collaboration in order to answer to user queries. They can change their ontology and/or extension of their knowledge independently from other peers and without any communication to other peers. In this way we intend to obtain very robust P2P systems, able to answer to user queries also when intended mappings between peers do not feet with the modified ontologies (relational database schemas) of peers, but also to have the possibility to map naturally P2P database systems into greed computation: having fully independent peers, which as we will see can be represented as ADTs (Abstract Data Types), it is enough to associate each pair (peer, query-formulae) to a particular resource of greed computing, in order to obtain known answer from such peer.

The Plan of this work is the following: In Section 2 we introduce the intensional logic and the intensional equivalence, which will be used to define intensionally equivalent views over two different peers. In Section 3 we define formally independent peer databases as ADT (Abstract Data Types) which encapsulate the semantics of a Data Integration System. Finally, in Section 4 we define the query-answering semantics, context-dependent, of the P2P system with intensional mapping semantics, which distinguish the certain answers of interrogated peer from the possible answers of other peers.

2   Intensional Equivalence

Tarski's elaboration of a semantics for formal languages, Kripke's invention of a possible-world semantics in connection with modal logic and Montague's semantics for Intensional logic provided powerful tools by means of which natural languages could be analyzed rigorously. Indeed, between 1968 and 1970, Montague, a logician from Tarski school, wrote three papers [20,21,22] the goal of which was to show that no important theoretical difference exist between natural languages and the formal languages of logic. Montague's research started where Davidson's work on recursive semantics left of [23].

Since 'meaning' is not synonymous with 'truth', a definition of truth is not necessarily a definition of the meaning. The recursive semantics (dual to the recursive syntax of the language) is to show how the *meaning* of a complex sentence depends upon the *meaning* of the elementary sentences of which it is composed. Here, a major difficulty appears: the meaning of a syntactic constituent which is not a sentence (a formula without free variables, whereas *formulae* may contain also free occurrences of variables) cannot be identified to its truth conditions, because *only sentences* may be said to be true or false. Tarski discovered how to overcome this difficulty: first, he recursively defines a notion more general than that of truth, the notion of *satisfaction*, and, next, he defines the notion of truth by way of the notion of satisfaction.

Montague's intensional logic develops Frege's distinction between *sense* and *reference* and Carnap's distinction between *intension* and *extension*, to treat phenomenon of referential opacity, pervasive in belief-sentences. Thus, in his semantic analysis of meaning, Montague distinguishes two elements: *intension* (or sense) and *extension* (or reference). The intension of a predicate is identified with the property it express; its extension is the class of objects which posses the property or which stand in the relation expressed by the predicate. For instance, the extension of a sentence is its truth value; its intension is the proposition it expresses whose extension can vary from one to other possible world (i.e., it can be true in some possible world and false in some other possible world). So, the intension (meaning) is something which needs to be defined in all possible worlds and not in some particular world: Motague defined the *intension of a sentence* as a function from possible worlds to truth values.

The correspondence between syntactic and semantic rules which *work in parallel* constitutes a formalization of Frege's *compositionality principle* that can be stated as follows: The meaning of a sentence is a function of the meaning of its parts and their mode of combinations.

For instance, the denotation (or semantic value) of the expression $\neg A$ in any possible world depends only on the denotation of A in the same world, i.e., $[\neg A] = [\neg][A]$, where $[\_]$ denotes the extension (reference) of an expression ($[\neg]$ is the set-complement function). Sentences of the form 'Necessarily A' (or $\Box A$) are a first example of a type of sentence whose reference (extension), at a given world, cannot be described as a function of the references of its parts (here $\Box$ and A), i.e., $[\Box A] \neq [\Box][A]$), but holds $[\Box A]_{in} = [\Box]_{in}[A]_{in}$ (where $[\_]_{in}$ denotes the intension of an expression).

2.1 Montague's Modal Logic Framework

In what follows we will use one simplified modal logic framework (we will not consider the time as one independent parameter as in Montague's original work) with a model $\mathcal{M} = (\mathcal{W}, \mathcal{R}, S, V)$, where $\mathcal{W}$ is the set of possible worlds, $\mathcal{R}$ is the accessibility relation between worlds ($\mathcal{R} \subseteq \mathcal{W} \times \mathcal{W}$), S is a non-empty domain of individuals, while V is a function defined for the following two cases:

1. $V : \mathcal{W} \times F \to \bigcup_{n < \omega} S^{S^n}$, with F a set of functional symbols of the language, such that for any world $w \in \mathcal{W}$ and a functional symbol $f \in F$, we obtain a function $V(w, f) : S^{arity(f)} \to S$.
2. $V : \mathcal{W} \times P \to \bigcup_{n < \omega} 2^{S^n}$, with P a set of predicate symbols of the language and $\mathbf{2} = \{t, f\}$ is the set of truth values (true and false, respectively), such that for any world $w \in \mathcal{W}$ and a predicate symbol $p \in P$, we obtain a function $V(w, p) : S^{arity(p)} \to \mathbf{2}$, which defines the extension $[p] = \{\mathbf{a} | \mathbf{a} \in S^{arity(p)}$ and $V(w, p)(\mathbf{a}) = t\}$ of this predicate p in the world w.

The extension of an expression α, w.r.t. a model $\mathcal{M}$, a world $w \in \mathcal{W}$ and assignment g is denoted by $[\alpha]^{\mathcal{M}, w, g}$. Thus, if $c \in F \bigcup P$ then for a given world $w \in \mathcal{W}$ and the assignment function for variables g, $[c]^{\mathcal{M},w,g} = V(w,c)$, that is, for any set of terms $t_1, .., t_n$, where n is the arity of c, we have $[c(t_1, .., t_n)]^{\mathcal{M},w,g} = V(w,c)([t_1]^{\mathcal{M},w,g}, .., [t_n]^{\mathcal{M},w,g})$; with terms defined by:

1. All variables $v \in Var$ and the constants $d \in S$ are terms;
2. If $f \in F$ is a function symbol of arity n, and $t_1, .., t_n$ are terms, then a functional form $f(t_1, .., t_n,)$ is a term.

For any formula A, $\mathcal{M} \vDash_{w,g} A \equiv ([A]^{\mathcal{M},w,g} = t)$, means 'A is true in the world w of a model $\mathcal{M}$ for assignment g'.

Montague defined the *intension* of an expression α as follows:

$$[\alpha]_{in}^{\mathcal{M},g} =_{def} \{w \mapsto [\alpha]^{\mathcal{M},w,g} \mid w \in \mathcal{W}\},$$

i.e., as graph of the function $[\alpha]_{in}^{\mathcal{M},g} : \mathcal{W} \to \bigcup_{w \in \mathcal{W}_N} [\alpha]^{\mathcal{M},w,g}$.

One thing that should be immediately clear is that intensions are more general that extensions: if the intension of an expression is given, one can determine its extension with respect to a particular world but not viceversa, i.e., $[\alpha]^{\mathcal{M},w,g} = [\alpha]_{in}^{\mathcal{M},g}(w)$.

In particular, if c is a non-logical constant (individual constant or predicate symbol), the definition of the extension of c is, $[c]^{\mathcal{M},w,g} =_{def} V(w,c)$. Hence, the intensions of the non-logical constants are the following functions: $[c]_{in}^{\mathcal{M},g} : \mathcal{W} \to \bigcup_{w \in \mathcal{W}} V(w,c)$.

The extension of variable is supplied by the value assignment g only, and thus does not differ from one world to the other; if x is a variable we have $[x]_{in}^{\mathcal{M},g} = g(x)$.

Thus the intension of a variable will be a constant function on worlds which corresponds to its extension.

2.2 Intensional Equivalence

Carnap suggested that the intension of an expression is nothing more than all the varying extensions the expression can have. In the next we will take this definition in order to define that two expressions (or concepts) α, β are *intensionally equivalent*, in the following two cases: the basic *flat-accumulation* case where varying world-dependent extensions are simply accumulated, and the *world-correspondent* case where we require that for a given extension S_E of the first expression in some possible world w there is an other possible world w' where the second expression has the same extension S_E.

Definition 1. *Any two expressions, α, β, are intensionally equivalent (in the* flat- accu- mulation *or the* world-correspondent *case, respectively) denoted by* $\alpha \approx_{in} \beta$, *if and only if:*

1. *flat-accumulation case:* $lub^{\mathcal{M},g}(\alpha) = lub^{\mathcal{M},g}(\beta)$, *where for a given expression δ, its lub (Least Upper Bound) is defined by:* $lub^{\mathcal{M},g}(\delta) =_{def} \bigcup_{w \in \mathcal{W}} [\delta]_{in}^{\mathcal{M},g}(w)$.
2. *world-correspondent case:* $\forall w \exists w'.([\alpha]_{in}^{\mathcal{M},g}(w) = [\beta]_{in}^{\mathcal{M},g}(w'))$, *and viceversa,* $\forall w' \exists w.([\alpha]_{in}^{\mathcal{M},g}(w) = [\beta]_{in}^{\mathcal{M},g}(w'))$, *so that for any two conjunctive queries, $q_i(x)$, $q_j(x)$ over peers P_i, P_j respectively, we define:* $q_i(x) \approx q_j(x)$ *if and only if* $K_i\, q_i(x) \approx_{in} K_j\, q_j(x)$.

It is easy to verify that the world-correspondent case of intensional equivalence is stronger then the flat-accumulation case (i.e., each world-correspondent intensional equivalence is also a flat- correspondent intensional equivalence: so, as first approach we will use the basic flat-accumulation intensional equivalence. In the context of this work we will consider each temporary instance (in a some time t_k) of the P2P database system as a particular possible world w: the dynamic changes of any local peer knowledge will result in one other possible world.

3   Abstract Object Types for Peer Databases

The current World-Wide Web has well over billions pages, but the vast majority of them are in human-readable format only (e-g., HTML). As a consequence software agents cannot understand and process this information, and much of the potential of the Web has so far remained untapped. In response, researches have created the vision of the *Semantic Web* [24], where data has structure and *ontologies* describe the semantics of the data. An ontology specifies a conceptualization of a domain in terms of concepts, attributes, and relations [25], thus introduce the *mediator schema* for user queries, and, consequently, *Data Integration Systems*. When data is marked up using mediator schemas (ontologies) software query-agents can better understand the semantics and therfore more intelligently locate and integrate data for a wide variety of tasks, [10,26].

Information integration is the problem of combining the data residing at different sources, and providing the user with a unified view of these data, called *global schema*.

The global schema is therefore a reconciled view of the information, which can be queried by the user. It can be thought of as a set of virtual relations, in the sense that their extensions are not actually stored anywhere. A data integration system frees the user from having to locate the sources relevant to a query, interact with each source in isolation, and manually combine the data from different sources.

Two basic approaches have been used to specify the mapping between sources and the global schema. The first approach, called query-centric or global-as-view (GAV), requires that the global schema is expressed in terms of the data sources. More precisely, to every concept of the global schema, a view over the data sources is associated, so that its meaning is specified in terms of the data residing at the sources. The second approach, called source-centric or local-as-view (LAV), requires the global schema to be specified independently of the sources. The relationships between the global schema and the sources are established by associating each element of the sources with a view over the global schema. Thus, in the LAV approach, we specify the meaning of the sources in terms of the concepts in the global schema.

The natural way to make more modular structure of a data-intensive Internet system, and to open up the possibility of effective query answering techniques is to organize a number of application-domain Data integration systems as a P2P system. The most important advantage of organizing a peer as a Data integration system is that it enables users to focus on specifying *what* they want, rather then thinking about *how* to obtain the answers: so that we can see it as an *Abstract Object Type* (AOT) which hides internal integration structure with data sources, and offers to users only a mediator schema with the standard query language in order to be able to formulate the questions in a declarative way.

As result, it frees the users from the tedious tasks of finding the relevant data sources, interacting with each source in isolation using a particular interface, and combining data from multiple sources.

The main characteristic distinguishing Data Integration systems from distributed and parallel database systems is that data sources underlying the system are autonomous. In particular, a data integration system provides access to *pre-existing* sources, which were created independently.

The aim of the encapsulation of a Data Integration system into an Abstract Object Type (AOT) is to hide the internal structure of such complex object and to offer to user the rich ontology of the global (mediator) schema in order to focus on specifying *what* they want, by ordinary conjunctive queries.

The main point is that every peer can be seen as an AOT (*Abstract Object Type*) which acts at the same level, with no unifying structure above it: in order to respond to the complex user queries (union of conjunctive queries). Thus we assume that expressive power of peers can be generally given by single-encapsulated Data Integration Semantic. In this way considering the (incomplete) sources extracted by wrappers we may enrich the peer database schema by integrity constraints in order to overcome incompleteness of heterogenous Web information: we assume that each AOT peer has a unique model or, otherwise, a *canonical (universal)* [27,28] global database, and that responds to user queries by *certain* (i.e., known [29]) answers.

- **Query reformulation:** A user of an AOT poses queries in terms of the mediated schema, rather than directly in the data sources which are encapsulated and hidden by AOT. As a consequence, the AOT must contain a module that uses the source descriptions in order to reformulate a user query that refers directly to the schemas of the sources. Clearly, we would like the reformulation to be sound, (i.e., the answers to the reformulated query should all be correct answers to the input query), and complete (i.e., all the answers that can be extracted from the data sources should be in the result of applying the reformulated query): the methods of this AOT which satisfy these requirements give to users the *known answers*.
- **Wrappers:** The other layer of an AOT that does not exist in a traditional system is the (hidden) wrapper layer. Unlike a traditional query execution engine that communicates with a local storage manager to fetch the data, the query execution plan in the AOT must obtain data from remote sources. An encapsulated into AOT wrapper is a program (method) which is specific to a data source, whose task is to translate data from the source to a form that is usable by the query processor (agent) of the system.

Dually to the theory of *algebraic specifications* where an Abstract Data Type (ADT) is specified by a set of operations (constructors), the *coagebraic specification* of a class of systems, i.e., Abstract Object Types (AOT), is characterized by a set of operations (destructors) which tell us what can be *observed* out of a system-*state* (i.e., an element of the carrier), and how can a state be transformed to successor state.

We start introducing the class of coalgebras for database query-answering systems. They are presented in an algebraic style, by providing a co-signature. In particular, sorts include one single "hidden sort", corresponding to the carrier of the coalgebra, and other "visible" sorts for inputs and outputs, which are given a fixed interpretation.

Visible sorts will be interpreted as sets without any algebraic structure defined on them. Coalgebraic terms, built only over destructors, have for us a precise interpretation as the basic *observations* that one can make on the states of a coalgebra. Input sorts are considered as the set $\mathcal{L}_Q$ of modal conjunctive queries, $K_i q(\mathbf{x})$, while output sorts are "valuations", that is, the set of a resulting "views", for each query $q(\mathbf{x})$ over a database $\mathcal{A}$ (considered as a carrier of the coalgebra).

Definition 2. *A co-signature for Database query-answering system is a triple $\mathcal{D}_\Sigma = (S, OP, [\_])$, where S, the sorts, OP, the operators, and $[\_]$ the interpretation of visible sorts are as follows:*

1. *$S = (X_A, \mathcal{L}_Q, \Upsilon)$, where X_A is the hidden sort (a set of states of a database A), $\mathcal{L}_Q$ is an input sort (set of conjunctive queries), and Υ is an output sort (set of all views of databases).*
2. *OP is set of operations: a method $Next_q : X_A \times \mathcal{L}_Q \to X_A$, which corresponds to an execution of a next query $q(\mathbf{x}) \in \mathcal{L}_Q$ in a current state of a database A, such that a database A pass to the next state; and $Out_Q : X_A \times \mathcal{L}_Q \to \Upsilon$ is an attribute which returns with an obtained view of a database for a given query $K_i q(\mathbf{x}) \in \mathcal{L}_Q$.*
3. *$[\_]$ is a function mapping each visible sort to a non-empty set.*

The Abstract Object Type (AOT) for a query-answering system is given by a coalgebra
$$< \lambda Next_Q, \lambda Out_Q >: X_A \to X_A^{\mathcal{L}_Q} \times \Upsilon^{\mathcal{L}_Q} ,$$ *of the polynomial endofunctor $(\_)^{\mathcal{L}_Q} \times \Upsilon^{\mathcal{L}_Q} : Set \to Set$, where λ denotes the lambda abstraction (Curring) for functions of two variables into functions of one variable (Z^Y is a set of all functions from Y to Z).*

In object-oriented terminology, the coalgebras just introduced are expressive enough to specify parametric methods and attributes for a database (conjunctive) query answering systems. In what follows , we conceive a peer P_i as a AOT software module characterized by a network ontology G_i expressed in a language $\mathcal{L}_\mathcal{O}$ over an alphabet $\mathcal{A}_{G_i}$. The internal structure of a peer database is hidden to the user, encapsulated in the way that only its logical relational schema $\mathcal{G}_{T_i}$ can be seen by users, and is able to respond to the union of conjunctive queries by *known* answers [9].

- **Example:** Let us consider the following scenario: a Data integration system, encapsulated into an AOT , be a triple [9] $\mathcal{I}_i = (\mathcal{G}_i, \mathcal{S}_i, \mathcal{M}_i)$, where $\mathcal{G}_i = (\mathcal{G}_{T_i}, \Sigma_{T_i})$. The Σ_{T_i} are the integrity constraints, $\mathcal{S}_i$ is a source schema and $\mathcal{M}_i$ is a set of mappings between a global schema $\mathcal{G}_{T_i}$ and a source schema $\mathcal{S}_i$.

  We can enrich the global schema $\mathcal{G}_{T_i}$ by a new unary predicate $Val(\_)$ such that $Val(c)$ is true if $c \in \mathbf{dom}$ is a constant of the local ontology of this peer. User query $q_C(\mathbf{x})$, where $\mathbf{x} = x_1, .., x_k$ is a non empty set of variables, over the global schema is a *conjunctive query*. The AOT module of a peer transforms every original query $q_C(\mathbf{x})$ into a **lifted query** over the global schema, denoted by q, such that $q := q_C(\mathbf{x}) \wedge Val(x_1) \wedge ... \wedge Val(x_k)$.

  The universal (canonical) database $can(\mathcal{I}, \mathcal{D})$, of the encapsulated Data integration system with the source database $\mathcal{D}$, has the interesting property of faithfully representing all legal databases (the construction of the canonical database is similar to the construction of the *restricted chase* of a database described in [30]).

  Thus, theoretically, the lifted query will filter only known answers from $can(\mathcal{I}, \mathcal{D})$. In practice we do not use this canonical database in order to give the answer to the query, and we use a *query rewriting technics under constraints* in data integration systems (for example, a data integration systems with key and inclusion integrity constraints [27]) to submit the rewritten query directly to source databases, extracted by wrappers from World-Wide Web.

P2P Network Definition

In order to be able to share the knowledge with other peer P_j in the network $\mathcal{N}$, each peer P_i has also an export-interface module $\mathcal{M}_{EXP}^{ij}$ composed by groups of ordered pairs of intensionally-equivalent logical views (conjunctive queries over peer's ontologies), denoted by (q_i, q_j), or equivalently, by $q_i \approx q_j$, that is, $K_i q_i(x) \approx_{in} K_j q_j(x)$. Notice that (q_i, q_j) does *not* mean that q_i logically implicates q_j or vice versa, as in *extensional* mapping definitions, based on material implication.

Definition 3. *[8] The P2P network system $\mathcal{N}$ is composed by $2 \leq N$ independent peers, where each peer module P_i is defined as follows: $P_i := \langle \mathcal{O}_i, \bigcup_{i \neq j \in N} \mathcal{M}_{EXP}^{ij} \rangle$, where $\mathcal{M}_{EXP}^{ij}$ is a (possibly empty) interface to other peer P_j in the network, defined as a group of intensionally-equivalent query-connections, denoted by $(q_{1k}^{ij}, q_{2k}^{ij})$ where q_{1k}^{ij} is a conjunctive query defined over $\mathcal{O}_i$, while q_{2k}^{ij} is a conjunctive query defined over the ontology $\mathcal{O}_j$ of the connected peer P_j :*

$$\mathcal{M}_{EXP}^{ij} = \{(q_{1k}^{ij}, q_{2k}^{ij}) \mid 1 \leq k \leq \mid ij \mid\},$$

and $\mid ij \mid$ is the total number of query-connections of the peer P_i toward a peer P_j.

Intuitively, when an user defines a conjunctive query over the ontology $\mathcal{O}_i$ of the peer P_i, the intensionally equivalent concepts between this peer and other peers will be used in order to obtain the answers from a P2P system.

They will be the "bridge" which a query agent can use to rewrite the original user query over a peer P_i into *intensionally-equivalent* query over other peer P_j which has different (and independent) ontology from the peer P_i.

The answers of other peers will be epistemically considered as *possible* answers because they are based on the *belief* which has the peer P_i about the knowledge of a peer P_j: this belief is formally represented by the supposition of a peer P_i that the pair of queries $(q_{1k}^{ij}, q_{2k}^{ij}) \in \mathcal{M}_{EXP}^{ij}$ is intensionally-equivalent.

Example: Let us consider the acyclic P2P system in a Fig.1, with a peers: P_i, with the ontology $\mathcal{O}_i$ and the interface $\mathcal{M}_{EXP}^{ij} = \{(v_{im}, v_{jm}) \mid v_{im} \approx v_{jm}, and$ $1 \leq m \leq k\}$ toward the peer P_j, and the peer P_j, with the ontology $\mathcal{O}_j$. We denote by $v_{im} \approx v_{jm}$ the intensional equivalence . The idea is the following: given a query $q_i(\mathbf{x})$ over a peer P_i, a query agent will rewrite (if it is possible) the *identical* query $\Psi(v_{i1}, ..., v_{ik})$ over the set of views $\{v_{i1}, ..., v_{ik}\}$ of a peer P_i, then it will use the set of intensional equivalences $v_{im} \approx v_{jm}, 1 \leq m \leq k$, to obtain the *intensionally equivalent* query $\Psi(v_{j1}, ..., v_{jk})$ over the set of views $\{v_{j1}, ..., v_{jk}\}$ of a peer P_j, and than it will rewrite this query into the *identical* query $q_j(\mathbf{x})$ over the ontology $\mathcal{O}_j$ of the peer P_j. The *known answers* of both peers P_i, P_j to the queries $q_i(\mathbf{x})$ and $q_j(\mathbf{x})$ will constitute the subset of the global P2P answer to the original user query; other possible answers to the same user query can be obtained

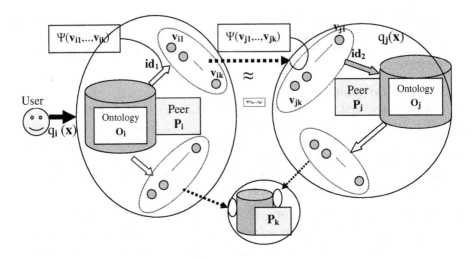

Fig. 1. P2P query answering

by the similar method from the intensionally equivalent queries over a peer P_k obtained from intensional mappings from P_i to P_k and from P_j to P_k respectively.

4   Query Answering with Intensional P2P Mappings

The intensional mapping between peers is given by couples of equivalent queries $(q_i(x), q_j(x))$, denoted by $q_i(x) \approx q_j(x)$, where a conjunctive query $q_i(x)$ over a peer P_i and a conjunctive query $q_j(x)$ over a peer P_j are intensionally equivalent, w.r.t. the *known* answers from peers, that is, $K_i q_i(x) \approx_{in} K_j q_j(x)$. Notice that for any given world w, both relationships
$[K_i q_i(x)]_{in}^{\mathcal{M}, g}(w) \subseteq [K_j q_j(x)]_{in}^{\mathcal{M}, g}(w)$, and $[K_j q_j(x)]_{in}^{\mathcal{M}, g}(w) \subseteq [K_i q_i(x)]_{in}^{\mathcal{M}, g}(w)$
need not to be satisfied. Moreover, if $\triangle_i$ and $\triangle_j$ are local universes for a peer P_i and P_j respectively (a local universe is the set of all the values that are elements of the domains used in the local schema of a peer), we do not require that for any $c \in \triangle_i \bigcap \triangle_j$, the sentences $K_i q_i(c)$ and $K_j q_j(c)$ have the same truth value as required in [15].

Proposition 1. *Let us consider the class of peers with the integrity constraints which does not contain negative clauses of the form* $\neg A_1 \vee \ldots \vee \neg A_m$, $m \geq 2$. *Then, the intensional equivalence is preserved by conjunction logic operation, that is,*
if $\varphi \equiv (b_1 \wedge \ldots \wedge b_k)$, $k \geq 1$, *and* $b_i \approx_{in} c_i$, $1 \leq i \leq k$, *then* $\varphi \approx_{in} \psi$
where $\equiv$ *is a logic equivalence and* $\psi \equiv (c_1 \wedge \ldots \wedge c_k)$.

Proof: By structural induction on the number of conjuncts in the expression: it is enough to prove for expression of two conjuncts. Let b_1 be $q_{i1}(x, y)$ and b_2 be $q_{i2}(y, z)$ any two (virtual) predicates over a peer P_i, and to them intensionally equivalent, c_1, c_2, (virtual) predicates $q_{j1}(x, y)$ and $q_{j2}(y, z)$ over a peer P_j.
We have to prove that $lub^{\mathcal{M}, g}(\varphi(x, z)) = lub^{\mathcal{M}, g}(\psi(x, z))$, where
$\varphi(x, z) \equiv K_i(q_{i1}(x, y) \wedge q_{i2}(y, z))$ and $\psi(x, z) \equiv K_j(q_{j1}(x, y) \wedge q_{j2}(y, z))$.

From the facts that $q_{i1}(x,y) \approx_H q_{j1}(x,y)$ and $q_{i2}(y,z) \approx_H q_{j2}(y,z)$, we define the set
$$S_L = \{(a,c) \mid \exists b.((a,b) \in lub^{\mathcal{M},g}(K_iq_{i1}(x,y)) \wedge (b,c) \in lub^{\mathcal{M},g}(K_iq_{i2}(y,z)))\} = \{(a,c) \mid \exists b.((a,b) \in lub^{\mathcal{M},g}(K_jq_{j1}(x,y)) \wedge (b,c) \in lub^{\mathcal{M},g}(K_jq_{j2}(y,z)))\}.$$

Let us prove that
$$lub^{\mathcal{M},g}(\varphi(x,z)) = \bigcup_{w \in \mathcal{W}}\{(a,c) \mid \exists b.((a,b) \in [K_iq_{i1}(x,y)]_{in}^{\mathcal{M},g}(w) \wedge (b,c) \in [K_iq_{i2}(x,y)]_{in}^{\mathcal{M},g}(w))\} \text{ is equal to } S_L.$$

First, from $[K_iq_{i2}(x,y)]_{in}^{\mathcal{M},g}(w) \subseteq lub^{\mathcal{M},g}(K_iq_{i1}(x,y)$ holds that $lub^{\mathcal{M},g}(\varphi(x,z)) \subseteq S_L$. Let us prove, that also $lub^{\mathcal{M},g}(\varphi(x,z)) \supseteq S_L$, i.e. that for any $(a,b) \in S_L$ also $(a,b) \in lub^{\mathcal{M},g}(\varphi(x,z))$.

Let us suppose that there is one (a,c) such that $(a,c) \in S_L$ but $(a,c) \notin lub^{\mathcal{M},g}(\varphi(x,z))$, i.e., that for all possible worlds for this P2P system, $w \in \mathcal{W}$, holds that
$$\pi_2([x = a \wedge K_iq_{i1}(x,y)]_{in}^{\mathcal{M},g}(w)) \cap \pi_1([z = c \wedge K_iq_{i2}(y,z)]_{in}^{\mathcal{M},g}(w)) = \{\}$$
(is empty), where π_1, π_2 are the first and the second projections. That is, the following logic formula must hold $\neg K_iq_{i1}(a,y) \vee \neg K_iq_{i2}(y',c) \vee \neg(y = y')$,
(which is equivalent to the formula $\neg K_i(q_{i1}(a,y) \wedge q_{i2}(y',c) \wedge y = y')$, from the fact that in a modal logic $K_i(A \wedge B)$ is logically equivalent to $K_iA \wedge K_iB$ and that for built-in predicates (as '=') holds that K_iA is logically equivalent to A).

But such constraint (negative clause) cannot exist in this class of peers, thus the supposition is false, and we conclude that $S_L = lub^{\mathcal{M},g}(\varphi(x,z))$.

By the same way we obtain that $S_L = lub^{\mathcal{M},g}(\psi(x,z))$, thus $\varphi(x,z) \approx_{in} \psi(x,z)$.

$\square$

This proposition is very important in order to be able to define the semantics for conjunctive-query answering in P2P database systems.

For example, all currently used integrity constraints (as the key and the foreign key constraints) in a global schema are valid integrity constraints in order to use also intensional semantics for the mapping between peer databases.

There is a number of different *context-dependent* scenarios for a query-answering with intensional semantics, as in human society: for example, the *confidential* scenario where an interviewer can interview a single person at time (we will denominate it as a *pure* P2P context), or a *conference* scenario where an interviewer can interact with a number of persons at time and possibly integrate partial knowledge of them in order to obtain the answer.

Let us consider the simplest scenario: the *pure* P2P context. Informally, given a conjunctive query $\varphi(x)$ over a peer P_i, the answer to this query of the whole P2P system, w.r.t. *intensional semantics* is the union of known answers from this peer, and (known) answers of all other peers which have intensionally equivalent to $\varphi(x)$ virtual predicates. That corresponds to the query-answering paradigm in a society of individuals: given a question $\varphi(x)$ to some person P_i, and its beliefs about the knowledge of other persons in this society, the interviewer can obtain the answer from P_i and from other persons who know something about the same concept $\varphi(x)$. In the real-world environment, the answer of other persons (in different languages) can be considered certain also, but in the virtual P2P database framework their answer is mediated by the belief of the P_i w.r.t. the knowledge of other peers, which may be imperfect, so the answers of other peers are epistemically different, i.e., they can be epistemically considered as *possible* answers.

4.1   Context-Dependent Query Answering

Let us consider now the semantics of this intensional mapping between a given peer P_i and other peers $P_{j_k}, 1 \leq k \leq N, j_k \neq i$, based on their intensionally equivalent views. Let us denote such a view by a conjunctive query $q_{i_1}(x)$ over peer P_i and, intensionally-equivalent to it, the views (conjunctive queries) $q_{j_k}(x)$ over other peers, so that $K_i q_{i_1}(x) \approx_{in} K_{j_1} q_{j_1}(x) \approx_{in} .. \approx_{in} K_{j_N} q_{j_N}(x)$, where K_i, K_{j_k} are local epistemic modal operators of the peers, such that the set $[K_i q_{i_1}(x)]_{in}^{\mathcal{M},g}(w)$ is the set of *known* answers of a peer P_i to the conjunctive query $q_{i_1}(x)$.

Definition 4. *The P2P network system $\mathcal{N}$ is composed by $2 \leq N$ independent peers. Each peer is defined by*

$P_i := \langle \mathcal{I}_i, \bigcup_{i \neq j \in N} \mathcal{M}_{EXP}^{ij} \rangle$, *where $\mathcal{I}_i$ is the encapsulated Data Integration System. $\mathcal{M}_{EXP}^{ij}$ is a (possibly empty) interface to other peer P_j in the network, defined by $\mathcal{M}_{EXP}^{ij} = \{(q_{1k}^{ij}, q_{2k}^{ij}) \mid q_{1k}^{ij} \approx q_{2k}^{ij}, \text{ and } 1 \leq k \leq \mid ij \mid\}$, where q_{1k}^{ij} and q_{2k}^{ij} are the conjunctive queries over the global schema of P_i and P_j, respectively; $\mid ij \mid$ denotes the total number of query-connections from P_i to P_j.*

Let, for any conjunctive query $q_{i_1}(x)$ over a peer P_i, the set of intensionally-equivalent concepts be

$$Q(q_{i_1}(x)) = \{K_{j_1} q_{j_1}(x), .., K_{j_N} q_{j_N}(x)\}.$$

We can introduce a peer-context, *$\mathcal{C}(P_i)$, for any given set of* contextual views *of a peer P_i, $\mathcal{V}(P_i) = \{q_{i_1}(x_1), ..., q_{i_M}(x_M)\}$, by the following set*

$$\mathcal{C}(P_i) = \{ (K_i q_{i_l}(x_l), Q(q_{i_l}(x_l))) \mid q_{i_l}(x_l) \in \mathcal{V}(P_i)\}.$$

The context of a peer P_i represents the whole information contribution of other peers to the local knowledge of this peer, and, consequently, can be used during the query-answering: given a conjunctive query $\varphi(y)$ over a peer P_i in a world w, first, we compute the set of *known* answers $[K_i \varphi(x)]_{in}^{\mathcal{M},g}(w)$, and after that also the set of *intensionally-possible answers* obtained from the information contribution from other peers, i.e., from the context $\mathcal{C}(P_i)$ of the considered peer: thus, the answer to a query over a peer is *context-dependent*. By changing the context of a peer we will obtain different set of possible answers: the interface module of a peer is the syntax of a specification for such context. Obviously, the aim of query-answering is to obtain the maximal set of answers for a given context of one peer.

There are two modalities in order to obtain intensionally-possible answers:

- *pure* P2P query answering: the query-agent has to try to completely reformulate the original query $\varphi(y)$ (over a peer P_i) for any peer P_j which has some view in the interface module of P_i. If it is possible then a peer P_j will be able to respond with possible answers. In this case we define the context as follows:
  $\mathcal{C}(P_i) = \{ (K_i q_{i_l}(x_l), K_j q_{j_l}(x_l)) \mid (q_{i_l}(x_l), q_{j_l}(x_l)) \in \mathcal{M}_{EXP}^{ij}\}$
- *Data integration* P2P query answering: we can consider partial answers from all contextual peers of a given peer P_i, defined in its interface module. The query

agent will assemble (join) the partial answers from them in order to obtain possible answers.In this case we define the context as follows:

$$\mathcal{C}(P_i) = \{\ (K_i q_{i_l}(x_l), \{\ K_j q_{j_l}(x_l)) \mid (q_{i_l}(x_l), q_{j_l}(x_l)) \in \mathcal{R}\}) \mid q_{i_l}(x_l) \in \pi_1(\mathcal{R})\}$$

where $\mathcal{R} = \bigcup_{1 \leq j \leq N} \mathcal{M}_{EXP}^{ij}$, and π_1 is the first projection.

In [8] is presented an answering algorithm for the pure P2P scenario. We define the set of contextual views as follows: $\mathcal{V}(P_i) = \{\ q_{i_l}(x_l) \mid K_i q_{i_l}(x_l) \in \pi_1(\mathcal{C}(P_i))\}$.

Definition 5. *Let $\phi(y)$ be a conjunctive query over a peer P_i in a world w, and $\varphi(y) = \mathcal{F}_{rew}(\mathcal{C}(P_i), \phi(y))$ be its complete (otherwise $\varphi(y)$ is empty formula) rewriting over the set of contextual views $\mathcal{V}(P_i)$, with the body $body(\varphi)$ a sequence $b_1, b_2, ..., b_m$, where each $b_j \in \mathcal{V}(P_i)$ is a contextual view of P_i.*

(the function $\mathcal{F}_{rew}$ is taken from [31], where the extension of $\phi(y)$ does not need necessarily to be contained in the extension of the set of views in $\mathcal{V}(P_i)$).

Than, for any set of intensional equivalences $b_i \approx c_i$, from the context of P_i, the answer to the query $\psi(x)$, obtained from $\phi(x)$ by substitution of b_k with c_k ($1 \leq k \leq m$), is called "the set of intensionally-possible answers for a query $\varphi(y)$ over a peer P_i in a world w".

(from Prop.1 we have that $\varphi(y)$ and $\psi(x)$ are intensionally equivalent).

Let us consider now the problem of how to obtain such possible answers from a network of peer databases: as first step we will define the kind of semantic mappings between one peer P_i and the information contribution of other peers to the local knowledge of this peer, by the usual first-order semantic modelling.

Definition 6. *(**Global semantics**) Let $\mathcal{N}$ be a P2P system with $\Delta = \biguplus_{P_i \in \mathcal{N}} \Delta_i$, where each Δ_i is a non empty set of constants of a peer P_i and '$\biguplus$' is the disjoint union operation. An interpretation of $\mathcal{N}$ over Δ is a $N - tuple$ $m = <m_1, m_2, ..., m_N>$ where each m_i is a classical first-order logic interpretation of the data-integration system $\mathcal{I}_i$ of a peer P_i on the local domain Δ_i.*

Let m_i denote the ith element of m. A (global) model M for $\mathcal{N}$, written $M \vDash_{global} \mathcal{N}$, is a non empty set of interpretations such that the model locally satisfies the conditions of each database integration system $\mathcal{I}_i$ of a peer P_i, i.e., $\forall m \in M.(m_i \vDash \mathcal{I}_i)$.

Now we can define a query answer in this global semantics for P2P system.

Definition 7. *(**Query answer**) Let $\phi(y)$ be a local query over a peer P_i with free variables $y = \{y_1, ..y_n\}$. The answer to ϕ is the union of:*

- known *answer from P_i, obtained as the set of substitutions of x with local constants $c \in \Delta_i$ of a peer P_i, such that any model M of $\mathcal{N}$ satisfies the query $\phi(y)$, i.e.,*
  $\{\{c_1, .., c_n\} \in \Delta_i^n \mid \forall M.(M \vDash_{global} \mathcal{N} \rightarrow \forall m \in M.(m_i \vDash \phi(c_1, .., c_n)))\}$,
  that is, locally to the set of known answers of a peer P_i
  $\{\{c_1, .., c_n\} \in \Delta_i^n \mid \forall m' \in \bigcup_{m \in M, M \vDash_{global} \mathcal{N}} m_i.(m' \vDash \phi(c_1, .., c_n))\}$.
- *1. In a pure scenario: possible answers from each peer $P_j, j \neq i$, such that $\psi(y) \approx \mathcal{F}_{rew}(\mathcal{C}(P_i), \phi(y)) \neq \{\}$, obtained as the set of substitutions of $y = \{y_1, ..y_n\}$ with local constants $\boldsymbol{d} = \{d_1, .., d_n\} \in \Delta_j^n$ of a peer P_j, such that any model M of $\mathcal{N}$ satisfies the query $\psi(y)$, i.e., $\{\boldsymbol{d} \mid \forall M.(M \vDash_{global} \mathcal{N} \rightarrow \forall m \in M.(m_j \vDash \psi(\boldsymbol{d})))\}$, that is, locally to the set of known answers of a peer P_j $\{\boldsymbol{d} \mid \forall m' \in \bigcup_{m \in M, M \vDash_{global} \mathcal{N}} m_j.(m' \vDash \psi(\boldsymbol{d}))\}$.*

- 2. *In a data-integration scenario:* possible *answers from other peers, to the query $\psi(y)$ which is intensionally equivalent to the expression $\mathcal{F}_{rew}(\mathcal{C}(P_i), \phi(y)) \neq \{\}$, obtained as the set of substitutions of $y = \{y_1, ..y_n\}$ with constants $\boldsymbol{d} = \{d_1, .., d_n\} \in \Delta^n$, such that any model M of $\mathcal{N}$ satisfies the query $\psi(y)$, i.e., $\{\boldsymbol{d} \in \Delta^n \mid \forall M.(M \vDash_{global} \mathcal{N} \rightarrow \forall m \in M.(m \vDash \psi(\boldsymbol{d})))\}$.*

Thus, in the case of an intensional-mapping semantics, the query answer to a given query $\phi(y)$ over a peer P_i is the union of answers to the set of all intensionally equivalent queries to $\phi(y)$, determined by peer-to-peer interfaces, with the epistemic distinction from the certain answer of the interrogated peer P_i and the possible answers of other peers. This epistemic distinction comes from the fact that, when we design the P2P intensional mappings and put the intensional equivalence $q_{1k}^{ij} \approx q_{2k}^{ij}$ of these two views, of P_i and P_j respectively, we do not know if actually $lub^{\mathcal{M},g}(K_i q_{1k}^{ij}) = lub^{\mathcal{M},g}(K_j q_{2k}^{ij})$, but we only *believe* that it has to be true. So that, while the answer of the interrogated peer to a query defined over its proper ontology (global schema) is semantically certain answer, the answer of other peers to the intensionally-equivalent query, obtained by the given P2P mappings, theoretically may be inadequate, that is, the *possible* (or plausible) answers.

5   Conclusion

We have presented a formal framework for representing interschema knowledge in Peer-to-peer database systems based on intensional equivalence between concepts of autoepistemic database peers. Such interschema mappings is not invasive w.r.t. the local epistemic knowledge of any single peer: each database-peer knows only its local extension of proper knowledge and is completely free to change its local knowledge. It does not import the extensional knowledge from other peer-databases of a P2P information system, but specify only which part of its own knowledge has the same meaning as correspondent knowledge of other actors.

For any given conjunctive query (virtual concept) submitted to some database peer, the query-agent obtains as answer the set of certain (known) answers from this interrogated peer, and the set of possible answers from other peers which are able to define the intensionally equivalent virtual concepts to the original user query. This query answering is *context sensitive*, and can be modeled in different context scenarios for P2P systems. We believe that the intensional mapping semantics presented in this paper constitutes a sound basis for studying the various issues related to interschema knowledge representation and reasoning, especially for P2P database systems in Web environment, where the peers can be considered as complex database agents.

References

1. M.Ushold, "Where is the semantics in the semantic web," *In Workshop on Ontologies in Agent Systems (OAS) at the 5th International Conference on Autonomous Agents*, 2001.
2. S.Gribble, A.Halevy, Z.Ives, M.Rodrig, and D.Suciu, "What can databases do for Peer-to-Peer?," *WebDB Workshop on Databases and the Web*, 2001.

3. L.Serafini, F.Giunchiglia, J.Mylopoulos, and P.A.Bernstein, "The local relational model: Model and proof theory," *Technical Report 0112-23, ITC-IRST*, 2001.

4. C.Ghidini and F.Giunchiglia, "Local models semantics or contextual reasoning = locality + compatibility," *Artificial Intelligence*, vol. 127, pp. 221–259, 2001.

5. Raymond Reiter, "Towards a logical reconstruction of relational database theory," in *On Conceptual Modeling: Perspectives from Artificial Intelligence Databases and Programming Languages*, M. L. Brodie, J. Mylopoulos, and J. W. Schmidt, Eds. Springer, 1984.

6. E.Franconi, G.Kuper, A.Lopatenko, and L.Serafini, "A robust logical and computational characterization of Peer-to-Peer data systems," *Technical Report DIT-03-051, University of Trento, Italy, September*, 2003.

7. D.Calvanese, G. De Giacomo, M.Lenzerini, and R.Rosati, "Logical foundations of Peer-to-Peer data integration," *PODS 2004, June 14-16, Paris, France*, 2004.

8. Z.Majkić, "Weakly-coupled ontology integration of P2P database systems," *1st Int. Workshop on Peer-to-Peer Knowledge Management (P2PKM), August 22, Boston, USA*, 2004.

9. Maurizio Lenzerini, "Data integration: A theoretical perspective.," in *Proc. of the 21st ACM SIGACT SIGMOD SIGART Symp. on Principles of Database Systems (PODS 2002)*, 2002, pp. 233–246.

10. M.Lenzerini and Z. Majkić, "General framework for query reformulation," *Semantic Webs and Agents in Integrated Economies, D3.1, IST-2001-34825, February,*, 2003.

11. D.Calvanese, E.Damaggio, G. De Giacomo, M.Lenzerini, and R.Rosati, "Semantic data integration in P2P systems," *Proc. of the Int. Workshop On Databases, Inf.Systems and P2P Computing, Berlin, Germany, September*, 2003.

12. D.Calvanese, G.De Giacomo, D.Lembo, M.Lenzerini, and R.Rosati, "Inconsistency tollerance in P2P data integration: an epistemic approach," *In Proc. 10th Int. Workshop on Database Programming Language*, 2005.

13. Z.Majkić, "Weakly-coupled P2P system with a network repository," *6th Workshop on Distributed Data and Structures (WDAS'04), July 5-7, Lausanne, Switzerland*, 2004.

14. Z.Majkić, "Massive parallelism for query answering in weakly integrated P2P systems," *Workshop GLOBE 04, August 30-September 3,Zaragoza, Spain*, 2004.

15. Tiziana Catarci and Maurizio Lenzerini, "Representing and using interschema knowledge in cooperative information systems," *J. of Intelligent and Cooperative Information Systems*, vol. 2, no. 4, pp. 375–398, 1993.

16. Z. Majkić, "Intensional logic and epistemic independency of intelligent database agents," *2nd International Workshop on Philosophy and Informatics (WSPI 2005), April 10-13, Kaiserslautern, Germany*, 2005.

17. Marcelo Arenas, Leopoldo E. Bertossi, and Jan Chomicki, "Consistent query answers in inconsistent databases," in *Proc. of the 18th ACM SIGACT SIGMOD SIGART Symp. on Principles of Database Systems (PODS'99)*, 1999, pp. 68–79.

18. Gianluigi Greco, Sergio Greco, and Ester Zumpano, "A logic programming approach to the integration, repairing and querying of inconsistent databases," in *Proc. of the 17th Int. Conf. on Logic Programming (ICLP'01)*. 2001, vol. 2237 of *Lecture Notes in Artificial Intelligence*, pp. 348–364, Springer.

19. Z.Majkić, "Autoepistemic logic programming for reasoning with inconsistency," *International Symposium on Logic-based Program Synthesis and Transformation (LOPSTR), September 7-9, 2005, Imperial College, London,UK*, 2005.

20. R.Montague, "Universal grammar," *Theoria*, vol. 36, pp. 373–398, 1970.

21. R.Montague, "The proper treatment of quantification in ordinary English," *Approaches to Natural Language, in J.Hintikka et al.(editors), Reidel, Dordrecht*, pp. 221–242, 1973.

22. R.Montague, "Formal philosophy. selected papers of Richard Montague," *in R.Thomason (editor), Yale University Press, New Haven, London*, pp. 108–221, 1974.

23. D.Davidson, "Truth and meaning," *Philosophical Logic, Reidel, Dodrecht*, 1969.
24. T.Berners-Lee, J.Hendlar, and O.Lassila, "The semantic web," *Scientific American*, vol. 279, 2001.
25. Dieter Fensel, *Ontologies: A Silver Bullet for Knowledge Management and Electronic Commerce*, Springer, 2001.
26. M.Lenzerini and Z. Majkić, "First release of the system prototype for query management," *Semantic Webs and Agents in Integrated Economies, D3.3, IST-2001-34825*, 2003.
27. A.Calì, D.Calvanese, G.De Giacomo, and M.Lenzerini, "Data integration under integrity constraints," in *Proc. of the 14th Conf. on Advanced Information Systems Engineering (CAiSE 2002)*, 2002, pp. 262–279.
28. R.Fagin, P.G.Kolaitis, R.J.Miller, and L.Popa, "DATA Exchange: Semantics and query answering," in *Proc. of the 9th Int. Conf. on Database Theory (ICDT 2003)*, 2003.
29. Raymond Reiter, "What should a database know?," *J. of Logic Programming*, vol. 14, pp. 127–153, 1990.
30. David S. Johnson and Anthony C. Klug, "Testing containment of conjunctive queries under functional and inclusion dependencies," *J. of Computer and System Sciences*, vol. 28, no. 1, pp. 167–189, 1984.
31. A.Levy, A.Mendelzon, and Y.Sagiv, "Answering queries using views," *Proc. 14th ACM Symp. on Principles of Database Systems*, pp. 95–104, 1995.

Integrating and Exchanging XML Data Using Ontologies*

Huiyong Xiao and Isabel F. Cruz

Department of Computer Science
University of Illinois at Chicago
{hxiao, ifc}@cs.uic.edu

Abstract. While providing a uniform syntax and a semistructured data model, XML does not express semantics but only structure such as nesting information. In this paper, we consider the problem of data integration and interoperation of heterogeneous XML sources and use an ontology-based framework to address this problem at a semantic level. Ontologies are extensively used for domain knowledge representation, by virtue of their conceptualization of the domain, which carries explicit semantics. In our approach, the global ontology is expressed in RDF Schema (RDFS) and constructed using the global-as-view approach by merging individual local ontologies, which represent XML source schemas. We provide a formal model for the mappings between XML schemas and local RDFS ontologies and those between local ontologies and the global RDFS ontology. We consider two cases of query processing, specifically for data integration and for data interoperation. In the first case, the user poses an RDF query on the global ontology, which is answered using all the mapped XML sources. In the second case, a query is posed on a single source and then is mapped to the XML sources that are connected to that source. For each case, we discuss the problem of query containment and present an equivalent query rewriting algorithm for queries expressed in two languages: conjunctive RDQL and conjunctive XQuery.

1 Introduction

1.1 Problem Description

Data integration is the problem of combining data residing at different sources, and providing the user with a unified view of these data [25]. It is relevant to a number of applications including data warehousing, enterprise information integration, geographic information systems, and e-commerce applications. Data integration systems are usually characterized by an architecture based on a global schema, which provides a reconciled and integrated view of the underlying sources. These systems are called *central data integration systems*, and a large number of such systems have been proposed [3,5,11,14,24,27,30,34,36].

---

* A preliminary version of this paper was presented at the 8th International Database Engineering & Applications Symposium (Isabel F. Cruz, Huiyong Xiao, Feihong Hsu: An Ontology-Based Framework for XML Semantic Integration. IDEAS 2004: 217-226). This research was partially supported by the National Science Foundation under Awards ITR IIS-0326284 and IIS-0513553.

There are two key issues in central data integration, namely system modeling and query processing. For modeling the relation between the sources and the global schema, two basic approaches have been proposed [10,25,36]. The first approach, called Global-as-View (GaV), expresses the global schema in terms of the data sources. The second approach, called Local-as-View (LaV), requires the global schema to be specified independently from the sources, and the relationships between the global schema and the sources are established by defining every source as a view over the global schema.

Query processing in central data integration may require a query reformulation step: the query over the global schema has to be reformulated in terms of a set of queries over the sources. In the GaV approach, every entity in the global schema is associated with a view over the source local schema, therefore query processing in this case uses a simple "unfolding" strategy [25]. In contrast, query processing in LaV can be complex, since the local sources may contain incomplete information. In this sense, query processing in LaV, called *view-based query processing* [1,12,18], is similar to query answering with incomplete information [37]. It can also be the case that two data sources communicate in a peer-to-peer (P2P) way either through the global schema or directly. Data exchange or query processing may occur in this case, which requires data translation or query rewriting when heterogeneities are present between the communicating sources [16,23,27,30,32].

The heterogeneities between distributed data sources can be classified as *syntactic*, *schematic*, and *semantic* heterogeneities [6]. Syntactic heterogeneity is caused by the use of different models or languages (e.g., relational and XML). Schematic heterogeneity results from the different data organizations (e.g., aggregation or generalization hierarchies). Semantic heterogeneity is caused by different meanings or interpretations of data. All these heterogeneities have to be resolved, to achieve the goal of integration or interoperation. In this paper, we consider the semantic integration of XML data and data exchange between heterogeneous XML sources, using ontologies.

XML documents that represent data with similar semantics may conform to different schemas. Therefore, a user must construct queries in accordance to the different XML document's structures even if to retrieve fragments of information that have the same meaning. This fact makes the formulation of queries over heterogeneous XML sources a nontrivial burden to the user. Furthermore, this shortcoming of XML impedes the interoperation between XML sources since the reformulation of XML queries from one source to another has to eliminate the structural differences of the queries while presenting the same semantics. Let us illustrate this problem using a running example.

Example 1. Figure 1 shows two XML schemas (S_1 and S_2) with their instances (i.e., XML documents D_1 and D_2), which are represented as trees. It is obvious that S_1 and S_2 both represent a many-to-many relationship between two concepts: book and author (equivalently denoted article and writer in S_2). However, structurally speaking, they are different: S_1, which is a book-centric schema, has the author element nested under the book element, whereas S_2, which is an author-centric schema, has the article element nested under the writer element. Suppose our query target is "Find all the authors of the publication b_2." The XML path expressions that are used to define the search patterns in the two schema trees can be respectively written as /books/book[booktitle.text()="b2"]/author/name and /writers/writer[article/title.text()="b2"]/fullname, where the contents in

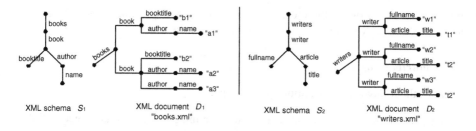

Fig. 1. Two XML sources with structural heterogeneities

the square brackets specify the constraints for the search patterns. We notice that although the above two search patterns refer to semantically equivalent concepts, they follow two distinct XML paths.

1.2 Semantic Integration of XML Documents

The structural diversity of conceptually equivalent XML schemas leads to the fact that XML queries over different schemas may represent the same semantics even though they are formulated using two different alphabets and structures. In comparison, the schema languages used for conceptual modeling are *structurally flat* so that the user can formulate a determined conceptual query without worrying about the structure of the source. RDF Schema (RDFS) [26], DAML+OIL, and OWL are examples of languages used to create ontologies, which represent a shared, formal conceptualization of the domain of knowledge [17]. There are currently many attempts to use conceptual schemas (or ontologies) [3,4,16] or conceptual queries [14,15] to overcome the problem of structural heterogeneities among XML sources.

In this paper, we propose an ontology-based approach for the integration of XML sources. We use the GaV approach to model the mappings between the source schemas and the global ontology, which is, therefore, an integrated view of the source schemas. The global ontology is expressed in terms of RDFS, which is at the core of several ontology languages (e.g., OWL and DAML+OIL). In order to facilitate the mappings between the XML source schemas and the global RDFS ontology, their syntactic disparity needs to be reconciled. To this end, we first transform the heterogeneous XML sources into local RDFS ontologies (defined using the RDFS space [9]), which are then merged into the global ontology. This transformation process encodes the mapping information between each concept in the local ontology and the corresponding element in the XML source. The ontology merging process can be semi-automatically performed (e.g., by using the PROMPT algorithm [29]). In addition to the global ontology, the merging process also produces a *mapping table*, which contains the mapping information between concepts in the global ontology and concepts in the local ontologies. In our approach, we can translate a query posed against the global ontology into subqueries over the sources. We can also translate a query posed against an XML source to an equivalent query against any other XML source. We call the query rewriting in the first case *global-to-local query rewriting* and that in the second case *local-to-local query rewriting*. Given that we choose a GaV approach, the global ontology is a view over the local ontologies, therefore the process of mapping a query over the global ontology to queries over the local ontologies is straightforward.

1.3   Contributions

We make the following contributions in this paper:

- We propose an ontology-based approach to the integration of heterogeneous XML sources. The global ontology takes into account both the XML nesting structure and the domain structure, which are expressed in RDFS, so as to enable semantic interoperation between the XML sources. This integration process is *lossless* with respect to the nesting structure of the XML sources, so that XML structural queries can be correctly rewritten.
- We extend the RDFS space by defining additional metadata, which enables the encoding of the nesting structure of the XML Schema in the RDF schema. We convert each of the XML source schemas into a local RDFS ontology while preserving their structure, so that they share a uniform representation with the global ontology.
- Finally, we refine the concepts of *certain answers* and of *query containment*, in two querying modes: global-to-local query rewriting and local-to-local query rewriting. Furthermore, a query rewriting algorithm that guarantees equivalence is provided for each case of query rewriting.

The paper is organized as follows. Section 2 describes related work. Section 3 describes the framework for the integration of XML sources. Data integration and query processing, which are the two key points in our approach, are discussed respectively in Sections 4 and 5. We draw conclusions and discuss future work in Section 6.

2   Related Work

There are a number of approaches addressing the problem of data integration or interoperation among XML sources. We classify those approaches into three categories, depending on their main focus, namely *semantic integration*, *query languages*, and *query rewriting*.

2.1   Semantic Integration

High-Level Mediator. Amann *et al.* propose an ontology-based approach to the integration of heterogeneous XML Web resources in the C-Web project [3,4]. The proposed approach is very similar to our approach except for the following differences. The first difference is that they use a local-as-view (LaV) approach [10] with a hypothetical global ontology that may be incomplete. The second difference is that they do not retain the XML documents' structures in their conceptual mediator so they cannot deal with the reverse query translation (from the XML sources to the mediator). Our previous work involved a layered approach for the interoperation of heterogeneous web sources, but the nesting structure associated with XML was lost in the mapping from XML data to RDF data [16].

Direct Translation. Klein proposes a procedure to transform XML data directly into RDF data by annotating the XML documents via external RDFS specifications [22]. The procedure makes the data in XML documents available for the Semantic Web. However, since the proposed approach does not consider the document structure of XML sources, it can not propagate queries from one XML source to another XML source.

Semantics Encoding. The Yin/Yang Web approach proposed by Patel-Schneider and Siméon address the problem of incorporating the XML and RDF paradigms [31]. They develop an integrated model for XML and RDF by integrating the semantics and inferencing rules of RDF into XML, so that XML querying can benefit from their RDF *reasoner*. But the Yin/Yang Web approach does not solve the problem of query answering across heterogeneous sources, that is, sources with different syntax or data models. It also cannot process higher-level queries such as RDQL. Lakshmanan and Sadri also propose an infrastructure for interoperating over XML data sources by semantically marking up the information contents of data sources using application-specific common vocabularies [23]. However, the proposed approach relies on the availability of an application-specific standard ontology that serves as the global schema. This global schema contains information necessary for interoperation, such as key and cardinality information for predicates. This approach has the same problem as the Yin/Yang Web approach, that is, higher-level queries can not be processed downward to XML queries.

2.2 Query Languages

CXQuery is a new XML query language proposed by Chen and Revesz, which borrows features from both SQL and other XML query languages [15]. It overcomes the limitations of the XQuery language by allowing the user to define views, explicitly specify the schema of the query answers, and query through multiple XML documents. However, CXQuery does not solve the issue of structural heterogeneities among XML sources. The user has to be familiar with the document structure of each XML source to formulate queries. Heuser *et al.* also present a new language (CXPath) based on *XPath* for querying XML sources at the conceptual level [14]. CXPath is used to write queries over a conceptual schema that abstracts the semantic content of several XML sources. However, they do not consider the situation of query translation from the XML sources to the global conceptual schema.

2.3 Query Rewriting

Query rewriting is often a key issue for both mediator-based integration systems and peer-to-peer systems. The Clio approach, which provides an example for the former case, mainly addresses schema mapping and data transformation between nested schemas and/or relational databases [32]. It focuses on how to take advantage of schema semantics to generate the consistent translations from source to target by considering the constraints and structure of the target schema. It uses queries to express the mappings from the data to the target schema. The Piazza system is a peer-to-peer system that aims to solve the problem of data interoperation between XML and RDF [19]. The system achieves its interoperation in a low-level (syntactic) way, i.e., through the interoperation of XML and the XML serialization of RDF, whereas we aim to achieve the same objective at the semantic level. For example, our approach supports a conceptual view of XML sources (to facilitate the formulation of queries) and allows for conceptual queries (e.g., RDF queries).

3   Framework

In this section, we present the framework for the integration of XML data sources and in particular we describe the integration of XML source schemas and query processing in the integrated system.

As shown in Figure 2, we generate for each local XML source a local RDFS ontology, which represents the source schema. These local RDFS ontologies are then merged into the global RDFS ontology, which provides an overview of all the local ontologies and a mediation between each pair of XML sources. In this merging process, a mapping table is also produced to contain all the mappings, which are correspondences between the global ontology and local ontologies.

The ontology-based XML data integration framework $\mathcal{I}$ can be formalized as a quadruple $\langle \mathcal{G}, \mathcal{S}, \mu, \mathcal{M} \rangle$, where

- $\mathcal{G}$ is the global ontology expressed in RDFS over the alphabet $\mathcal{A_G}$. The alphabet comprises the name of the classes and properties of $\mathcal{G}$.
- $\mathcal{S}$ is the XML source schema expressed in a language $\mathcal{L_S}$ over the alphabet $\mathcal{A_S}$, which comprises the XML element names in $\mathcal{S}$.
- μ is a schema transformation function, which generates a local RDFS ontology $\mathcal{R}$ for $\mathcal{S}$, such that $\mathcal{R}$ encodes the nesting structure specified by $\mathcal{S}$.
- $\mathcal{M}$ is the mapping table consisting of a set of mappings between the global ontology $\mathcal{G}$ and a set of n XML sources $\mathcal{S}_i$, where $i \in [1..n]$. Each entry in $\mathcal{M}$ is of the form $(g, s_1, ..., s_n)$, where $g \in \mathcal{A_G}$ and $s_i \in \mathcal{A}_{\mathcal{S}_i} \cup \{\epsilon\}$ for $i \in [1..n]$. Note that ϵ is used when a source schema has no corresponding elements to an element of $\mathcal{G}$.

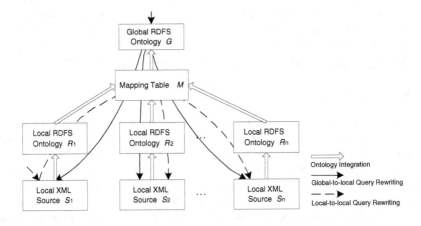

Fig. 2. The ontology-based framework for the integration of XML sources

3.1   Integration of XML Source Schemas

The first task of the framework is the integration of the distributed and heterogeneous XML sources. Here, we are mainly concerned with the issue of schematic heterogeneity, that is, with the different schema structures among the sources. The process of data integration contains two steps: *schema transformation* and *ontology merging*.

In the first step, we use a local RDFS ontology to represent each XML source schema so as to achieve a uniform representation for the next step. In other words, the schema transformation function μ takes as input the source schema S, and the output is the local ontology R. The key operation in this schema transformation is the preservation of the nesting structure of S. To this end, we have to extend the RDFS space since it does not have a property to encode the nesting structure between elements. In particular, we add a new RDF property, `contained`, in the namespace of "http://www.example.org/rdf-extension" (abbreviated as `rdfx`), The RDF/XML syntax for this property is described below.

```
<rdf:RDF
   xmlns:rdf="http://www.w3.org/1999/02/22-rdf-syntax-ns#"
   xmlns:rdfs="http://www.w3.org/2000/01/rdf-schema#"
   xmlns:rdfx="http://www.example.org/rdf-extension#">
<rdf:Property rdf:about=
        "http://www.example.org/rdf-extension#contained">
   <rdfs:isDefinedBy rdf:resource=
        "http://www.example.org/rdf-extension#"/>
   <rdfs:label>contained</rdfs:label>
   <rdfs:comment> The containment between two classes.
   </rdfs:comment>
   <rdfs:range rdf:resource=
        "http://www.w3.org/2000/01/rdf-schema#Class"/>
   <rdfs:domain rdf:resource=
        "http://www.w3.org/2000/01/rdf-schema#Class"/>
</rdf:Property>
```

The second step is the merging (or integration) of all local ontologies, which generates the global ontology as well as the mapping table. The merging is performed based on the semantics of classes and properties from each of the local ontologies. In particular, the classes or properties that have similar or same (equivalent) semantics are merged into a class or a property of the global ontology. Then, each of these correspondences are recorded as an entry in the mapping table. Different kinds of mappings can be established between two schemas or ontologies [38]. For this paper, however, we consider only the *equivalence* type of mapping. We also do not consider the different degrees to which two concepts may be equivalent. For instance, we simply take `book` and `article` as equivalent concepts, although we could further refine such equivalence. Additional domain-related knowledge (e.g., inheritance) may be considered. We discuss these issues in more detail in Section 4.

It is worth mentioning that the global ontology in our system has two roles: (1) It provides the user with access to the data with a uniform query interface to facilitate the formulation of a query on all the XML sources; (2) It serves as the mediation mechanism for accessing the distributed data through any of the XML sources.

3.2 Query Processing

Our framework handles user queries using a query rewriting strategy. More specifically, query processing in our framework may occur in the following two directions, as shown in Figure 2:

Global-to-Local Query Rewriting. When the user poses a query q on the global ontology, the system rewrites q into the union q' of subqueries, one for each XML source. The subqueries are then executed over the XML sources to get the answers, which are then integrated (by using union) to produce the answer to q.

Local-to-Local Query Rewriting. Given a query q posed on a local source, its answers then include not only those retrieved from the local source, but also those from all the other sources in the system. For the purpose of getting answers from the other sources, it requires that q be rewritten (through the global ontology) into a union q' of queries, one on each of the other sources. Query rewriting in this direction is performed similarly to that in peer-to-peer systems [33].

Query rewriting in both directions is based on the mapping information contained in the mapping table. Each entry contains a element (RDF class or property) of the global ontology and its corresponding elements in the local source schemas. Given that query rewriting is from a query over one alphabet to that over another alphabet, the mapping table provides a convenient way to finding the mapping between alphabets, in both rewriting directions. In addition, the query languages used to formulate the queries have to be taken into consideration, since they may have different expressiveness. We consider a subset of XQuery [7], called *conjunctive XQuery* (*c-XQuery*), for queries over the XML sources and a subset of RDQL [20], namely *conjunctive RDQL* (*c-RDQL*), for queries over the global RDFS ontology. We discuss in detail query processing and related issues in Section 5.

4   Integrating Structure and Semantics

4.1 Local XML Schemas and Local RDFS Ontologies

To integrate heterogeneous XML data sources, we first transform the local XML schema into a local RDFS ontology while preserving the XML document structure. By *document structure*, we mean the structural relationship of objects specified in *data-centric* documents [8] by a schema language (such as DTD, XML Schema, or RelaxNG[1]). In this paper, we only focus on the nesting structure (i.e., hierarchy). Other structural properties include order. A consequence of not including order in our framework is that we cannot consider a query that involves the order of the subelements of an element. However, this kind of query is of little interest in a framework where we are mostly concerned with the semantics of the data.

---

[1] http://relaxng.sourceforge.net

Elements and attributes are the two basic building blocks of XML documents. Elements can be defined as *simple types*, which cannot have element content and cannot carry attributes, or *complex types*, which allow elements in their content and/or contain attributes. On the other hand, all attribute declarations must reference simple types since attributes cannot contain other elements or other attributes. From the perspective of XML Schema, these nesting relationships are defined in terms of *datatypes* (simple or complex). An XML schema can be formalized as an edge-labeled tree, namely an *XML schema tree*, as depicted in Figure 1. We overlook the distinction between XML elements and attributes by considering both of them as vertices in the XML schema tree.

Definition 1. *An XML schema S over alphabet $\mathcal{A}_S$ is an edge-labeled tree $S = (V, E, \lambda)$, where V is a set of vertices, $E = \{(v_i, v_j)|v_i, v_j \in V\}$ is a set of edges, and λ is a labeling function $\lambda : E \mapsto \mathcal{A}_S$.*

Before we discuss schema transformation, let us look at the formalization of ontologies. Both the global ontology and local ontologies are actually RDF schemas defined in the RDFS space, which is extended with the RDF property "rdfx:contained". An RDF schema can be formalized as a labeled graph, called *RDF schema graph*, as defined in Definition 2. We do not elaborate on the data types of RDF properties and assume that they are all of type *literal*. Also, we do not take into account the notion of namespace in the definition of both XML and RDF schemas.

Definition 2. *An RDF schema graph $\mathcal{R}$ over alphabet $\mathcal{A}_\mathcal{R}$ is a directed labeled graph $\mathcal{R} = (V, E, \lambda)$, where V is a set of labeled vertices consisting of classes C, properties P, and data types L, $E = \{(v_i, v_j)|v_i, v_j \in V\}$ is a set of labeled edges, and λ is a labeling function $\lambda : V \cup E \mapsto \mathcal{A}_\mathcal{R}$, such that*

- *$\forall v \in P$, we have $domain(v) \in C$, $range(v) \in C \cup L$, and $\lambda((v, domain(v))) = $ "rdfs:domain" and $\lambda((v, range(v))) = $ "rdfs:range";*
- *$\forall e = (v_i, v_j) \in E$, we have $\lambda(e) = $ "rdfs:subClassOf" (or "rdfx:contained") if v_i and $v_j \in C$, or $\lambda(e) = $ "rdfs:subPropertyOf" if v_i and $v_j \in P$.*

Now we are able to define the schema transformation function μ. Formally speaking, the *schema transformation function* μ is a function $\mu : S \mapsto \mathcal{R}$, where $S = (V_S, E_S, \lambda_S)$, $\mathcal{R} = (V_\mathcal{R}, E_\mathcal{R}, \lambda_\mathcal{R})$, and $V_\mathcal{R} = C \cup P$, such that $\forall e_{ij} = (v_i, v_j) \in E_S$, we have $\mu(v_j) \in V_\mathcal{R}$, $\lambda_\mathcal{R}(\mu(v_j)) = \lambda_S(e_{ij})$, and furthermore:

(1) if $\exists(v_j, v_k) \in E_S$, then $\mu(v_j) \in C$, $(\mu(v_j), \mu(v_i)) \in E_\mathcal{R}$, and $\lambda_\mathcal{R}(\mu(v_j), \mu(v_i)) = $ "rdfx:contained";
(2) if $\nexists(v_j, v_k) \in E_S$, then $\mu(v_j) \in P$, $(\mu(v_j), \mu(v_i)) \in E_\mathcal{R}$, and $\lambda_\mathcal{R}(\mu(v_j), \mu(v_i)) = $ "rdfs:domain".

The transformations thus defined fall into two categories:

Element-Level Transformation. The element-level transformation converts from XML complex-type elements to RDF classes and from XML simple-type elements to properties. For example, for S_1 in Example 1, we define the RDF classes Books, Book, and Author, while taking booktitle and name as RDF properties of Book and Author, respectively, as depicted in the resulting local RDFS ontology of Figure 3.

Structure-Level Transformation. The structure-level transformation encodes the nesting structure of the XML schema into the local RDFS ontology. In particular, the nesting may occur between two complex-type elements or between a complex-type element and its child (simple) element. Following the element-level transformation, the nesting structure in the former case corresponds to a *class-to-class* relationship between two RDFS classes, which are connected by the property rdfx:contained, The first item that defines μ formalizes this case. In the latter case, the XML nesting structure corresponds to the *class-to-literal* relationship in the local ontology, with the class and the literal connected by the corresponding property. The second item that defines μ formalizes this case.

By applying the schema transformation function to the two XML schemas in Figure 1, we can get the resulting local ontologies as shown in Figure 3. We see that rdfx:contained enables the representation of the nesting relationship. Specifically, by following the edges of rdfx:contained from Books to Author in $\mathcal{R}_1$, we actually get the corresponding path /books/book/author in $\mathcal{S}_1$. In terms of the alphabets, the schema transformation function specifies a mapping between the alphabet of the source schema and that of the local ontology. Table 1 lists the mapping between the XML schema $\mathcal{S}_1$ and the local RDFS ontology $\mathcal{R}_1$. For simplicity, we use XPath to specify the XML elements. Also, the properties in the mapping table are in the form of an RDF expression $c.p$, where c is the class associated with p.

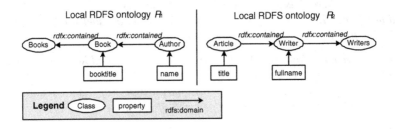

Fig. 3. Local RDFS ontologies transformed from $\mathcal{S}_1$ and $\mathcal{S}_2$

Table 1. Mappings between $\mathcal{S}_1$ and $\mathcal{R}_1$

XPath expressions in $\mathcal{S}_1$	RDF expressions in $\mathcal{R}_1$
/books	Books
/books/book	Book
/books/book/booktitle	Book.booktitle
/books/book/author	Author
/books/book/author/name	Author.name

4.2   Global RDFS Ontology

Now that the source schemas are represented by local RDFS ontologies, we are able to merge them to construct the global RDFS ontology. In other words, the process of ontology merging takes as input the multiple local ontologies and returns a merged ontology as the output [35].

Ontology merging and ontology alignment, which require the mapping of ontologies, are widely pursued research topics. Readers can be referred to a thorough survey of the state-of-the-art of ontology mapping [21]. In this paper we do not intend to introduce a new technique for ontology merging. Instead, we utilize existing techniques to generate the integrated ontology from the local ontologies. In particular, we use an approach (such as PROMPT [29]) that provides the following functionalities:

– *Merging of classes:* Multiple conceptually equivalent classes of the local ontologies are combined into one class in the global ontology.
– *Merging of properties:* Multiple conceptually equivalent properties of the equivalent classes in the local ontologies are combined as one property of the combined class in the global ontology.
– *Merging relationships between classes:* Given two conceptually equivalent relationships, e.g., p_1 from a class c_1 to another class c'_1 and p_2 from c_2 to c'_2, we combine p_1 and p_2 into one relationship p between the combined class c (of c_1 and c_2) and c' (of c'_1 and c'_2).
– *Copying a class or a property:* If there does not exist a conceptually equivalent class or property for a class c (or a property p of c), we simply copy c (or p, as a property of the target class of c) into the global ontology.
– *Generalizing semantically related classes into a superclass:* The superclass can be obtained by searching an existing knowledge domain (e.g., the DAML Ontology Library) or reasoning over a thesaurus such as WordNet.[2] For example, we can find in the semantic network of terms (consisting of terms and their semantic relations) that two classes (Author and Writer) have the same hypernym (Person), which is then taken as a superclass of both classes.

Figure 4 shows the global ontology that results from merging the two local RDF ontologies of Figure 3. The greyed classes and properties are merged classes and properties from the original ontologies. For instance, Book in $\mathcal{R}_1$ and Article in $\mathcal{R}_2$ are merged into Book, whereas booktitle in $\mathcal{R}_1$ and title in $\mathcal{R}_2$ are merged into title. The classes Book and Author are also respectively extended with the superclasses Publication and Person.

Besides the global ontology, the process of ontology merging also yields as an output the mapping table that contains the mappings between the local RDFS ontologies and the global RDFS ontology. In general, if a class, property, or relationship between classes p in the global ontology is the result of merging p_i and p_j from different local ontologies, then a tuple of the form (p, p_i, p_j) is generated. If a class or property p in the global ontology is only copied from p_i in a local ontology, then a tuple (p, p_i) is produced. For instance, for the class Book.title (in the global ontology), which is merged from Book.booktitle in $\mathcal{R}_1$ and Article.title in $\mathcal{R}_2$, we generate a tuple in the mapping table: (Book.title, Book.booktitle, Article.title). Table 2 lists all the mappings in our example.

---

[2] http://wordnet.princeton.edu

Table 2. Mapping table between the global ontology and local RDF ontologies

RDF expressions in the global ontology	RDF expressions in $\mathcal{R}_1$	RDF expressions in $\mathcal{R}_2$
Books	Books	-
Book	Book	Article
Book.title	Book.booktitle	Article.title
Authors	-	Writers
Author	Author	Writer
Author.name	Author.name	Writer.fullname

Table 3. Mapping table between the global ontology and XML source schemas

RDF expressions in the global ontology	XPath expressions in $\mathcal{S}_1$	XPath expressions in $\mathcal{S}_2$
Books	/books	-
Book	/books/book	/writers/writer/article
Book.title	/books/book/booktitle	/writers/writer/article/title
Authors	-	/writers
Author	/books/book/author	/writers/writer
Author.name	/books/book/author/name	/writers/writer/article/fullname

Now that we have the one-to-one mappings $\mathcal{M}_1$ between the XML source schemas and their local ontologies and the one-to-one mappings $\mathcal{M}_2$ between the local ontologies and the global ontology, we can compose $\mathcal{M}_1$ and $\mathcal{M}_2$ to get the mappings $\mathcal{M}$ between the source schemas and the global ontology. Table 3 shows the results.

4.3 Data Integration Semantics

In this subsection, we discuss the semantics of the data integration in our proposed framework including the semantics of the XML (local) databases, the mapping table, and the RDFS (global) database. The discussion of the syntax and semantics of queries is postponed until Section 5. In what follows, we refer to a fixed, finite set Γ of constants, which is shared by all data sources. We also refer to a finite set U of URIs.

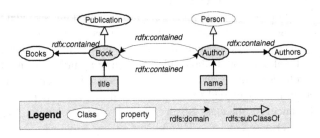

Fig. 4. The global ontology $\mathcal{G}$ that results from merging $\mathcal{R}_1$ and $\mathcal{R}_2$

There are two types of databases in the framework, i.e., the local XML databases and the global RDF database. An XML database is an *XML instance tree*, and an RDF database is an *RDF instance graph*.

Definition 3 (XML instance tree). *Given an XML schema* $S = (V_S, E_S, \lambda_S)$, *an instance of* S *is an XML instance tree* $G = (V_G, E_G, \tau, \lambda_G)$, *where* V_G *is a set of vertices,* E_G *is a set of edges, and*

(1) τ *is a typing function* $\tau : V_G \mapsto V_S$, *such that (a)* $\forall v \in V_G$, $\tau(v) \in V_S$, *and (b)* $\forall (v_i, v_j) \in E_G$, $(\tau(v_i), \tau(v_j)) \in E_S$.
(2) λ_G *is a labeling function, such that (a)* $\forall v \in V_G$, $\lambda_G(v) \in \Gamma \cup \{\epsilon\}$, *and (b)* $\forall (v_i, v_j) \in E_G$, $\lambda_G((v_i, v_j)) = \lambda_S((\tau(v_i), \tau(v_j)))$.

Definition 4 (RDF instance graph). *Given an RDF schema* $S = (V_S, E_S, \lambda_S)$, *where* $V_S = C \cup P$, *an instance of* S *is an RDF instance graph* $G = (V_G, E_G, \tau, \lambda_G)$, *where* V_G *is a set of vertices,* E_G *is a set of edges,* λ_G *is a labeling function* $\lambda_G : V_G \cup E_G \mapsto A_S \cup U \cup \Gamma$, *and* τ *is a typing function* $\tau : V_G \cup E_G \mapsto V_S \cup \{$"rdf:Property"$\} \cup \{$"rdfs:literal"$\}$, *such that* $\forall e = (v_i, v_j) \in E_G$, *we have*

(1) if $\tau(e)=$"rdf:Property", *then* $\lambda_G(e)=$"rdfx:contained" *or* "rdfs:subClassOf", $\lambda_G(v_i)$ *and* $\lambda_G(v_j) \in U$, $\tau(v_i)$ *and* $\tau(v_j) \in C$, *and* $(\tau(v_i), \tau(v_j)) \in E_S$;
(2) if $\tau(e) \in P$, *then* $\lambda_G(e) = \lambda_S(\tau(e))$, $\lambda_G(v_i) \in U$, $\tau(v_i) \in C$, $\lambda_S((\tau(e), \tau(v_i))) =$ "rdfs:domain", $\lambda_S((\tau(e), \tau(v_j)))=$"rdfs:range", *and*
  - $\lambda_G(v_j) \in U$, *when* $\tau(v_j) \in C$;
  - $\lambda_G(v_j) \in \Gamma$, *when* $\tau(v_j)=$"rdfs:literal";

The semantics of the mappings depends on the assumptions adopted. In the view-based approach, there are three assumptions for the inter-schema mappings, namely *soundness*, *completeness*, and *exactness* [25]. In particular, given a database D, a set of view definitions V over D, and view extensions E of V, we say the views V are *sound* if $V^D \supseteq E$, *complete* if $V^D \subseteq E$, and *exact* if $V^D = E$. It is common to use the soundness assumption for view-based data integration [25]. Given that our framework adopts a GaV approach, it is natural to assume an exact semantics, that is, the sources are complete with respect to the global database. However, the definition for these assumptions differs from our framework, where mappings are represented by element correspondences in the mapping table.

Given an entry $t_i = (g_i, s_{i,1}, ..., s_{i,n})$ in the mapping table $\mathcal{M}(G, S_1, ..., S_n)$, where $g_i \in G$ and $s_{i,j} \in S_j$ $(1 \leq j \leq n)$, the semantics of the mappings can be captured by the concept of valuation. Given the global database B of G and local databases D_j of S_j $(1 \leq j \leq n)$, a *valuation* of t_i is a function σ, which maps t_i to a tuple $(v_i, v_{i,1}, ..., v_{i,n})$, where $v_i \in B$, and $v_{i,j} \in D_j$ $(1 \leq j \leq n)$, such that $\tau_B(v_i) = g_i$ and $\tau_{D_j}(v_{i,j}) = s_{i,j}$ for $j \in [1..n]$. Under the exact assumption, the semantics of the mapping table $\mathcal{M} = \{t_1, ..., t_m\}$ is captured by a conjunction of all the equalities (between the valuation of each global element and the union of the valuations of its mapped local elements), that is:

$\bigwedge_{1 \leq i \leq m} [\sigma(g_i) = \sigma(s_{i,1}) \cup ... \cup \sigma(s_{i,n})]$, such that for $1 \leq k, l \leq m$,
(1) $(g_k, g_l) \in E_G \Leftrightarrow (\sigma(g_k), \sigma(g_l)) \in E_B$, and
(2) $(s_{k,j}, s_{k,l}) \in E_{S_k} \Leftrightarrow (\sigma(s_{k,j}), \sigma(s_{k,l})) \in E_{D_k}$, for each $j \in [1..n]$.

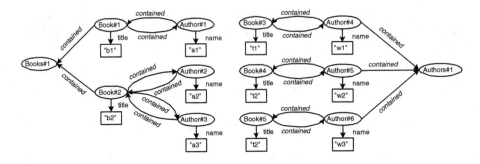

Fig. 5. The global database of $\mathcal{G}$

The definition of the semantics of sound (or complete) mappings is the same as the above definition, except for the substitution of = by $\supseteq$ (or $\subseteq$). For simplicity, we abbreviate the preceding assertion to $\sigma(\mathcal{G}) = \sigma(\mathcal{S}_1) \cup ... \cup \sigma(\mathcal{S}_n)$. The *global database* $\mathcal{B}$ is then any database such that $\sigma(\mathcal{G}) = \sigma(\mathcal{S}_1) \cup ... \cup \sigma(\mathcal{S}_n)$ holds for the local databases $\mathcal{D}_1, ..., \mathcal{D}_n$. Figure 5 shows the global database (instances) for the data sources of Example 1.

5   Query Processing

5.1   Query Languages

RDQL (RDF Data Query Language) uses an SQL-like syntax. More specifically, the Select clause identifies the variables to be returned to the application. The From clause specifies the RDF model using an URI. The Where clause specifies the graph pattern as a list of triple patterns. The And clause specifies the Boolean expressions. Finally, the Using clause provides a way to shorten the length of the URIs. By overlooking the notion of namespace (i.e., URI) and the And clause, we get a *conjunctive RDQL* (c-RDQL) expression, which can be expressed in a conjunctive formula:

$$ans(X) :- p_1(X_1), ..., p_n(X_n).$$

where $X_i = (x_i, x_i')$ and p_i is an RDF property of x_i having the value x_i'.

XQuery is a typed functional language that has an FLWR (i.e., For, Let, Where, Return) syntax. For simplification, we assume that the XML query posed by the user is formulated only in the form of *FLWR expressions* [7]. In other words, we do not consider nesting FLWR expressions, although they are allowed in XQuery. In particular, a *conjunctive XQuery* (c-XQuery) is of the form:

$$ans(X) :- p_1(X_1), ..., p_n(X_n).$$

where $X_i = (x_i, x_i')$ and p_i is an XPath $/e_1/.../e_n$ connecting x_i to x_i'. That is, each predicate represents an expression $x_i/e_1/.../e_n/x_i'$, where $e_i(1 \leq i \leq n)$ is an edge label along the path from x_i to x_i'.

In both query definitions, $ans(\boldsymbol{X})$ is the *head* of the query, denoted $head_q$, and the remaining part is the *body* of the query, denoted $body_q$. We say that the query is *safe* if $\boldsymbol{X} \subseteq \boldsymbol{X_1} \cup ... \cup \boldsymbol{X_n}$.

The answer $q^{\mathcal{D}}$ to a query q over a database $\mathcal{D}$ is the result of evaluating q over $\mathcal{D}$. The query evaluation is based on the concept of *valuation* and depends on the data model and the query language used. Informally, a *valuation* ρ over the variables $var(q)$ of a query q is a total function from $var(q)$ to constants (or URIs for RDF queries) in the domain Γ of the database, where q is evaluated [2], as follows:

– In the XML model: given a c-XQuery q of the form $ans(\boldsymbol{X}) :\text{-} p_1(\boldsymbol{X_1}), ..., p_n(\boldsymbol{X_n})$ over an XML instance graph $\mathcal{D}$, we have

$$q^{\mathcal{D}} = \{\rho(\boldsymbol{X}) | \rho \text{ is a valuation over } var(q) \text{ and } p_i = (\rho(x_i), \rho(x_i')) \text{ is a fact in } \mathcal{D},$$
$$\text{for each } \boldsymbol{X_i} = (x_i, x_i'), \text{ where } i \in [1..n]\}.$$

– In the RDF model: given a c-RQL query q of the form $ans(\boldsymbol{X}) :\text{-} p_1(\boldsymbol{X_1}), ...,$ $p_n(\boldsymbol{X_n})$ over an RDF instance graph $\mathcal{D}$, we have

$$q^{\mathcal{D}} = \{\rho(\boldsymbol{X}) | \rho \text{ is a valuation over } var(q) \text{ and } p_i \text{ is a path connecting } \rho(x_i) \text{ and}$$
$$\rho(x_i') \text{ in } \mathcal{D}, \text{ for each } \boldsymbol{X_i} = (x_i, x_i'), \text{ where } i \in [1..n]\}.$$

Example 2. Consider two queries q_1 and q_2. In particular, q_1 is expressed over the global ontology $\mathcal{G}$ in c-RDQL, to retrieve all the (Author, Book) pairs. The c-XQuery query q_2 is issued on local XML source $\mathcal{S}_1$, to retrieve all (Author, Book) pairs.

q_1: $ans(x, y) :\text{-} name(u, x), title(v, y), contained(u, v)$.
q_2: $ans(x, y) :\text{-} /name(u, x), /booktitle(v, y), /author(v, u)$.

By evaluating q_1 over the global database $\mathcal{B}$ (shown in Figure 5) and q_2 over $\mathcal{D}_1$ (shown in Figure 1), we obtain the following answer sets to both queries.

$q_1^{\mathcal{B}} = \{(a1, b1), (a2, b2), (a3, b2), (w1, t1), (w2, t2), (w3, t2)\}$,
$q_2^{\mathcal{D}_1} = \{(a1, b1), (a2, b2), (a3, b2)\}$.

We finally assume that all the concepts in the local ontologies are mapped to the concepts in the global ontology during the ontology integration process. That is, the mappings are total, one-to-one mappings from the local RDF ontologies to the global ontology. However, it is possible that some concept c or property p in the global ontology gets mapped to a local ontology but not to another local ontology. This may lead to null values when a query involves c or p. However, we do not consider this case in our discussion.

5.2 Certain Answers and Query Containment

The concept of *certain answers* has been introduced in view-based query processing to represent the results of answering a global query (the query over the global schema) using view extensions [1]. In our framework, where the mappings are correspondences between elements of the global ontology and elements of the source schemas, the concept of *certain answers* is redefined. We call the query posed on the global ontology a *global query*, and the query posed over a local data source a *local query*. As previously discussed, these

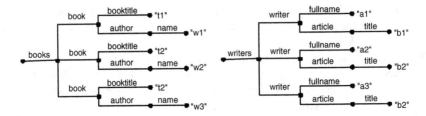

Fig. 6. The retrieved database on S_1 w.r.t. S_2 and that on S_2 w.r.t. S_1

two queries are processed in two different directions, i.e., the global-to-local direction and the local-to-local direction. The certain answers to a global query are called *global certain answers*, while those to a local query are called *local certain answers*.

Before we discuss the formalism for these two types of certain answers, we revisit the concept of *global database*, from which we retrieve the global certain answers, and we introduce the concept of *retrieved database*, where the local certain answers are computed.

Given the local data sources $D_1, ..., D_n$ and the mapping table $M(G, S_1, ..., S_n)$ between the global ontology G and local source schemas $S_1, ..., S_n$. The *global database* B is such that $\sigma(G) = \bigcup_{(1 \leq i \leq n)} \sigma(S_i)$ holds on $D_1, ..., D_n$. Likely, the *retrieved database* B_k on a local source S_k w.r.t. all the other local sources is the one satisfying $\sigma(S_k) = \bigcup_{(1 \leq i \leq n, i \neq k)} \sigma(S_i)$, whereas, the retrieved database $B_{k,l}$ on S_k w.r.t. a particular local source S_l is the one satisfying $\sigma(S_k) = \sigma(S_l)$ (refer to Section 4 for the semantics of σ). Figure 6 shows an example of the retrieved database on S_1 w.r.t. S_2 (on the left side) and the one on S_2 w.r.t. S_1 (on the right side), for S_1 and S_2 as presented in Figure 1.

Based on the concept of global database and that of retrieved database, we formally define both types of certain answers next.

Definition 5 (Certain answers). *Let G be the global ontology of n XML source schemas $S_1, ..., S_n$ respectively with databases $D_1, ..., D_n$, M be the mapping table, q be a global query posed over G, and q_k be a local query on S_k. The **global certain answers** to q with respect to $D_1, ..., D_n$ based on M are the results of evaluating q over the global database B, denoted $cert_M(q) = q^B$. The **local certain answers** to q_k with respect to $D_1, ..., D_{k-1}, D_{k+1}, ..., D_n$ based on M are computed by evaluating q_k over the retrieved database B_k on S_k, denoted $cert_{M,k}(q_k) = q^{B_k}$.*

While the global certain answers constitute the answer to a global query, the answer to a local query q_k contains both the local certain answers and those retrieved from the local database D_k, that is, $ans(q_k) = cert_{M,k}(q_k) \cup q^{D_k}$.

Query containment is a fundamental problem in database research. In general, query containment checks whether two queries are contained in each other. This problem has been studied in the following three cases.

The first case is query containment in a single database D, over which the two queries are posed, that is, $D_1 = D_2 = D$. Given a single database schema S over which q_1 and q_2 are posed, we say q_1 is *contained* in q_2, denoted $q_1 \sqsubseteq q_2$, if they have the same output schema and $q_1^{\mathcal{D}} \subseteq q_2^{\mathcal{D}}$ for every database $\mathcal{D}$ of $\mathcal{S}$. The two queries q_1 and q_2 are said to be *equivalent*, denoted $q_1 \equiv q_2$, if $q_1^{\mathcal{D}} \subseteq q_2^{\mathcal{D}}$ and $q_2^{\mathcal{D}} \subseteq q_1^{\mathcal{D}}$ [2].

The second case is query containment in data integration systems, where both queries are posed over the global database. The data sources are usually *homogeneous* in the sense that the same syntax is used. Given that the sources are expressed as views over the global database, two queries are said to be equivalent relative to the same set of data sources, if for any source databases they have the same set of certain answers. The query containment problem in this case is called *relative query containment* [28].

The third case is also in homogeneous data integration systems, where data sources are defined as views of the global schema, but the two queries are formulated in terms of different alphabets. In particular, there are two kinds of queries, i.e., the queries q^{Σ} over the alphabet Σ of the global schema and the queries $q^{\mathcal{V}}$ over the alphabet $\mathcal{V}$ of the view definitions. The query containment in this case is called *view-based containment* and is discussed for different situations such as containment between q_1^{Σ} and q_2^{Σ}, between q_1^{Σ} and $q_2^{\mathcal{V}}$, between $q_1^{\mathcal{V}}$ and q_2^{Σ}, and between $q_1^{\mathcal{V}}$ and $q_2^{\mathcal{V}}$ [13].

In our case, we are interested in two kinds of containment, specifically the containment between a global query q and a union of local queries $q_1, ..., q_n$, and the containment between two local queries q_k and q_l. The first kind of containment, which we call *global query containment*, is the same as the containment between q_1^{Σ} and q_2^{Σ}. Whereas the second kind differs from the containment between $q_1^{\mathcal{V}}$ and $q_2^{\mathcal{V}}$, in the sense that q_k and q_l refer to different alphabets but $q_1^{\mathcal{V}}$ and $q_2^{\mathcal{V}}$ are expressed over the same alphabet. We call the containment between q_k and q_l *P2P query containment*, because of its likeness to query processing in a P2P system. Next we give the formal definitions for these two containments in our framework.

Definition 6 (Global query containment). *Let $\mathcal{G}$ be the global ontology over n XML source schemas $\mathcal{S}_1, ..., \mathcal{S}_n$, $\mathcal{M}$ be the mapping table, q be a global query posed over $\mathcal{G}$, and q' be a union of local queries $q_1, ..., q_n$ respectively over $\mathcal{S}_1, ..., \mathcal{S}_n$. We say q is* **globally contained** *in q', denoted $q \subseteq_{\mathcal{M}} q'$, if for any databases $\mathcal{D}_1, ..., \mathcal{D}_n$, we have $cert_{\mathcal{M}}(q) \subseteq q_1^{\mathcal{D}_1} \cup ... \cup q_n^{\mathcal{D}_n}$. We say q and q' are* **globally equivalent**, *denoted $q \equiv_{\mathcal{M}} q'$, if $q \subseteq_{\mathcal{M}} q'$ and $q \supseteq_{\mathcal{M}} q'$.*

Definition 7 (P2P query containment). *Let $\mathcal{G}$ be the global ontology over n XML source schemas $\mathcal{S}_1, ..., \mathcal{S}_n$, $\mathcal{M}$ be the mapping table, q_i be a local query posed over $\mathcal{S}_i$, and q_j be a local query over $\mathcal{S}_j$. We say q_i is* **P2P contained** *in q_j, denoted $q_i \subseteq_{\mathcal{M}} q_j$, if for any databases $\mathcal{D}_1, ..., \mathcal{D}_n$, we have $cert_{\mathcal{M},i}(q_i) \cup q_i^{\mathcal{D}_i} \subseteq cert_{\mathcal{M},j}(q_j) \cup q_j^{\mathcal{D}_j}$. We say q and q' are* **P2P equivalent**, *denoted $q_i \equiv_{\mathcal{M}} q_j$, if $q_i \subseteq_{\mathcal{M}} q_j$ and $q_i \supseteq_{\mathcal{M}} q_j$.*

Example 3. Consider the following three queries q, q_1, and q_2 respectively on the global ontology $\mathcal{G}$, local XML source $\mathcal{S}_1$, and local XML source $\mathcal{S}_2$. Also consider the mapping table $\mathcal{M}$ shown in Table 3.

    q: $ans(x, y) \text{ :- } name(u, x), title(v, y), contained(u, v)$.
    q_1: $ans(x, y) \text{ :- } /name(u, x), /booktitle(v, y), /author(v, u)$.
    q_2: $ans(x, y) \text{ :- } /fullname(u, x), /title(v, y), /article(u, v)$.

By executing q on the global database $\mathcal{B}$, q_1 on $\mathcal{D}_1$ and on the retrieved database $\mathcal{B}_1$, and q_2 on $\mathcal{D}_2$ and on the retrieved database $\mathcal{B}_2$, we obtain the following answers to the three queries.

$cert_{\mathcal{M}}(q) = q^{\mathcal{B}}: \{(a1, b1), (a2, b2), (a3, b2), (w1, t1), (w2, t2), (w3, t2)\}$
$q_1^{\mathcal{D}_1}: \{(a1, b1), (a2, b2), (a3, b2)\}$
$cert_{\mathcal{M},1}(q_1) = q_1^{\mathcal{B}_1}: \{(w1, t1), (w2, t2), (w3, t2)\}$
$q_2^{\mathcal{D}_2}: \{(w1, t1), (w2, t2), (w3, t2)\}$
$cert_{\mathcal{M},2}(q_2) = q_2^{\mathcal{B}_2}: \{(a1, b1), (a2, b2), (a3, b2)\}$

Therefore, by Definition 6 and Definition 7, we have $q \equiv_{\mathcal{M}} (q_1 \cup q_2)$ and $q_1 \equiv_{\mathcal{M}} q_2$.

5.3 Query Rewriting

In a data integration system where the sources are described as views over the global schema, query processing is called *view-based query processing*, which has two approaches, i.e., *view-based query answering* and *view-based query rewriting* [12,18]. Likewise, there are two approaches to answering a query in our framework, where mappings are expressed by correspondences. The first approach utilizes the notion of (global or local) certain answers, as previously discussed.

The alternative approach is by query rewriting. Specifically, to answer a global (or local) query q, the query is rewritten into a union of the queries over all the sources, using the mappings. The integration of the answers retrieved from each source constitutes the answer to q.

As mentioned before, there are two directions of query processing in our framework. We expect that query rewriting in both directions is equivalent, in the sense that the rewriting is *globally* (or *P2P*) *equivalent* to the original query. We present next two query rewriting algorithms, i.e., GLREWRITING for global-to-local query rewriting and LLREWRITING for local-to-local rewriting, which will ensure the equivalence of the rewritten queries.

Algorithm GLREWRITING
Input: 1. q_1 over the global ontology $\mathcal{G}$: $ans(\boldsymbol{X})$:- $p_1(\boldsymbol{X_1}), ..., p_m(\boldsymbol{X_m})$;
      2. $\mathcal{M}$ between the global ontology $\mathcal{G}$ and local XML schemas $\mathcal{S}_1, ..., \mathcal{S}_n$.
Output: q_2: Union of the c-XQueries over $\mathcal{S}_1, ..., \mathcal{S}_n$.
1. $q_2 = null$;
2. **For** $i = 1$ **to** n **do**
3. $head_q = head_{q_1}$; $body_q = null$;
4.   **For** $j = 1$ **to** m **do**
5. (c_1, c_2) = name of the class/property bound to (x_1, x_2), for $\boldsymbol{X_j} = (x_1, x_2)$;
6.   Search $\mathcal{M}$ to find (d_1, d_2) such that $\{(c_1, d_1), (c_2, d_2)\} \subseteq \pi_{\mathcal{G}, \mathcal{S}_j}(\mathcal{M})$;
7.   **If** a path p exists from d_1 to d_2 in $\mathcal{S}_j$ **then**
8.   add $p(x_1, x_2)$ to $body_q$;
9.   **Else if** a path p exists from d_2 to d_1 in $\mathcal{S}_j$ **then**
10.   add $p(x_2, x_1)$ to $body_q$;
11.   **Else add** $p(\hat{x}, x_1)$ and $p'(\hat{x}, x_2)$ to $body_q$, where $\hat{x}$ is a new variable bound to the lowest ancestor d of d_1 and d_2, and p (p') is the path from d to d_1 (d_2);
12. $q_2 = q_2 \cup q$;

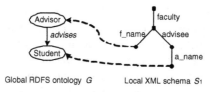

Fig. 7. A part of XML data integration setting

We see that the algorithm GLREWRITING adopts a strategy similar to the "unfolding" strategy used by query processing in a GaV-based relational data integration system [25]. However, instead of substituting the predicates in a query q with the corresponding views, the substitution of predicates in GLREWRITING is guided by the correspondences in the mapping table $\mathcal{M}$, as stated in Lines 5 to 11. The calculation of the class or property (Line 5) bound to different variables in q_1 is as follows. For each predicate $p(x_1, x_2)$: (1) if p is a property connecting two classes c_1 and c_2, we say that x_1 is bound to c_1 and that x_2 is bound to c_2; (2) if p connects a class c to a value (or literal) v, we say that x_1 is bound to c and that x_2 is bound to p. Also, we note that the algorithm uses the relational algebra *projection* operator π (Line 6).

Example 4. Given a global query

$$q : ans(x, y) :\text{-} name(u, x), title(v, y), contained(u, v).$$

we use GLREWRITING to rewrite q into a union of subqueries, each on a local XML source (refer to the mapping table $\mathcal{M}$ of Table 3). For illustration, we only look at the rewriting of q into a subquery q_1 over the local source $\mathcal{S}_1$.

In particular, Line 5 computes the bound classes or properties of the variables (u, v, x, y) as (Author, Book, Author.name, Book.title). By looking into $\mathcal{M}$, we find the corresponding element sequence of (Author, Book, Author.name, Book.title) in $\mathcal{S}_1$ to be (/books/book/author, /books/book, /books/book/author/name, /books/book/booktitle). From Lines 7 to 11, we compute the predicates in the body of q_1 as follows.

$$q_1 : ans(x, y) :\text{-} /name(u, x), /booktitle(v, y) /author(v, u).$$

Note that for the predicate $contained(u, v)$ in q, we generate in q_1 a predicate/ $author(v, u)$, where the order of the two variables is switched. This results from the computation performed by Lines 9 and 10. In particular, u and v are respectively bound to Author and Book, which respectively correspond to XML paths /books/book/ author and /books/book. From $\mathcal{S}_1$, we find that /author is the path from v to u, not the path from u to v.

Example 5. We give one more example to illustrate query rewriting when Line 11 is used. Consider the following setting, where a local XML schema $\mathcal{S}_1$ (on the right side) is mapped to the global RDFS ontology $\mathcal{G}$ (on the left side), as indicated by the dashed lines. The two classes Advisor and Student are respectively instantiated with the name of faculty and the name of advisee, that is, the mapping table contains two correspondences:

(Advisor, /faculty/f_name)
(Student, /faculty/advisee/a_name).

Now we consider rewriting a global c-RDQL query q: $ans(x, y)$:- $advises(x, y)$. into a local c-XQuery query q' over $\mathcal{S}_1$. It is apparent that x and y are bound to Advisor and Student, thus corresponding to /faculty/f_name and /faculty/advisee/a_name, respectively. Because /faculty/f_name and /faculty/ advisee/a_name share the same ancestor /faculty, by using Line 11 we add two predicates /f_name(u, x) and /advisee/a_name(u, y) to the body of q', generating the following local c-XQuery query q':

$$ans(x, y) :- /f\_name(u, x), /advisee/a\_name(u, y).$$

Algorithm LLREWRITING
Input: 1. q_1 over a local XML schema $\mathcal{S}_1$: $ans(\boldsymbol{X})$:- $p_1(\boldsymbol{X_1}), ..., p_m(\boldsymbol{X_m})$;
     2. $\mathcal{M}$ between the global ontology $\mathcal{G}$ and local XML schemas $\mathcal{S}_1, ..., \mathcal{S}_n$.
Output: q: A query over local XML schema $\mathcal{S}_2$.
1. $head_q = ans(\boldsymbol{X})$; $body_q = null$;
2.   **For** $j = 1$ **to** m **do**
3. (c_1, c_2) = name of the element bound to (x_1, x_2), for $\boldsymbol{X_j} = (x_1, x_2)$;
4.   Search $\mathcal{M}$ to find (d_1, d_2) such that $\{(c_1, d_1), (c_2, d_2)\} \subseteq \pi_{\mathcal{S}_1, \mathcal{S}_2}(\mathcal{M})$;
5.   **If** a path p exists from d_1 to d_2 in $\mathcal{S}_2$ **then**
6.   add $p(x_1, x_2)$ to $body_q$;
7.   **Else if** a path p exists from d_2 to d_1 in $\mathcal{S}_2$ **then**
8.   add $p(x_2, x_1)$ to $body_q$;
9.   **Else** add $p(\hat{x}, x_1)$ and $p'(\hat{x}, x_2)$ to $body_q$, where $\hat{x}$ is a new variable bound to the lowest ancestor d of d_1 and d_2, and p (p') is the path from d to $d_1(d_2)$;

Algorithm LLREWRITING differs from GLREWRITING only in finding the elements bound to the variables (Line 3) and in finding the corresponding elements from the mapping table (Line 4). Unlike in global-to-local rewriting, the result of using LLREWRITING is a single c-XQuery.

Taking into account the definitions of *global* and *P2P query containment*, we prove below that the algorithms GLREWRITING and LLREWRITING yield equivalent queries.

Theorem 1. *Given a global query q over the global ontology $\mathcal{G}$, its rewriting q' as computed by* GLREWRITING *is globally equivalent to q, that is, $q \equiv_\mathcal{M} q'$.*

PROOF SKETCH. To prove $q \equiv_\mathcal{M} q'$, where $q' = q_1 \cup ... \cup q_n$, we will check whether $cert_\mathcal{M}(q) = q_1^{\mathcal{D}_1} \cup ... \cup q_n^{\mathcal{D}_n}$, given the mapping table $\mathcal{M}(\mathcal{G}, \mathcal{S}_1, ..., \mathcal{S}_n)$. Taking into account the semantics of $\mathcal{M}$, given any sequence u of values from the global database $\mathcal{B}$, which makes $body_q$ true, we can always have a sequence v of values from $\mathcal{D}_1, ..., \mathcal{D}_n$, since $\sigma(\mathcal{G}) = \sigma(\mathcal{S}_1) \cup ... \cup \sigma(\mathcal{S}_n)$. By GLREWRITING, the sequence v is exactly the one that makes $body_{q_i}$ true, where $i \in [1..n]$. Therefore, we have $q^\mathcal{B} \subseteq q_1^{\mathcal{D}_1} \cup ... \cup q_n^{\mathcal{D}_n}$. Similarly, we can show that $q^\mathcal{B} \supseteq q_1^{\mathcal{D}_1} \cup ... \cup q_n^{\mathcal{D}_n}$. By the definition of certain answers, we conclude that $cert_\mathcal{M}(q) = q_1^{\mathcal{D}_1} \cup ... \cup q_n^{\mathcal{D}_n}$. □

Similarly, we have:

Theorem 2. *Given a local query q_1 over a local XML source S_1, its rewriting q_2 over the local XML source S_2 computed by* LLREWRITING *is P2P equivalent to q_1, that is, $q_1 \equiv_M q_2$.*

We discuss here an interesting property, namely *reversibility*, of the local-to-local query rewriting. Informally, consider a local query q_1, which is rewritten into another local query q_2. If q_2 can be rewritten back to a query q_1' (on the same source as q_1) such that $q_1 \equiv q_1'$, we say q_1' is a *reverse* query of q_1. In the case that q_2 and q_1' are computed using the same rewriting algorithm, we say that the algorithm is *reversible*, if every query that is rewritable by the algorithm has a reverse rewriting.

More generally, we consider a P2P data integration system with a cyclic path of P2P mappings, informally annotated as $p_1, \mathcal{M}_{12}, p_2, ..., \mathcal{M}_{(n-1)(n)}, p_n, \mathcal{M}_{n1}, p_1$, and an equivalent query rewriting algorithm translating a query q_1 (over p_1) along this path until it comes back to p_1 with the resulting query q_1'. In the spirit of equivalent query rewriting, we expect that it is the case that $q_1 \equiv q_1'$, and furthermore, $(q_1 \equiv_M q_2), ..., (q_n \equiv_M q_1') \Rightarrow q_1 \equiv q_1'$ and $q_1 \equiv q_1' \Rightarrow (q_1 \equiv_M q_2), ..., (q_n \equiv_M q_1')$. In other words, we expect that there exists a logical relationship between P2P query containment/equivalence and a reversible rewriting algorithm.

6   Conclusions and Future Work

XML and its schema languages do not express semantics but rather the document structure, such as information about nesting. Therefore, semantically-equivalent documents often present different document structures when they originate from different applications. In this paper, we provide an ontology-based framework that aims to make XML documents interoperate at the semantic level while retaining their nesting structure. The framework consists of two key aspects: data integration and query processing.

For data integration, a global RDFS ontology is generated by merging the local RDFS ontologies that are generated from each of the XML documents. At the same time, the mappings between the global ontology and local XML schemas are manually established. We extend RDFS by defining additional metadata that can encode the nesting structure of an XML document. For query processing, we propose two query rewriting algorithms: one algorithm translates an RDF query (posed on the global ontology) to an XML query; the other algorithm translates an XML query (posed on one of the individual XML data sources) to another XML query (posed on a different XML data source). In doing so, we discuss the problem of query containment for two query languages, namely conjunctive RDQL (c-RDQL) and conjunctive XQuery (c-XQuery). It is shown that both query rewriting algorithms are equivalent, in terms of both global and P2P query equivalence.

In the future, we will extend query processing in our framework, by taking into account other data models, such as relational and RDF data sources. We will further study query containment in the case of more expressive query languages, e.g., the complete RDQL and XQuery. The concept of reversibility of query rewriting, especially in P2P data integration systems, is also a direction for future research.

References

1. S. Abiteboul and O. M. Duschka. Complexity of Answering Queries Using Materialized Views. In *Proceedings of the 17th ACM SIGACT-SIGMOD-SIGART Symposium on Principles of Database Systems (PODS 1998)*, pages 254–263, 1998.
2. S. Abiteboul, R. Hull, and V. Vianu. *Foundations of Databases*. Addison-Wesley, 1995.
3. B. Amann, C. Beeri, I. Fundulaki, and M. Scholl. Ontology-Based Integration of XML Web Resources. In *Proceedings of the 1st International Semantic Web Conference (ISWC 2002)*, pages 117–131, 2002.
4. B. Amann, I. Fundulaki, M. Scholl, C. Beeri, and A.-M. Vercoustre. Mapping XML Fragments to Community Web Ontologies. In *Proceedings of the 4th International Workshop on the Web and Databases (WebDB 2001)*, pages 97–102, 2001.
5. Y. Arens, C. A. Knoblock, and C. Hsu. Query Processing in the SIMS Information Mediator. In *The AAAI Press*, May 1996.
6. Y. A. Bishr. Overcoming the semantic and other barriers to GIS interoperability. *International Journal of Geographical Information Science*, 12(4):229–314, 1998.
7. S. Boag, D. Chamberlin, M. F. Fernández, J. R. Daniela Florescu, and J. Siméon. XQuery 1.0: An XML Query Language. http://www.w3.org/TR/xquery, W3C Working Draft, April 2005.
8. R. Bourret. XML and Databases. http://www.rpbourret.com/xml/XMLAndDatabases.htm, December 2004.
9. D. Brickley and R. Guha. RDF Vocabulary Description Language 1.0: RDF Schema. http://www.w3.org/TR/rdf-schema, W3C Working Draft, February 2004.
10. A. Calì, D. Calvanese, G. D. Giacomo, and M. Lenzerini. On the Expressive Power of Data Integration Systems. In *Proceedings of the 21st International Conference on Conceptual Modeling (ER 2002)*, pages 338–350, 2002.
11. A. Calì, D. Calvanese, G. D. Giacomo, M. Lenzerini, P. Naggar, and F. Vernacotola. IBIS: Semantic Data Integration at Work. In *Proceedings of the 15th Conference on Advanced Information Systems Engineering (CAiSE 2003)*, pages 79–94, 2003.
12. D. Calvanese, G. D. Giacomo, M. Lenzerini, and M. Y. Vardi. View-Based Query Processing and Constraint Satisfaction. In *The 15th Annual IEEE Symposium on Logic in Computer Science (LICS 2000)*, pages 361–371, 2000.
13. D. Calvanese, G. D. Giacomo, M. Lenzerini, and M. Y. Vardi. View-based Query Containment. In *Proceedings of the 22rd ACM SIGACT-SIGMOD-SIGART Symposium on Principles of Database Systems (PODS 2003)*, pages 56–67, 2003.
14. S. D. Camillo, C. A. Heuser, and R. dos Santos Mello. Querying Heterogeneous XML Sources through a Conceptual Schema. In *Proceedings of the 22nd International Conference on Conceptual Modeling (ER 2003)*, pages 186–199, 2003.
15. Y. Chen and P. Revesz. CXQuery: A Novel XML Query Language. In *Proceedings of International Conference on Advances in Infrastructure for Electronic Business, Science, and Medicine on the Internet (SSGRR 2002w)*, 2002.
16. I. F. Cruz and H. Xiao. Using a Layered Approach for Interoperability on the Semantic Web. In *Proceedings of the 4th International Conference on Web Information Systems Engineering (WISE 2003)*, pages 221–232, Rome, Italy, December 2003.
17. T. R. Gruber. A Translation Approach to Portable Ontology Specifications. *Knowledge Acquisition*, 5(2):199–220, 1993.
18. A. Y. Halevy. Answering Queries Using Views: A Survey. *VLDB Jounal*, 10(4):270–294, 2001.
19. A. Y. Halevy, Z. G. Ives, P. Mork, and I. Tatarinov. Piazza: Data Management Infrastructure for Semantic Web Applications. In *Proceedings of the 12th International World Wide Web Conference (WWW 2003)*, pages 556–567, 2003.
20. HP Labs. RDQL - RDF Data Query Language. http://www.hpl.hp.com/semweb/rdql.htm, 2005.

21. Y. Kalfoglou and M. Schorlemmer. Ontology Mapping: the State of the Art. *The Knowledge Engineering Review*, 18(1):1–31, 2003.
22. M. C. A. Klein. Interpreting XML Documents via an RDF Schema Ontology. In *Proceedings of the 13th International Workshop on Database and Expert Systems Applications (DEXA 2002)*, pages 889–894, 2002.
23. L. V. S. Lakshmanan and F. Sadri. Interoperability on XML Data. In *Proceedings of the 2nd International Semantic Web Conference (ICSW 2003)*, pages 146–163, 2003.
24. P. Lehti and P. Fankhauser. XML Data Integration with OWL: Experiences and Challenges. In *2004 Symposium on Applications and the Internet (SAINT 2004)*, pages 160–170, 2004.
25. M. Lenzerini. Data Integration: A Theoretical Perspective. In *Proceedings of the 21st ACM SIGACT-SIGMOD-SIGART Symposium on Principles of Database Systems (PODS 2002)*, pages 233–246, Madison, Wisconsin, June 2002. ACM.
26. F. Manola and E. Miller. RDF Primer. http://www.w3.org/TR/rdf-primer, W3C Working Draft, February 2004.
27. E. Mena, V. Kashyap, A. P. Sheth, and A. Illarramendi. OBSERVER: An Approach for Query Processing in Global Information Systems based on Interoperation across Pre-existing Ontologies. In *Proceedings of the 1st IFCIS International Conference on Cooperative Information Systems (CoopIS 1996)*, pages 14–25, 1996.
28. T. D. Millstein, A. Y. Halevy, and M. Friedman. Query Containment for Data Integration Systems. *Journal of Computer and System Sciences*, 66(1):20–39, 2003.
29. N. F. Noy and M. A. Musen. PROMPT: Algorithm and Tool for Automated Ontology Merging and Alignment. In *Proceedings of the 17th National Conference on Artificial Intelligence and 12th Conference on Innovative Applications of Artificial Intelligence (AAAI/IAAI 2000)*, pages 450–455, 2000.
30. Y. Papakonstantinou, H. Garcia-Molina, and J. Widom. Object Exchange Across Heterogeneous Information Sources. In *Proceedings of the 11th International Conference on Data Engineering (ICDE 1995)*, pages 251–260, 1995.
31. P. F. Patel-Schneider and J. Siméon. The Yin/Yang Web: XML Syntax and RDF Semantics. In *Proceedings of the 11th International World Wide Web Conference (WWW 2002)*, pages 443–453, July 2002.
32. L. Popa, Y. Velegrakis, R. J. Miller, M. A. Hernández, and R. Fagin. Translating Web Data. In *Proceedings of the 28th International Conference on Very Large Data Bases (VLDB 2002)*, pages 598–609, 2002.
33. O. D. Sahin, A. Gupta, D. Agrawal, and A. E. Abbadi. Query Processing Over Peer-To-Peer Data Sharing Systems. Technical Report CSD-2002-28, University of California at Santa Barbara, 2002.
34. L. A. Shklar, A. P. Sheth, V. Kashyap, and K. Shah. InfoHarness: Use of Automatically Generated Metadata for Search and Retrieval of Heterogeneous Information. In *Proceedings of the 7th Conference on Advanced Information Systems Engineering (CAiSE 1995)*, pages 217–230, 1995.
35. G. Stumme and A. Maedche. Ontology Merging for Federated Ontologies for the Semantic Web. In *Proceedings of the International Workshop on Foundations of Models for Information Integration (FMII 2001)*, pages 16–18, 2001.
36. J. D. Ullman. Information Integration Using Logical Views. In *Proceedings of the 6th International Conference on Database Theory (ICDT 1997)*, pages 19–40, 1997.
37. R. van der Meyden. Logical Approaches to Incomplete Information: A Survey. In *Logics for Databases and Information Systems*, pages 307–356, 1998.
38. H. Xiao, I. F. Cruz, and F. Hsu. Semantic Mappings for the Integration of XML and RDF Sources. In *Proceedings of the VLDB Workshop on Information Integration on the Web (VLDB-IIWeb 2004)*, 2004.

Managing Uncertainty in Schema Matching
with Top-K Schema Mappings

Avigdor Gal

Technion – Israel Institute of Technology
Technion City, Haifa 32000, Israel

Abstract. In this paper, we propose to extend current practice in schema matching with the simultaneous use of top-K schema mappings rather than a single best mapping. This is a natural extension of existing methods (which can be considered to fall into the top-1 category), taking into account the imprecision inherent in the schema matching process. The essence of this method is the simultaneous generation and examination of K best schema mappings to identify useful mappings. The paper discusses efficient methods for generating top-K methods and propose a generic methodology for the simultaneous utilization of top-K mappings. We also propose a concrete heuristic that aims at improving precision at the cost of recall. We have tested the heuristic on real as well as synthetic data and anlyze the emricial results.

The novelty of this paper lies in the robust extension of existing methods for schema matching, one that can gracefully accommodate less-than-perfect scenarios in which the exact mapping cannot be identified in a single iteration. Our proposal represents a step forward in achieving fully automated schema matching, which is currently semi-automated at best.

1 Introduction

Matching concepts describing the meaning of data in heterogeneous distributed data sources (*e.g.*, HTML form tags and database and XML schemata) is one of the basic operations of data integration. Due to the cognitive complexity of this matching process [8], it has traditionally been performed by human experts (Web designers, database analysts, and even lay users, depending on the context of the application) [32,20]. As data integration has been made more automated, the ambiguity in concept interpretation, also known as *semantic heterogeneity*, has become one of the main obstacles to this process. For obvious reasons, manual concept reconciliation in dynamic environments (with or without computer-aided tools) is inefficient to the point of being infeasible, and so cannot provide a general solution. Introduction of the Semantic Web vision [4] and the shift towards machine-understandable Web resources have underscored the importance of automatic matching between sets of elements, also known as *schema matching*.

As a result, several tools for automated schema matching, such as GLUE [11] and OntoBuilder [15], have been developed in recent years. Given two data schemata (*e.g.*, two sets of attributes), these tools output a single *mapping* from

S. Spaccapietra et al. (Eds.): Journal on Data Semantics VI, LNCS 4090, pp. 90–114, 2006.

elements of one schema to elements of the other. The outputted mapping is considered to be the *best* of all possible mappings between these schemata.

Although these tools comprise a significant step towards fulfilling the vision of automated schema matching, it has become obvious that the user must accept a degree of imperfection in this process [14]. A prime reason for this is the enormous ambiguity and heterogeneity of data description concepts: It is unrealistic to expect a single mapping engine to identify the correct mapping for any possible concept in a set. Another (and probably no less crucial) reason is that "the syntactic representation of schemas and data do not completely convey the semantics of different databases" [26]; *i.e.*, the description of a concept in a schema can be semantically misleading. Therefore, managing uncertainty in schema matching has been recognized as the next issue on the research agenda in the realm of data integration [24].

In this work, we offer an uncertainty management tool, using top-K mappings. We propose to extend current practice in schema matching by using top-K schema mappings rather than a single best mapping. This is a natural extension of existing methods (which can be considered to fall into the top-1 category), taking into account the uncertainty described above. The essence of this method is the **simultaneous** generation of K schema mappings and the use of heuristics on them to improve the matching process. We demonstrate our approach using a heuristic, dubbed *stability analysis*, to analyze top-K mappings. The usefulness of the heuristic is demonstrated through an empirical analysis of real-world schemata as well as synthetic data.

1.1 Motivating Example

Figure 1 presents two Web sites that offer matchmaking services. In each of these sites, one has to fill in personal information (*e.g.*, name, country of residence, and birthdate). We have applied a schema matcher called *Combined*, which is

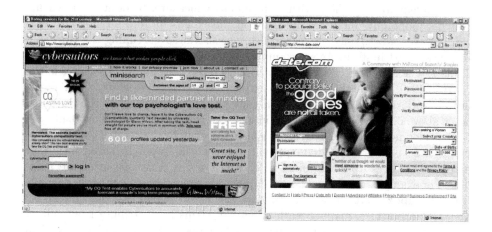

Fig. 1. Motivating example

Table 1. Best mapping of the motivating example

www.cybersuitors.com	www.date.com
select: Country: (cboCountries)	select: Select your Country (countrycode)
select: Birthday: (cboDays)	select: Date of Birth (dob_day)
select: Birthday: (cboMonths)	select: Date of Birth (dob_month)
select: Birthday: (cboYears)	select: Date of Birth (dob_year)
checkbox: (chkAgreement2)	image: ()
checkbox: (chkAgreement1)	checkbox: Date.com - Join Now for Free! (over18)
select: State (if in USA): (cboUSstates)	select: I am a (i_am)

part of the toolkit of OntoBuilder [15]. The matcher returned the best mapping, containing a set of possible attribute mappings. We shall present a formal model of the matching process in Section 2.

A list of these mappings appear in Table 1. Each column in the table contains information about one field in a registration form in one of the Web sites. The information consists of the type of field (*e.g.*, select field and checkbox), the label as appears at the Web site, and the name of the field, given here in parentheses and hidden from the user. Each row in the table represents an attribute mapping, as proposed by the matcher. The top part of the table contains four correct mappings. The bottom part of the table contains three incorrect mappings.

Schema matchers face two obstacles in providing the best mapping. First, correct mappings should be identified and provided to the user. Second, incorrect mappings should be avoided. These two tasks can be measured by the classical IR metrics of recall and precision. The former judges how many correct mappings the matcher identifies, while the latter measures how many incorrect mappings the matcher has managed to avoid. Separating correct from incorrect mappings is a hard task. One technique that is often used is that of a threshold. Using a threshold, a matcher can discard attribute mappings that do not reach sufficient similarity, assuming that those attribute mappings with low similarity measures are less adequate than those with high similarity measure. By doing so, a schema matcher (hopefully) increases precision, at the expense of recall. Using a threshold, however, works only in clear-cut scenarios. Moreover, tuning the threshold becomes an art in itself. As an example, consider the case study in Figure 1 and Table 1. The four correct attribute mappings received similarity measures in the range $[0.49, 0.7]$ while the other similarity measures ranged from 0 to 0.5. Any arbitrary apriori selection of a threshold may yield false negatives (if the threshold is set above 0.49) or false positives, in case the threshold is set below 0.49.

Consider now an alternative, in which the matcher generates top-10 mappings, that is, the best 10 mappings between the two schemata, such that mapping i differs from mappings $1, 2, ...i - 1$ by at least one attribute mapping. For example, the second best mapping maps checkbox: (chkAgreement2) with checkbox: Date.com - Join Now for Free! (over18) and checkbox: (chkAgreement1) is mapped with image: () (this last attribute is actually a button and has no associated label or field name). The method proposed in this paper assumes that such a scenario represents a "shaky" confidence in this mapping to start with and removes it from the set of proposed attribute mappings (see Section 3.2). Simultaneous analysis of the top-10 mappings reveals that the four correct attribute mappings did not change throughout the 10 mappings, while the other attributes were mapped with different attributes in different mappings. Stability analysis, the heuristic proposed in this paper, suggests that the four mappings, for which consistent attribute mappings were observed in the top-10 mappings, should be proposed as the "best mapping," yielding a precision of 100% without adversely affecting recall.

1.2   Related Work

Schema matching has been an active field of study for many years now. In this section, we review past research in two areas, heterogeneous databases and ontology design.

Heterogeneous Databases. The evolution of organizational computing, from "islands of automation" to enterprise-level systems, has created the need to homogenize heterogeneous databases. More than ever before, companies are seeking integrated data that go well beyond a single organizational unit. In addition, a high percentage of organizational data is now supplied by external resources (*e.g.*, the Web and extranets). Data integration is thus becoming increasingly important for decision support in enterprises [5]. This development also implies that databases with heterogeneous schemata increasingly face the prospect that their data integration process will not effectively manage semantic differences. This may result, at least to some degree, in the mismatching of concepts. Hence, methods for schema matching should take into account a certain level of uncertainty.

Many matchers have been proposed over the past two decades, by researchers in both academia and industry (*e.g.*, [33,6,13,10,28,24]) to increase automation of the matching process and reduce semantic mismatch problems. A useful classification of the various solutions can be found in [31]. A few other systems (MOMIS [3] and Clio [27], to name a couple) aim at resolving semantic heterogeneity in heterogeneous databases using manual intervention. For example, MOMIS input includes manual specification of concept semantic meaning and context as a prerequisite to the matching process.

Several systems offer facilities for iteratively scanning the search space, which can be considered an iterative variation of top-K. Clio presents the user with the best mapping and revises it if the user rejects the mapping. LSD [10] exploits domain constraints to produce the best mapping. A user then examines each concept mapping in the best mapping. If a user specifies a concept mapping as incorrect, it is fed to LSD as an additional constraint, and LSD then produces the next best mapping. Other matchers, such as similarity flooding [25] can be easily adapted to provide such top-K facilities. What is common to all these works is the manual involvement in the iterative process. We aim, in this work, at reducing manual involvement. Therefore, we suggest a heuristic for automatic analysis of information that can be generated from simultaneous (rather than iterative) analysis of top-K mappings.

Another variation of top-K exists [25,19], in which the user is presented with top-K ($K = 3$ as a default in [25]) concept level mappings. That is, for **each concept** the user is presented with the best top-K concept mappings, out of which it can choose the one that fits best its needs. While top-K here is simultaneous, there are two main differences with our work. First, it ignores concept inter-relationships, and burdens the user with enforcing matching constraints (such as cardinality constraints). Secondly, there is no automatic reasoning involved in deciding which of the top-K is preferred.

There is sparse academic literature on the imprecision of automatic schema matching. A study of representations and reasoning about mappings between domain models was presented in [24]. The paper provides a model representation and inference analysis. It recognizes managing uncertainty as the next step on the research agenda in this area, and leaves this issue open for future research. The research described in [14] fills this gap by providing a model that represents uncertainty (as a measure of imprecision) in the matching process outcome. In the current paper, we build on the results of [14] in extending the current "best mapping" approach into one that considers top-K mappings as an uncertainty management tool.

Ontology Design. The second body of literature concerned with schema matching is that of ontology design. Ontologies have been widely accepted as the model of choice for modeling heterogeneous data sources by various communities, including the areas of databases [11,21,15] and knowledge representation [13], to name just two.

The realm of information science has produced an extensive body of literature and practice in ontology construction, using tools such as thesauri, and in terminology rationalization and matching of different ontologies (e.g., [1,35]). Elsewhere, as in the DOGMA project [21,34], an engineering approach to ontology management is taken. Finally, researchers in the area of knowledge representation have studied ontology interoperability, resulting in systems such as Protégé [13].

The body of research aiming at matching schemata by using ontologies has traditionally focused on interactive methods requiring human intervention, massive at times. However, the vision of the semantic Web makes it necessary to minimize human intervention, replacing it with measures of syntactic similarity designed to approximate semantic matching. Recent papers (e.g., [11,15]) have explored the idea of automatic semantic reconciliation using ontologies. It was observed previously that automatic matching is imperfect [26]. Our approach, focusing on top-K mappings rather than the best mapping, handles this imperfection well.

The QOM (Quick Ontology Mapping) approach [12] is the closest we are aware of to our proposed framework. In this work, an iterative matching process is proposed, in which the mapping of a previous iteration is utilized in determining (the equivalence of our top-K) ontology elements to consider in the next iteration (note the difference of this approach from other iterative approaches, e.g., similarity flooding, in which there is no selectivity between iterations). The decision is either manual (with the support of a user) or by using a threshold. As already discussed, both methods have disadvantages. In this work, we generalize this approach. One other limitation of QOM is that its top-K is computed per concept, as in [25,19], ignoring overall ontology constraints (such as $1:1$ mapping).

1.3 Contributions and Outline

The specific contributions of this paper are as follows:

- We formalize the notion of top-K schema mappings within the framework of schema matching.
- We provide a classification of top-K matchers according to cardinality constraints.
- We demonstrate that there exists a correlation between patterns in top-K mappings and the correctness of the mapping, which makes the case for the need for top-K mapping analysis.
- We present a heuristic that makes use of simultaneous top-K mappings to improve mapping precision.
- We show experimental results to substantiate the usefulness of top-K mappings in improving precision and evaluate the trade-offs of applying methods based on top-K mappings.

The rest of the paper is organized as follows. Section 2 presents a model for schema matching as a basis for the formal introduction of top-K mappings. Next, we provide a generic heuristic for using top-K mappings (verification) and instantiate it into a concrete heuristic (Section 3). Section 4 outlines our experiments with the verification heuristic. We conclude in Section 5.

2   The Model

This section introduces formally the concept of top-K mappings in the context of schema matching. A model for schema matching is presented in Section 2.1, followed by the modeling of top-K in Section 2.2.

2.1   A Model for Schema Matching

As a basis for this work we next layout a model for schema matching and explicitly specify the set of assumptions we shall use throughout the paper. Let S_1 and S_2 be two schemata, defined using some data model (*e.g.*, relational or ontological), with n_1 and n_2 attributes, respectively. Attributes can be joint into *elements*, sets of attributes. The process of schema matching yields schema mapping(s), in which elements of S_1 are mapped onto elements of S_2.

Generally speaking, the process of schema matching is performed in two steps [9]. First, a degree of similarity is computed **automatically** for all element pairs (one element from each schema in each pair), using such methods as name matching, domain matching, and structure (such as XML hierarchical representation) matching. Recall that an element may consist of more than a single attribute. For illustration purposes, consider Table 3 (Section 2.2) to be described in details later. Each entry in the table represents a degree of similarity of a single element pair. The degree of similarity is typically defined on a $[0, 1]$ scale, where 0 represents no similarity and 1 represents fully similar elements.

As a second step, a single mapping is chosen to be the *best mapping*. The best mapping is a mapping that optimizes some target function F, subject to matching constraints. For example, many schema matching tools aim at maximizing the sum (or average) of pair-wise weights of the selected elements. When deciding on a best mapping, a matcher should decide which elements from one schema are to be mapped with elements of another schema. Also, the matcher may decide that some elements do not satisfy some matching constraints (*e.g.*, minimal degree of similarity) and cannot be mapped. For further illustration, consider Table 3 once more. The bold-face entries in the table (jointly) represent the best mapping.

COMA [9], OntoBuilder, Cupid, and other schema matching tools apply variations of this model in their matching process. Others (such as Prompt and similarity flooding) also apply this two step methodology, yet do not support a mode that provides the user with all pairwise element mappings. However, it can be expected that making their internal representation of attribute similarity measures available for generating top-K mappings is feasible.

A convenient data structure for modeling the matching problem is to view it as an undirected bipartite graph, $G = (X, Y, E)$, with a node set $V = X \bigcup Y$ representing elements, where X and Y denote the sides of the graph (each side representing one schema), and an edge set E. Weights $w : E \to \mathrm{R}^+$ are assigned with edges, representing the degree of similarity between elements. G does not have to be a complete graph. Threshold constraints may result in the elimination of some edges. Also, some matchers (*e.g.*, similarity flooding) present only partial pairwise similarity measures. Again, such constraints are interpreted as an incomplete graph.

A mapping in G is a subset of pair-wise edges of E. We denote a mapping by $M \subseteq E$. $F(M)$ represents the target function value of M. Each edge $e \in M$ is an *element mapping*.

Using the proposed data structure, the matching problem becomes a problem of selecting an optimal mapping (*i.e.*, a subset of E that optimizes F). Given a matching problem and a set of matching constraints, we denote by A_{best} the best known algorithm for solving the bipartite graph matching problem, given the matching constraints. We denote by $C(A_{best})$ the complexity of A_{best}.

Typical classification of matching constraints partitions matching problems into either $1 : 1$ matching, $1 : n$ matching, $n : 1$ matching, and general $(n : m)$ matching [31]. We now discuss three special cases within this classification and the methods for solving the matching problem in these cases, using an undirected bipartite graph as the underlying data structure. Henceforth, we shall assume that $F(M) = \sum_{e \in M} k_e w(e)$, a weighted average where k_e is a parameter that can represent the relative importance of an edge e. The study of top-K using other target functions is left for future research.

$1 : 1$ **Matching.** When constraining the mapping to be $1 : 1$, the node set represents individual attributes, where the X node set contains all attributes of one schema ($|X| = n_1$) and the Y node set contains all attributes of the other schema ($|Y| = n_2$). A mapping in G is a subset of pair-wise **disjoint** edges of E. An efficient algorithm for identifying the best mapping in this case is given as a variation of the weighted bipartite graph matching problem [16]. Such an algorithm has a complexity of $C(A_{best}) = O(n^3)$ [23],[1] where $n = \max(n_1, n_2)$.

Before moving on to the next two cases, we would like to offer a refined categorization of matching constraints. Consider, for example, a $1 : n$ constraint. Such a constraint may indicate that a single attribute in one schema can be replicated to more than a single attribute in another schema (*e.g.*, a `Password` attribute in one schema vs. `Type Password` and `Retype Password` in another schema). Alternatively, such a constraint may indicate that an attribute in one schema is decomposed into several attributes in another schema (*e.g.*, `Name` in one schema is decomposed into `Given Name` and `Surname` in another schema). We denote the former a *replication* constraint and the latter a *decomposition* constraint.

When a replication constraint is applied, matching decisions of individual attributes are independent of one another. Therefore, matching `Password` with `Type Password` is independent of the matching of `Password` with `Retype Password`. However, a decomposition constraint cannot be evaluated by some aggregation of matching of individual attributes. For example, consider the attribute `Name` and the attribute pair `Given Name` and `Surname`. Machine learning techniques are likely to rate the comparison of concatenation of values from `Given Name` and `Surname` against `Name`, higher than comparing each of the attributes independently. Therefore, decomposition constraints require the evaluation of elements as well as individual attributes.

The bipartite graph can support the provision of such comparison by adding feasible attribute sets as elements (nodes) in the graph. Such enhancement entails, in many cases, higher complexity of the matching process. For example, if the matching constraint allows a single attribute in S_1 to be matched with up to 2 attributes in S_2, one needs to consider all possible pairs in a schema. Therefore, n_1 elements of S_1 are matched with $\binom{n_2}{2} = \frac{1}{2} n_2 (n_2 - 1)$ elements of S_2, which increases the number of nodes in G to $|V| = \mathcal{O}(n^2)$. This computation can be generalized to any (sufficiently small) constant c, constraining the number of attributes in an element. The complexity in this case is of $\mathcal{O}(n^c)$.

$1 : n$ **matching with replications.** Using the bipartite graph as a data structure, the following simple algorithm can be devised. Consider a matching constraint that allows an attribute in one schema to be replicated several times in another schema. Therefore, nodes on one side of the bipartite graph (say, the Y nodes) cannot have more than a single incidenting edge. Such a

---

[1] Here we consider the complexity of the best *sequential* algorithm for finding a maximum weight mapping in a bipartite graph. Likewise, an alternative algorithm for this problem is presented in [17], and its time complexity is $O(n^{2.5} \log(nW))$, where W stands for the highest edge weight in the graph.

constraint does not apply to the other side of the graph (X nodes). Therefore, all one has to do is to identify the best edge incidenting upon each node that requires unique mapping. Let $v \in Y$ be a node in the graph and v_e be the set of all edges incident on v. The following simple algorithm can thus be applied, where $argmax_{v_e} w(e)$ stands for the edge of v_e that maximizes w.

Algorithm 1

$S_e \leftarrow \emptyset$
  For each $v \in Y$ do
        $S_e \leftarrow S_e \cup \{argmax_{v_e} w(e)\}$
  Return S_e

The complexity of Algorithm 1 is $C\left(A_{best}\right) = \mathcal{O}\left(|E|\right) = \mathcal{O}\left((n^c)^2\right) = \mathcal{O}\left(n^{2c}\right)$.

$n : m$ **Matching with Decomposition.** When replacing single attributes with elements, traditional algorithms for solving matching problems in bipartite graphs can no longer ensure unique attribute selection. Therefore, two elements that contain the same attribute A can be chosen as part of a mapping, which means that A no longer has a unique mapping. Nevertheless, certain $n : m$ constraints can be supported by the bipartite graph data structure. As an example, consider a constraint enforcing each attribute in one schema to be mapped uniquely to a single combination of attributes. Therefore, if Name in S_1 is mapped to the combination of Given Name and Surname in S_2, no other attribute in S_1 can be mapped to this combination (although a different combination of Surname and OfficeNumber in S_2 may be the appropriate combination for InitialPassword in S_1). This special case can fall into the category of 1 : 1 global cardinality and $n : m$ local cardinality, according to the classification of [31].

Such a constraint is mapped into the data structure in the following way. The X set of nodes represent individual attributes of one schema. The Y set of nodes represent all legal elements of the other schema. We can then apply an algorithm for solving the weighted bipartite graph matching problem in this graph. The complexity of this algorithm can be defined in terms of attributes as followed.

$$C\left(A_{best}\right) = \mathcal{O}\left(|V|^3\right) = \mathcal{O}\left((n^c)^3\right) = \mathcal{O}\left(n^{3c}\right)$$

2.2   Modeling Top-K Mappings

Let $G = (X, Y, E)$ be an undirected bipartite graph with edges representing the degree of similarity between elements. Top-K can be defined recursively as follows. For $K = 1$, the K-th best mapping M_1^* is any maximum weight mapping in G. Let M_i^* denote the i-th best mapping, for any $i > 0$. Then, given the best $i - 1$ mappings $M_1^*, M_2^*, \ldots, M_{i-1}^*$, the i-th best mapping M_i^* is defined as a mapping of maximum weight over mappings that differ from each of

Table 2. Running example attributes

cybersuitors.com	date.com
101. select: Country: (cboCountries)	201. select: Select your Country (countrycode)
102. select: Birthday: (cboYears)	202. select: Date of Birth (dob_year)
103. select: Birthday: (cboMonths)	203. select: Date of Birth (dob_month)
104. .select: Birthday: (cboDays)	204. select: Date of Birth (dob_day)
105. checkbox: (chkAgreement1)	
106. checkbox: (chkAgreement2)	
107. text: Last name: (txtLastName)	
108. text: First name: (txtFirstName)	
109. text: Use this name instead of my first name: (cboPenName)	
110. text: Your city town village: (txtPlace)	
111. select: State (if in USA): (cboUSstates)	
112. password: Please choose a password This ... (txtPassword)	
113. password: Re-enter password: (txtPassword2)	
114. text: Your email address: (txtEmail)	
115. text: Please retype your email address to confirm it: (txtEmail2)	
	205. image: ()
	206. checkbox: Date.com - Join Now for Free! (over18)
	207. select: I am a (i_am)

$M_1^*, M_2^*, \ldots, M_{i-1}^*$. Therefore, given top-$K$ mappings, any mapping $M \subseteq E$ such that $M \notin \{M_1^*, M_2^*, \ldots, M_K^*\}$ satisfies $F(M) \leq \min_{1 \leq j \leq k} F(M_j^*) = F(M_k^*)$.

To illustrate the notion of top-K mappings, consider the following example.

Example 1 (Running example schemata). Table 2 is an extension of Table 1, presenting attributes of two schemata, `cybersuitors.com` and `date.com`. Matching attributes are presented in the same row.

Attribute names were extracted from the labels as appear on the Web site and the field names (in parentheses) of the form entries. Field names are used for matching the values returned by the client to the server's database schema, hence the condensed form. Attribute names are preceded by field type (*e.g.*, select, checkbox, *etc.*), also used to enhance the matching process. The field `image: ()` is an image field, used as a submit button, that is not associated with name or label. We refer the interested reader to [15] for a detailed description of the extraction process. Henceforth, we number vertices rather than using attribute names, for the sake of clarity.

The edge weights of the bipartite graph of the example are given in Table 3, as computed **automatically** by OntoBuilder. We refer the interested reader to [15] for a detailed description of OntoBuilder matching techniques. In this example, we constrain the matching process to result in 1 : 1 mappings.

The exact mapping (as determined by a human observer) is: $\{e_{101,201}, e_{102,202}, e_{103,203}, e_{104,204}\}$, while the outcome of A_{best} for the bipartite graph is the best mapping $M^* = \{e_{101,201}, e_{102,202}, e_{103,203}, e_{104,204}, e_{105,205}, e_{106,206}, e_{111,207}\}$. M^* contains the exact mapping, with additional three attribute mappings. As discussed in Section 1.1, the exact mapping cannot be found by setting a threshold. □

Table 3. Edge weights in the example

↓ cybersuitors.com/ date.com→	201	202	203	204	205	206	207
101	**0.5937**	0.0597	0.0639	0.0597	0	0.0597	0.0542
102	0.0575	**0.4944**	0.184	0.184	0	0.0618	0.0625
103	0.0620	0.1833	**0.6847**	0.1833	0	0.0611	0.0618
104	0.0620	0.2516	0.2507	**0.7042**	0	0.0627	0.0634
105	0.05774	0.0538	0.0577	0.0538	**0.4**	0.5038	0.0538
106	0.0577	0.0538	0.0577	0.0538	0.4	**0.5038**	0.0538
107	0.0075	0.0101	0.0101	0.0101	0	0.0473	0.0216
108	0.0071	0.0153	0.0153	0.0153	0	0.0469	0.0194
109	0.0085	0.009	0.009	0.009	0	0.034	0.014
110	0.051	0.0089	0.0089	0.0089	0	0.0115	0.0089
111	0.0649	0.0712	0.0712	0.0712	0	0.0629	**0.1101**
112	0.013	0.0052	0.0052	0.0052	0	0.0124	0.0124
113	0.01	0.0108	0.0108	0.0108	0	0.0125	0.0075
114	0.0563	0.0094	0.0094	0.0094	0	0.0118	0.0094
115	0.0599	0.0083	0.0083	0.0083	0	0.0083	0.0319

To motivate our research, we now offer an intuitive interpretation of top-K mappings. Suppose an edge weight represents the belief of a matcher in the correctness of an element mapping. A higher weight indicates a higher confidence in the element mapping correctness. When switching from the i-th best mapping to the $(i + 1)$ best mapping, the matcher is forced to give up at least one element mapping, while maintaining an overall high confidence in a schema mapping. To do so, the matcher cedes an element mapping in which it is less confident. Therefore, generating top-K mappings can be observed as a process in which a matcher iteratively abandons element mappings in which it is less confident.

We substantiate this intuitive interpretation with an empirical analysis, based on experiments with real world data. The details of the experiments are provided in Section 4, together with a thorough empirical analysis. Here, we provide an initial motivation to our work. Figure 2 provides an analysis of the attribute mapping stability. K is given at the x axis. For each K, we measure the percentage of correct (incorrect) attribute mappings that were not changed throughout the

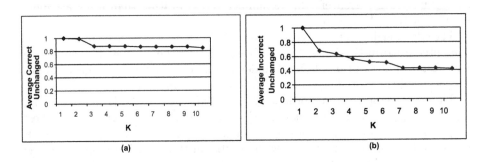

Fig. 2. Average unchaged attribute mappings

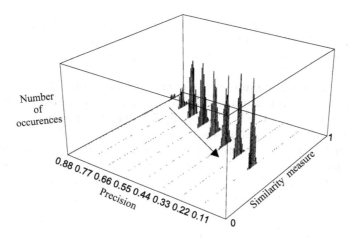

Fig. 3. Similarity measures distribution according to imprecision levels

K mappings. That is, those attribute pairs that appear in all top-K mappings. Figure 2(a) illustrates the results for correct attribute mappings. Figure 2(b) illustrates the results for incorrect mappings. It is easy to observe that correct attribute mappings were less subject to change (less than 16%) with K then incorrect attribute mappings (dropping 60%). Therefore, by analyzing top-K mappings, it is likely that correct attribute mappings will remain stable, while incorrect attribute mappings will keep on changing.

It can be argued that top-K mappings are not different from any K mappings. Therefore, by choosing **any** K mappings (and not necessarily the top ones), one can derive useful information on the quality of the schema matching process. We justify the decision to use top-K mappings in an earlier research [14]. A class of schema matchers (termed *monotonic*) was defined in [14], for which a higher similarity measure is an indication of a more precise mapping. For completeness sake, we now provide an illustrative example of one form of monotonicity, dubbed *statistical monotonicity* in [14]. Figure 3 presents a pictorial illustration of a distribution of similarity measure values of all possible mappings between two schemata, according to precision levels. These results are based on similarity measure, as assigned by the *Combined* matcher, already mentioned in Section 1.1. At each precision level, similarity measures seem to be normally distributed with a decreasing mean. Therefore, the higher the precision of a mapping is, the higher would be the similarity measure assigned by the matcher. In the absence of any variance, one would expect the top-1 mapping to be the exact mapping. However, as shown in [14] and illustrated here, the variance in each precision level allows mappings within any given precision level to overlap in their similarity measure with other precision levels. Therefore, monotonicity ensures that the top-K mappings are sufficiently "close" to the exact mapping.

The analysis in [14] shows that due to the uncertainty inherent in the matching process, no matcher can be expected to identify the exact mapping as the best mapping at all times. If a matcher were required to iterate over all possible permutations, the search would become infeasible. However, if the top-K mappings contain sufficient information to predict most of the correct mappings and K can be determined to be sufficiently small, precision may be increased at a negligible cost.

Based on the observations of this section, and the empirical analysis we have conducted, a reasonable approach involves a simultaneous analysis of possible mappings to determine the best mapping. This approach is in contrast to current practice, in which a system seeks the best mapping and resorts to manual intervention for additional input whenever using the best mapping fails. The most prominent drawback of the current approach has to do with the reliance on manual intervention. We aim at minimizing such intervention, and therefore we propose to enhance automatic reasoning on top-K mappings.

3   Schema Matching Verification

To overcome the uncertainty in mapping results, we propose the following generic methodology. Let S_1 and S_2 be two schemata. The methodology contains five steps as follows:

1. **Computing:** $G = (X, Y, E)$ =Generate similarity graph.
2. **Matching:** $\{M_1^*, M_2^*, \ldots, M_K^*\}$ =Generate top-K mappings, using G.
3. **Verifying:** $A = \{(a, a')\}$ =Analyze $\{M_1^*, M_2^*, \ldots, M_K^*\}$.
4. **Recomputing:** $G' = (X, Y, E')$ =compute $w(a, a')$ for each $(a, a') \in A$.
5. **Rematching:** M^* =Generate top-1 mapping, using G'.

According to this generic methodology, a similarity graph is generated and top-K mappings are generated and analyzed to identify element pairs that are worthy of further consideration (*i.e.*, verification). It then recomputes the similarity measures and generates the best mapping.

Three main differences exist between the proposed methodology and existing practice in schema matching. First, most of current methods do not use top-K mappings. For those who use top-K mappings (*e.g.*, [25,12]), it is done locally, on an attribute-based cases. Therefore, it can capture only local similarities, while ignoring global constraints, such as cardinality constraints, and global phenomenon, such as accumulation of elements from one schema around a single element from another schema. The reasoning behind local top-K mappings brings us to the second difference. Current methods assume the assistance of a user in the process, by refuting certain mappings, or setting new constraints. Clearly, cognitive limitations of users make it much harder to compare whole schemata, while attribute-based comparison is a much easier task. In contrast, our approach is aimed at fully-automatic schema matching, recognizing the inherent uncertainty in such a process. With humans outside the loop, there is no reason to simplify the task at the expanse of accuracy, whenever it can be avoided. Finally, the verification step analyzes all top-K mappings simultaneously, rather the iteratively, as was proposed in approaches such as Clio [27]. This difference can also be attributed to the presence of a user in the loop in current practice. In user presence, iterations provide an opportunity for incremental improvement, a process that fits human cognitive capabilities. With automatic matching, on the other hand, no feedback is given, and the use of simultaneous analysis can provide insights that are not necessarily evident with pairwise comparison. One final comment has to do with machine learning methods for schema matching. Such methods allow a training period on annotated data, to be followed by matching schemata, unknown beforehand. Feedback is only given during the learning phase. Therefore, the proposed approach can serve as a complementary method once the learning phase is completed.

The first step is beyond the scope of this paper. As discussed in Section 1.2, many worthy methods and heuristics have been proposed in generating G, and any that satisfy the monotonicity condition, as set in [14], would suffice. The last step has also been extensively discussed in the literature. In Section 2.1 we have discussed the use of bipartite graphs in representing the schema matching problem, and solving the top-1 problem.

In the rest of this paper we focus on steps 3-4. For completeness sake, we next introduce an analysis of existing algorithms for step 2, finding top-2 mappings and top-K mappings.

3.1   Algorithms for Finding Top-K Mappings

The assignment ranking problem involves the enumeration of K assignments with least cost. The first algorithm of $\mathcal{O}(K\,|V|^4)$ for ranking assignments was suggested by Murty in 1968 [29], where $|V|$ is the number of nodes in the assignment graph. In 1985/6, Hamachar and Queyranne proposed an alternative general algorithm for ranking solutions of combinatorial problems [18]. This algorithm was later specialized for bipartite matchings [7], in $\mathcal{O}(K\,|V|^3)$, using flow networks. In [30], another $\mathcal{O}(K\,|V|^3)$ algorithm was presented, using a specific order of analyzing assignments.

In [7] it was shown that finding the second best assignment is equivalent to finding the shortest cycle in a residual network relatively to the best assignment. This demands solving at most n shortest path problems, and therefore solving the top-2 problem is of $\mathcal{O}(|V|^3)$ complexity. Therefore, the top-2 problem can be solved for the case of $1:1$ mapping in $\mathcal{O}(n^3)$. The case of $m:n$ with decomposition is also reduced to $1:1$ mapping (see Section 2.1), yielding a solution to the top-2 problem in $\mathcal{O}(n^{3c})$.

For the case of $1:n$ with replication, an efficient algorithm for generating top-K mappings can be devised as follows, summarized in Algorithm 2 as a pseudo-code. Let $G = (X, Y, E)$ be the matching bipartite graph. First, for each node $v \in Y$, a sorted list of all edges $\{(u,v)\,|\,u \in X\}$ in a decreasing order of similarity is generated (Line 2). In the next step, we compute for each node $v \in Y$ the weight difference between the edge (u,v) with maximum similarity and the next edge in the list (Line 3). These values are then inserted into a minimum heap (Line 4). Lines 5-7 generate the best mapping. At an iteration i, we remove an edge (u,v) from M^*_{i-1} such that its weight difference is minimal (Line 9) and replace it by an edge (u',v), which precedes it in the sorted list of

v (lines 10 and 11). The weight difference between (u', v) and the next edge in the sorted list of v is then inserted into the heap (Line 12).

Algorithm 2

1 For each $v \in Y$ do
2   v^{sorted} =create a sorted list of $\{u \in X\}$ in a decreasing order of $w(u, v)$
3          $\Delta v_{\max} = w(u_{(1)}, v) - w(u_{(2)}, v)$
4 H =Build-Min-Heap($\{ (u_{(1)}, v), \Delta v_{\max} \,|v \in Y \}$)
5 $M_1^* = \{ (\max \{ v^{sorted} \}, v) \,|v \in Y \}$

6 For each $v \in Y$ do
7          $v^{sorted} = v^{sorted} \backslash \max \{ v^{sorted} \}$
8 For $i = 2$ to k do
9       $(u_{(l)}, v), \Delta v$=Heap-Extract-Min(H)
10       $M_i^* = M_{i-1}^* \backslash \{ (u_{(1)}, v) \} \cup (\max \{ v^{sorted} \}, v)$
11       $v^{sorted} = v^{sorted} \backslash \max \{ v^{sorted} \}$
12   Min-Heap-Insert$(H, (u_{(l+1)}, v), w(u_{(l+1)}, v) - w(u_{(l+2)}, v))$
13 Return $\{ M_i^* \}_{i=1}^k$

Sorting the edge weights for each node takes $\mathcal{O}(n \lg n)$. Therefore, the overall sorting takes $\mathcal{O}(n^2 \lg n)$. Building the heap is $\mathcal{O}(n)$ and the generation of the best mapping takes $\mathcal{O}(n)$. Each additional mapping requires $\mathcal{O}(\lg n)$, due to the heap operations. Therefore, the overall complexity is $\mathcal{O}(n^2 \lg n + K \lg n)$.

An adaptation of Murty's algorithm for top-K and Chegireddy's and Hamacher's algorithm for top-2 to the schema matching world is detailed in [2]. We have implemented the algorithms and embedded them in OntoBuilder [15], which was used for experimenting with the heuristic proposed in this paper.

3.2   Stability Analysis

We are now ready to introduce a concrete heuristic, instantiating the generic verification methodology presented earlier. Let S_1 and S_2 be two schemata and let $G = (X, Y, E)$ be a bipartite graph, modeling the matching alternatives between S_1 and S_2. Given a set $\{M_1^*, M_2^*, \ldots, M_K^*\}$ of K top mappings, and a user threshold $t \in [0, 1]$, the analysis step of the stability analysis heuristic first computes for each edge $e \in E$ the number of times it appears in $\{M_1^*, M_2^*, \ldots, M_K^*\}$, dubbed $\iota(e)$. It is worth noting that $0 \le \iota(e) \le K$. Then, it generates a set of edges $A = \{(a, a')\}$ such that $(a, a') \in A$ iff $\frac{\iota(e)}{K} \le t$. That is, the set A contains all edges that do not appear a sufficient number of times in the top-K mappings, $\{M_1^*, M_2^*, \ldots, M_K^*\}$. The recomputation phase revises G by setting $w(a, a') = 0$ for each $(a, a') \in A$.

Example 2 (Stability analysis example). Consider Example 1. Table 4 provides $\frac{\iota(e)}{K}$ values of all edges whose count in the top-10 mappings is non-zero, in a decreasing order. For $t > 0.6$, the only non-zero edges will be those of the exact mapping.   □

Table 4. Stability analysis of the motivating example

www.cybersuitors.com	www.date.com	$\frac{\iota(e)}{K}$
101	201	1.0
102	202	1.0
103	203	1.0
104	204	1.0
111	207	0.6
105	205	0.5
106	205	0.5
107	206	0.4
108	206	0.4
115	207	0.4
109	206	0.2

For the stability analysis to work, a schema matcher should be monotonic [14]. Therefore, our underlying assumption is that stable attribute mappings represent those mappings that are part of the exact mapping. Our empirical analysis show that this heuristic indeed works better for a matcher which was shown to be monotonic in [14].

4   Experiments

We now present an empirical evaluation of stability analysis, to support our hypothesis that simultaneous analysis of top-K mappings improves the quality of mapping. We report in details on our experimental setup (Section 4.1), the data that was used (Section 4.2), and the evaluation methodology (Section 4.3). We then present in Section 4.4 the experiment results and provide an empirical analysis of these results.

4.1   Experiment Setup

We have implemented several top-K algorithms (including Murty's, Chegireddy and Hamacher's, and our version of $1 : n$ mappings with replication) as part of the development of OntoBuilder. OntoBuilder runs under the Java 2 JDK version 1.4 or greater and is downloadable from http://ie.technion.ac.il/OntoBuilder. We chose for A_{best} (whenever $1 : 1$ mapping is applicable) the maximum weighted bipartite algorithm implementation suggested in LEDA ([22], pp. 132-150). The A_{best} algorithm was implemented in Java, and plugged in for use within our top-K algorithms. We have also generated a demo presentation showing execution of the top-K mappings. Figure 4 provides the visual output of the algorithm, with $K = 3$.

OntoBuilder specializes in extracting ontologies from Web forms, a feature we have used in our experiments. OntoBuilder accepts two ontologies as input, a candidate ontology and a target ontology. It attempts to match each attribute in the target ontology with an attribute in the candidate ontology. OntoBuilder

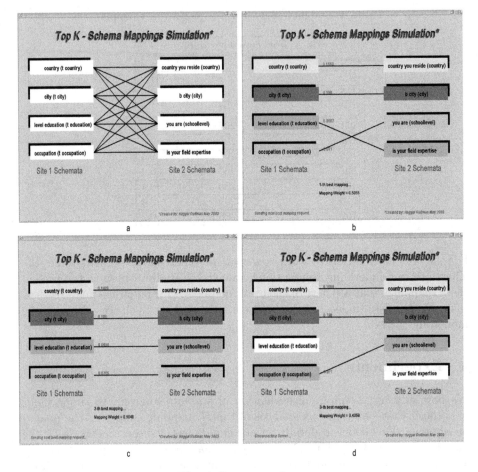

Fig. 4. Demo snapshots

supports an array of matching and filtering algorithms and can be used as a framework for developing new schema matchers which can be plugged-in and used via GUI or as an API. In our experiments we have used the following four matchers (detailed description of which can be found in [15]):

Term: A term is a combination of a label and a name. Term matching compares labels and names to identify syntactically similar terms. To achieve better performance, terms are preprocessed using several techniques originating in IR research. Term matching is based on either complete word or string comparison.

Value: Value matching utilizes domain constraints (*e.g.*, drop lists, check boxes, and radio buttons) to compute similarity measure among terms. The availability of constrained value-sets becomes valuable when comparing two terms that do not exactly match through their labels.

Composition: A composite term is composed of other terms (either atomic or composite). Composition can be translated into a hierarchy. This schema matcher assigns similarity to terms, based on the similarity of their neighbors.

Precedence: The precedence relationship is unique to OntoBuilder and therefore worth of a lengthier discussion. In any interactive process, the order in which data are provided may be important. In particular, data given at an earlier stage may restrict the availability of options for a later entry. For example, a car rental site may determine which car groups are available for a given session, using the information given regarding the pick-up location and time. Therefore, once those entries are filled in, the information is sent back to the server and the next form is brought up. Such precedence relationships can usually be identified by the activation of a script, such as (but not limited to) the one associated with a SUBMIT button. Precedence can be translated into a precedence graph. The matching algorithm is based on a technique we dub *graph pivoting*, as follows. When matching two terms, we consider each of them to be a pivot within its own ontology, thus partitioning the graph into semantically related subgraphs. The semantics of pivoting is taken from the ontological analysis, and in the case of precedence the graph it partitioned into a subgraph of all preceding terms and all succeding terms. By comparing preceding subgraphs and succeding subgraphs, we determine the confidence strength of the pivot terms.

4.2   Data

For our experiments with stability analysis, we have selected 86 Web forms from different domains, such as dating and matchmaking, job hunting, Web mail, hotel reservation, news, and cosmetics. We extracted each Web form ontology using OntoBuilder. We have matched the Web forms in pairs, where pairs were taken from the same domain. The ontologies vary in size, from 5 to 64 attributes with about half of the ontologies have between 10 and 20 attributes. They also vary in the proportion of number of attribute pairs in the exact mapping relative to the target ontology. This proportion ranges from 16.6% to 94.7%; the proportion in about half of the ontologies is more than 60%. Another dimension is the size difference between matched ontologies, ranging from equal size ontologies to about 3 times difference between ontologies. In about half of the pairs, the difference was less than 30% of the target ontology size. Finally, the best mapping precision results range from 5% to 100%, with about half the ontology pairs were mapped by both matchers (see below) with precision of more than 40%.

In addition to the real data, we generated 50 synthetic ontology pairs, as follows. We have selected the ontology pair taut.securesites.com and www1522.boca15-verio.com. Both ontologies are of medium size (18 and 19 attributes, respectively), strongly similar (the exact mapping contains 18 attributes), and close in size. The best mapping of the *Combined* matcher is the exact mapping. Based on the similarity matrix of these ontologies we have generated 50 similarity matrices, for which each value val is replaced with $val + val * f$

and f is randomly taken from $[-v, v]$. $v \in \{0.1, 0.2, 0.3, 0.4, 0.5\}$ (10 matrices for each v value).

We ran two schema matchers, namely *Term* and *Combined*, to generate the top-10 mappings. The *Combined* matcher aggregates the results of the four matchers, detailed in Section 4.1, using weighted average. We ran a total of 1860 experiments (93 ontology pairs, 2 schema matchers, and 10 best mappings). Note that in our experiments, generating top-1, top-2, *etc.* can be performed in one pass.

4.3   Evaluation Methodology

In order to evaluate the stability analysis heuristic, we measured its performance using two main metrics, namely precision and recall. Precision is computed as the ratio of correct element mappings, with respect to some exact mapping, out of the total number of element mappings suggested by a heuristic. Recall is computed as the ratio of correct element mappings, out of the total number of element mappings in the exact mapping. Both recall and precision are measured on a $[0, 1]$ scale. An optimal schema matching results in both precision and recall equal to 1. Lower precision means more false positives, while lower recall suggests more false negatives.

The independent variables of the experiments were K, the number of simultaneous mappings, and t, the threshold.

4.4   Results and Analysis

In our first experiment we have measured precision and recall for a fixed $K \in \{1, 2, ..., 10\}$, varying the threshold t. Figure 5 presents the average change to precision and recall for different thresholds over all 43 real data pairs. K was set to 10. Figure 5(left) illustrates the results for the *Term* matcher and Figure 5(right) illustrates the results for the *Combined* matcher. In both cases, precision increases (in general) up to $t = 0.9$ with the increased threshold. Recall demonstrates a monotonic decrease with the increased threshold. Such a phenomenon accords with our initial intuition and is expected for monotonic matchers. In [14] we have shown that both the *Term* and the *Combined* matchers are monotonic.

A closer look at the amount of improvements reveals that the precision of the *Term* matcher increases by up to 15.4% (with $t = 0.9$). The *Combined* matcher

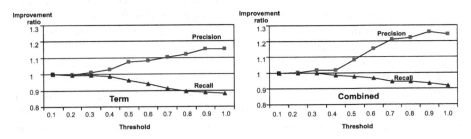

Fig. 5. Precision and Recall for Stability analysis with $K = 10$

provides an increase of 25.6% (again with $t = 0.9$). As for recall, it decreases to a maximum of 11.9% for the *Term* matcher and by a smaller 8% for the *Combined* matcher (for $t = 1$). Therefore, stability analysis works better for the *Combined* matcher than for the *Term* matcher. This conclusion can be aligned with the discussion in [14], where the exact mapping was found, on average, at $K = 7$ for the *Combined* matcher and for $K > 100$ for the *Term* matcher.

Looking at the shape of the graphs, it seems that with both matchers, the improvements (in terms of precision) levels off at about $t = 0.9$. We hypothesize that, in general, the increased demand of a higher threshold benefit the heuristic up to a point, from which it will become impossible for the top-K algorithm to keep even its stronger attribute mappings. We believe that the "break-even point" depends to a great extent on the size of the ontology, some evidence to which is given below. The *Term* matcher has a more wiggly precision result, with some decreases in precision for $t = 0.1, 0.6$, and 0.7. Therefore, the performance of the *Term* matcher is less predicted (although the difference is not statistically significant) than that of the *Combined* matcher. This conclusions was also reached in [14].

Next, we have partitioned the ontologies into two groups, based on ontology similarity. We define an ontology pair for which 60% or more of the terms in the target ontology can be matched to terms in the target ontology to be *strongly similar*. 22 pairs out of the 43 pairs were strongly similar, with similarity ranging from 60% to 94.7%. Table 5 summarizes the analysis for this and following partitions. Again, K was set to 10. The results show improvement over the whole group in the precision level, with smaller decrease in the recall level. The precision of the *Term* matcher increases by up to 19.8% (with $t = 1$). The *Combined* matcher provides an increase of 28.5% (again with $t = 1$). As for recall, it decreases by 10.1% for the *Term* matcher and by a smaller 5.8% for the *Combined* matcher. The main conclusion for this experiment is that stability analysis works better for strongly similar ontologies.

We also partitioned the ontologies based on size. We define an ontology to be big (relative to ontology sizes we have in our data set) if it has more than 20

Table 5. Stability analysis of ontology classes

Ontology class	Term								Combined							
	precision		recall		precision		recall	
	max increase	t	max decrease	t	max increase	t	max decrease	t
strongly similar	19.8%	1.0	10.1%	1.0	28.5%	1.0	5.8%	1.0
weekly similar	12.1%	0.9	13.7%	1.0	23.3%	0.9	10.3%	1.0
big	7.6%	1.0	8.5%	1.0	16.7%	1.0	3.6%	1.0
small	20.7%	1.0	14.3%	1.0	29.5%	1.0	11.1%	1.0
similar	8.9%	0.9	11.3%	1.0	19.9%	0.9	7%	1.0
disimilar	24.1%	1.0	12.6%	1.0	32.3	0.9	9%	1.0
low initial precision	11.4%	0.9	16.9%	1.0	27.6%	0.9	11.6%	1.0
high initial precision	19.2%	1.0	7.1%	1.0	24.5%	1.0	4.7%	1.0

attributes. There were 18 big target ontologies. The results show less improvement in the precision level for bigger ontologies, yet with smaller decrease in the recall level. The precision of the *Term* matcher increases by up to 7.6% (with $t = 1$). The *Combined* matcher provides an increase of 16.7% (again with $t = 1$). As for recall, it decreases by 8.5% for the *Term* matcher and by 3.6% for the *Combined* matcher. The smaller gain in precision and the smaller reduction in recall for bigger ontologies can be justified by the smaller marginal impact a single attribute has on the overall performance. Generally speaking, however, it seems that stability analysis is better suited for smaller ontologies.

We next experimented with ontologies that differ in size. Ontology pairs were considered similar if the difference between the number of attributes of the candidate and target ontologies was less then 30% of the target ontology (there were 23 such pairs). The results show less improvement in the precision level for similar-size ontologies. The precision of the *Term* matcher increases by up to 8.9% (with $t = 0.9$). The *Combined* matcher provides an increase of 19.9% (again with $t = 0.9$). As for recall, it decreases by 11.3% for the *Term* matcher and by 7% for the *Combined* matcher. We found no clear explanation to the phenomenon in which stability analysis is better suited for ontologies that differ in size.

The last partitioning is based on the best mapping precision level. Out of the 43 pairs, 21 pairs (20 pairs for the *Combined* schema matcher) had a precision level of less than 0.4 for the best mapping. Here, our analysis show different results for the *Term* matcher and the *Combined* matcher. The stability analysis heuristic using the *Term* matcher seem to be more effective for pairs which had high initial precision, increasing the precision by an average of 19.2%. Using the *Combined* matcher, the difference between the two groups is much smaller, showing slightly better performance (27.6% vs. 24.5%) for the ontology pairs with low initial precision. Recall, for both matchers, was significantly less affected by for ontologies with high initial precision.

Our final experiment was aimed at analyzing the impact of noise in schema matcher similarity measures. We have generated top-K mappings for the synthetic matrices (see Section 4.2), applied the stability analysis heuristic and measured precision and recall as before. Figure 6 illustrates the change of precision and recall, partitioned according to the various v (maximum deviation)

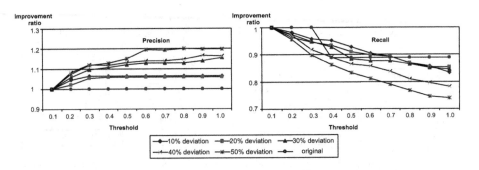

Fig. 6. Stability analysis on synthetic data: Combined algorithm

values. We present the results for the *Combined* matcher only since the results for the *Term* matcher share the same trends. The synthetic data demonstrates the same trends as the real data, increase of precision as the threshold increases, leveling off at around $t = 0.9$. Somewhat surprising, the heuristic becomes more effective, in terms of precision, as v increases. Clearly, the good starting point of the original mapping serves in the good performance, even with increased noise. When we applied the heuristic to randomly generated matrices (in which each attribute pair got a uniformly distributed value in $[0, 1]$) the result was a complete chaos, and the heuristic was practically useless. Recall deterioration (Figure 6(right)) serves as an indication to the impact of noise. With more noise, the heuristic throws out more attribute mappings, including good ones. Therefore, with $v = 0.5$, the matcher lost 26% in its recall level for $t = 10$ (compare this with an average of 12% recall loss for real data).

5   Discussion and Conclusion

In this paper, we have investigated a major shortcoming of standard methods for automatic semantic reconciliation: namely, that they commit to the best mapping, typically chosen as that which maximizes the sum (or average) of pair-wise similarities under certain constraints (*e.g.*, 1:1 mapping). The problem is that, due to uncertainty in concept interpretation, the best mapping chosen by the matcher can actually be an unsuccessful choice. To alleviate this shortcoming, we propose that instead of using just the best mapping, a set of top-K mappings should be generated and examined iteratively until a good mapping is found. Using this approach, the exact mapping is likely to be identified if the matcher ranks it sufficiently high (but not necessarily as the best).

We have proposed a generic framework for the simultaneous utilization of top-K mapping and provide a concrete heuristic, termed stability analysis, to utilize top-K mappings in improving mapping precision (at the cost of recall). Stability analysis was shown empirically to provide good results for monotonic schema matchers.

An ongoing research involves the investigation of efficient methods for utilizing input from multiple schema matchers. Choosing among the current variety of schema matchers is far from being trivial. First, the number of heuristics is continuously growing, and this diversity by itself complicates our decision making. Second, as one would expect, recent empirical analysis shows that there is no (and may never be) a single dominant schema matcher that performs best, regardless of the data model and application domain [14]. Bearing these observations in mind, we believe that customers of schema matching would expect some degree of robustness, despite the biases and shortcomings of individual heuristics. Therefore, tools for determining the best "cocktail" of schema matchers would seem to be the next natural step in schema matching research. Future work involves the identification of additional heuristics for top-K utilization. Such heuristics may be based on the separation of matchers into groups. For example, matchers can be partitioned into costly vs. cheap matchers. Cheap matchers are utilized in identifying potential points of failures and more costly matchers will be applied to this problem subset, thus reducing the overall cost of the matching process (hopefully) without hurting its accuracy.

Acknowledgement

The work of Gal was partially supported by Technion V.P.R. Fund - New York Metropolitan Research Fund, The Fund for the Promotion of Research at the Technion, and the IBM Faculty Award for 2003/2004 on "Self-Configuration in Autonomic Computing using Knowledge Management." We thank Haggai Roitman for his assistance in implementing the algorithms and Amir Taller for his assistance in running experiments.

References

1. J. Aitchison, A. Gilchrist, and D. Bawden. *Thesaurus construction and use: a practical manual.* Aslib, London, third edition, 1997.
2. A. Anaby-Tavor. Enhancing the formal similarity based matching model. Master's thesis, Technion-Israel Institute of Technology, May 2003.
3. S. Bergamaschi, S. Castano, M. Vincini, and D. Beneventano. Semantic integration of heterogeneous information sources. *Data & Knowledge Engineering,* 36(3), 2001.
4. T. Berners-Lee, J. Hendler, and O. Lassila. The semantic Web. *Scientific American,* May 2001.
5. M. Brodie. The grand challenge in information technology and the illusion of validity. Keynote lecture at the International Federated Conference 'On the Move to Meaningful Internet Systems and Ubiquitous Computing', 2002.
6. S. Castano, V. De Antonellis, M.G. Fugini, and B. Pernici. Conceptual schema analysis: Techniques and applications. *ACM Transactions on Database Systems (TODS),* 23(3):286–332, 1998.
7. C.R. Chegireddy and H.W. Hamacher. Algorithms for finding k-best perfect matchings. *Discrete Applied Mathematics,* 18:155–165, 1987.
8. B. Convent. Unsolvable problems related to the view integration approach. In *Proceedings of the International Conference on Database Theory (ICDT),* Rome, Italy, September 1986. In *Computer Science,* Vol. 243, G. Goos and J. Hartmanis, Eds. Springer-Verlag, New York, pp. 141-156.
9. H.H. Do and E. Rahm. COMA - a system for flexible combination of schema matching approaches. In *Proceedings of the International conference on very Large Data Bases (VLDB),* pages 610–621, 2002.
10. A. Doan, P. Domingos, and A.Y. Halevy. Reconciling schemas of disparate data sources: A machine-learning approach. In Walid G. Aref, editor, *Proceedings of the ACM-SIGMOD conference on Management of Data (SIGMOD),* Santa Barbara, California, May 2001. ACM Press.
11. A. Doan, J. Madhavan, P. Domingos, and A. Halevy. Learning to map between ontologies on the semantic web. In *Proceedings of the eleventh international conference on World Wide Web,* pages 662–673. ACM Press, 2002.
12. M. Ehrig and S. Staab. Qom quick ontology mapping. In *Proceedings of the Third International Semantic Web Conference (ISWC'2004),* pages 683 – 697, October 2004. Lecture Notes in Computer Science, Volume 3298.

13. N. Fridman Noy and M.A. Musen. PROMPT: Algorithm and tool for automated ontology merging and alignment. In *Proceedings of the Seventeenth National Conference on Artificial Intelligence (AAAI-2000)*, pages 450–455, Austin, TX, 2000.
14. A. Gal, A. Anaby-Tavor, A. Trombetta, and D. Montesi. A framework for modeling and evaluating automatic semantic reconciliation. *VLDB Journal*, 14(1):50–67, 2005.
15. A. Gal, G. Modica, H.M. Jamil, and A. Eyal. Automatic ontology matching using application semantics. *AI Magazine*, 26(1), 2005.
16. Z. Galil. Efficient algorithms for finding maximum matching in graphs. *ACM Computing Surveys*, 18(1):23–38, March 1986.
17. U. Güntzer, W-T. Balke, and W. Kießling. Optimizing multi-feature queries in image databases. In *Proceedings of the Twenty Sixth Very Large Databases (VLDB) Conference*, pages 419–428, Las Vegas, 2001.
18. H.W. Hamacher and M. Queyranne. K-best solutions to combinatorial optimization problems. *Annals of Operations Research*, 4:123–143, 1985/6.
19. A. Heß and N. Kushmerick. Learning to attach semantic metadata to web services. In *Proceedings of the Second Semantic Web Conference*, 2003.
20. R. Hull. Managing semantic heterogeneity in databases: A theoretical perspective. In *Proceedings of the ACM SIGACT-SIGMOD-SIGART Symposium on Principles of Database Systems (PODS)*, pages 51–61. ACM Press, 1997.
21. M. Jarrar and R. Meersman. Formal ontology engineering in the DOGMA approach. In *Proceedings International Federated Conference 'On the Move to Meaningful Internet Systems and Ubiquitous Computing'*, pages 1238–1254, October 2002.
22. K.Mehlhorn and S.Naher, editors. *LEDA, A platform for combinatorial and geometric computing*. Cambridge University Press, 1999.
23. B. Korte and J. Vygen. *Combinatorial Optimization: Theory and Algorithms*. Springer, second edition, 2002.
24. J. Madhavan, P.A. Bernstein, P. Domingos, and A.Y. Halevy. Representing and reasoning about mappings between domain models. In *Proceedings of the Eighteenth National Conference on Artificial Intelligence and Fourteenth Conference on Innovative Applications of Artificial Intelligence (AAAI/IAAI)*, pages 80–86, 2002.
25. S. Melnik, E. Rahm, and P.A. Bernstein. Rondo: A programming platform for generic model management. In *Proceedings of the ACM-SIGMOD conference on Management of Data (SIGMOD)*, pages 193–204, San Diego, California, 2003. ACM Press.
26. R.J. Miller, L.M. Haas, and M.A. Hernández. Schema mapping as query discovery. In A. El Abbadi, M.L. Brodie, S. Chakravarthy, U. Dayal, N. Kamel, G. Schlageter, and K.-Y. Whang, editors, *Proceedings of the International conference on very Large Data Bases (VLDB)*, pages 77–88. Morgan Kaufmann, 2000.
27. R.J. Miller, M.A. Hernàndez, L.M. Haas, L.-L. Yan, C.T.H. Ho, R. Fagin, and L. Popa. The Clio project: Managing heterogeneity. *SIGMOD Record*, 30(1):78–83, 2001.

28. G. Modica, A. Gal, and H. Jamil. The use of machine-generated ontologies in dynamic information seeking. In C. Batini, F. Giunchiglia, P. Giorgini, and M. Mecella, editors, *Cooperative Information Systems, 9th International Conference, CoopIS 2001, Trento, Italy, September 5-7, 2001, Proceedings*, volume 2172 of *Lecture Notes in Computer Science*, pages 433–448. Springer, 2001.

29. K.G. Murty. An algorithm for ranking all the assignments in order of increasing cost. *Operations Research*, 16:682–687, 1968.

30. M. Pascoal, M.E. Captivo, and J. Cl'imaco. A note on a new variant of Murty's ranking assignments algorithm. *4OR: Quarterly Journal of the Belgian, French and Italian Operations Research Societies*, 1(3):243–255, 2003.

31. E. Rahm and P.A. Bernstein. A survey of approaches to automatic schema matching. *VLDB Journal*, 10(4):334–350, 2001.

32. A. Sheth and J. Larson. Federated database systems for managing distributed, heterogeneous, and autonomous databases. *ACM Computing Surveys*, 22(3):183–236, 1990.

33. A.P. Sheth, S.K. Gala, and S.B. Navathe. On automatic reasoning for schema integration. *Intenational Journal on Intelligent Cooperative Information Systems (IJICIS)*, 2(1):23–50, June 1993.

34. P. Spyns, R. Meersman, and M. Jarrar. Data modelling versus ontology engineering. *ACM SIGMOD Record*, 31(4), 2002.

35. B.C. Vickery. *Faceted classification schemes.* Graduate School of Library Service, Rutgers, the State University, New Brunswick, N.J., 1966.

Semantic Data Management in Peer-to-Peer E-Commerce Applications

Yosi Ben-Asher and Shlomo Berkovsky[*]

Computer Science Department, University of Haifa
31905 Haifa, Israel
{yosi, slavax}@cs.haifa.ac.il

Abstract. Weakly organized structure of Peer-to-Peer systems may cause severe data management problems and high communication overheads. We partially resolve these problems by developing a novel semantic approach to efficiently create, search and organize data objects in E-Commerce Peer-to-Peer applications. The approach is based on the notion of Unspecified Ontology (UNSO). Unlike many existing systems using a global predefined ontology, UNSO approach assumes that the ontology is not fully defined, leaving some parts of it to be dynamically specified by the users. The data objects inserted to the system organize a multi-layered hypercube graph topology, providing a stable infrastructure for efficient semantic search and routing operations. The proposed method has a potential of becoming a practical infrastructure for Peer-to-Peer data management applications.

Keywords: Peer-to-Peer Systems, Data Management, Ontology, E-Commerce.

1 Introduction

Peer-to-Peer (P2P) [21] technology offers a solid alternative to the traditional Client-Server model of computing. While Client-Server model typically bases on a single or small number of servers, in P2P systems every user (peer) acts as both the client and the server at the same time, and provides a portion of the system capability. Thus, P2P technology allows a dynamic set of users to efficiently share resources without any centralized management. The shared resources are computing power (e.g., in distributed computation), data (e.g., in large-scale file sharing), bandwidth (e.g., data transfer from multiple sources) and others. As a result, the advantages of P2P technology over the Client-Server model include roughly unlimited scalability, high privacy and anonymity of the users, and low costs. Sharing and aggregation of the resources guarantees robustness and high availability of P2P systems.

In this work we examine the issue of developing a P2P infrastructure supporting a dynamic semantic management (i.e., insertion and search) of general-purpose E-Commerce advertisements (in short, *ads*). The infrastructure is capable of managing E-Commerce ads of both *supply* and *demand* types. Supply ads are ads, where the users offer a product or a service in exchange for a payment, whereas in demand ads

---

[*] This work was supported by a research grant from Caesarea Edmond Benjamin de Rothschild. Foundation Institute for Interdisciplinary Applications of Computer Science (CRI).

S. Spaccapietra et al. (Eds.): Journal on Data Semantics VI, LNCS 4090, pp. 115–142, 2006.

the users seek for a product or for a service provided by other users. The main functionality of the proposed system is to identify matching between appropriate demand and supply ads. This is further referred as publish-locate functionality. Note that we do not aim at performing higher functions, such as selecting the best offer, conducting public auctions or implementing market clearing (see [9] and [20] for a discussion on distributed systems performing these tasks).

In the state-of-the-art E-Commerce systems, a user publishing or searching an ad, is usually required to fill-in a predefined form describing the matter of the ad. For example, CarSmart (*http://www.carsmart.com*) users searching for a car are asked to fill-in a form containing the following fields: manufacturer name, geographical location, and price range. On the contrary, in another cars site, Motocar (*http://www.motocar.co.il*), the users are asked to fill-in a more complicated form, containing the following fields: producer name, model, range of production years, gearbox type, engine volume and number of previous owners. Although both sites refer to the same type of products, the forms (and even the names or parallel fields in the form) are different, such that a search query launched by the user in one site, is incompatible to the other.

This approach, exploiting predefined forms containing a set of attributes describing the objects, is further referred as ontology-based approach. According to [13], ontology is a formal explicit specification of a domain. Thus, the set of attributes, describing the objects from a particular domain, is considered as the ontology of a domain, whereas the attributes are the slots of the ontology.

HyperCuP [32] proposed a flexible ontology-based hypercube topology for P2P data management. It used a single predefined ontology to classify users as providers of particular information associated with the ontology slots. This classification determined the position of the user in the underlying hypercube and allowed location of any desired information in a bounded number of steps through a semantic routing (see [27] and [5] for a discussions on semantic routing in P2P systems). Thus, HyperCup formed an alternative to distributed hashing [29], [33], [26], network flooding [3], local routing tables [10], gossiping [2], and others fundamental search techniques in P2P systems. Additionally, HyperCuP proposed decentralized algorithms, capable of constructing and maintaining highly-connected hypercube graph, stable to dynamic joins and departures of users.

However, HyperCuP approach, requiring a single predefined ontology, is applicable only to a limited set of domains and is inappropriate for general-purpose E-Commerce systems, implying dynamic and a-priori unknown set of objects. A possible solution might be allowing users to add new types of ontological forms. However, this will flood the system with multiple (partially similar and overlapping) ontologies. As a negative example, consider a setting, where a user publishing an object and a user looking for the same object, are using slightly different ontologies. Another solution might be developing a global comprehensive ontology, comprising as many domain ontologies as possible. However, projecting this ontology on the underlying hypercube will result in a huge, sparse and barely manageable structure. Moreover, sharing of the single ontology by all the users will obstruct it from being expanded.

All these restrictions contradict the decentralized spirit of P2P networks and raise an issue of developing a flexible mechanism for managing a dynamic set of ontologies. Recent researches, e.g., [23] and [34], aim at resolving the ontologies management issue through integrating local ontologies used by various systems. These works try to overcome the autonomous nature of P2P systems and the resulted heterogeneity of the ontologies by developing semantic mappings between the ontologies. The mappings exploit semantic knowledge about the ontology slots for the purposes of identifying commonalities between the ontologies and matching different terms describing similar underlying data.

Conversely, in this work we developed a novel approach of an *UNSpecified Ontology* (UNSO) for the management of E-Commerce ads. Instead of trying to identify the matching between the ontologies, UNSO presumes that the ontology is not fully defined, and parts of it can be dynamically specified by the users. This broader notion of ontology allows UNSO to be exploited in different application domains, rather than just in the domains defined a-priori by the ontology experts.

To maintain the semantic routing, UNSO extends the original hypercube graph of HyperCuP to a *Multi-Layered Hypercube* (MLH). MLH can be schematically depicted as a hypercube where each node is recursively constructed of another hypercube. Hashing mechanism is used to deal with the unspecified nature of the ontology, and with the variety of terms mentioned in the ads. Besides that, hashing uniformly distributes the ads among the MLH to guarantee equivalent load partitioning.

The generated structure facilitates the semantic routing, similar to the routing of HyperCuP. To eliminate ambiguity and enhance the precision, the terms mentioned in the ads undergo simple semantic standardization using WordNet [11]. In summary, UNSO expands the traditional notion of ontological data management and provides a novel technique for a decentralized management of a dynamic set of ontology-based ads, while keeping the essential publish-locate functionality. The fact that the users are not forced to share any predefined ontology simplifies the use of the system by inexperienced users and increases the chance of successful searches.

The rest of the paper is organized as follows. In section 2 we review the research efforts in P2P computing, the major classes of P2P applications, their advantages and shortcomings. Section 3 discusses the works in the area of ontology-based management in P2P systems and particularly HyperCuP [32]. Section 4 presents the notion of unspecified ontology, and discusses the generalization of a fixed ontology to UNSO. Section 5 discusses the details of UNSO implementation. In section 6 we present the experimental results, showing the performance of UNSO. Finally, section 7 concludes the work and discusses the directions of further research.

2   Peer-to-Peer Data Management

P2P computing refers to a subclass of distributed computing, where the system functionality is achieved in a decentralized way by unifying a set of distributed resources, such as computing power, data and network traffic. P2P systems usually lack a designated centralized management, rather depending on the voluntary contribution of resources by the users. These systems are usually characterized by one or more of the following advantages: cost sharing/reduction, improved scalability/reliability, resource aggregation and operability, increased autonomy, dynamism, anonymity/privacy and ad-hoc communication and collaboration [21].

The first generation of P2P systems was based on three classical architectures: mediated P2P architecture (e.g., [30]), pure P2P architecture (e.g., [10] and [26]), and hybrid architecture (e.g., [38] and [22]). An elaborate comparison, advantages and shortcomings of the above architectures, and discussion on the typical applications of each architecture can be found in [6].

Basically, they all were designed for a large-scale data sharing. Applications, such as Napster [30], Freenet [10] and Gnutella [3], allowed users to download data (mainly multimedia files), shared by other users. Performance of these systems suffered from severe problems. For example, in Napster a cluster of central servers, called super-peers maintained the indices of the files shared by the users. Flooding search algorithm of Gnutella limited the scalability of the system and did not allow proper functioning over a heterogeneous set of users. Freenet, despite being fully decentralized and employing efficient routing algorithms, could not guarantee reliable data location. This led to a development of content-addressable P2P systems.

A number of similar fully decentralized content-addressable P2P systems, such as CAN [26], Pastry [29], Chord [33] and some others, are referred as the second generation of P2P systems. They implement highly scalable self-organizing infrastructure for a fault-tolerant routing over distributed hashing data management mechanism (DHT). In these systems, the users and the data objects are assigned unique identifiers (respectively, *user-ids* and *keys*) from a sparse space. Data objects are inserted and located through *put(key,user-id)* and *get(key)* primitives in a bounded number of routing network hops. An elaborate description of and survey of P2P content-addressable distribution technologies can be found in [4].

In Pastry [29], *user-ids* and keys are *128* bit vectors. Routing tables of the connected users contain $O(logN)$ rows and *16* columns, where N is the total number of users. The entries in the row n of the routing tables refer to the logical neighbors, whose *user-ids* share the first n digits with the *user-id* of the current users, whereas the digit $(n+1)$ of the *user-id* in column m of the row n is m. Unlike Pastry, Chord [33] uses a one-dimensional circular *160*-bit space and instead of the prefix-based neighbors table, Chord users maintain a finger table, containing *user-ids* and addresses of the other connected users. Entry number i in the table of a user n refers to another user with the smallest *user-id*, clockwise from $n+2^{i-1}$. The first entry in the table points to the direct successor of user n, whereas the following entries point to the users at repeatedly doubling distances from n. CAN [26] is operated over d-dimensional toroidal space, where each user is associated with a hypercubal zone of the space, and its neighbors are the other users managing the adjacent hypercube zones.

The routing algorithm of content-addressable systems is based on Plaxton routing algorithm, developed in [25]. Plaxton algorithm was not designed for P2P systems, rather for graphs with a static nodes' population. The main idea of Plaxton algorithm is correcting a single digit of address in every routing step. Consider the following example. User *1234* receives a message, addressed to user *1278* (note that the first two digits of the address already match). The message is forwarded to user *1275* (since there the first three digits will match). To support this routing, each user maintains a data structure of logical neighbors that match i-digits length prefix of its own *user-id*, but differ in the $(i+1)th$ digit. To maintain a connected system with N users, each user is connected to $O(logN)$ neighbors. Since a single digit of address is corrected each time the message is routed, the total length of the routing path is $O(logN)$ hops.

In P2P implementations of Plaxton routing algorithm, the routed message is continuously forwarded to the user, whose *user-id* is closer to the *user-id* of the addressee than the current user. Although each one of the above DHT-based systems (Pastry, CAN, and Chord) employs slightly different variant of Plaxton routing algorithm, they all outperform the routing algorithms used in the first generation of P2P systems. Their communication overhead is significantly lower due to the fact that the messages are routed to the relevant users only.

However, DHT-based system rely on the hashing primitives of *put(key,user-id)* and *get(key)*. Thus, one of their major limitations is their support in exact-match searches only. For example, consider two similar, but not identical keys: key_1 and key_2. The results of their insertions into the system through hashing-based *put* primitive will usually be absolutely different. Therefore, only the searches, specifying the exact *key* that was used when the *key* was inserted, will succeed to find it, and an approximated search can not be operated.

Possible solutions for this issue are discussed in [15]. The paper compares various approaches facilitating complex range queries in DHT-based P2P networks. An architecture for relational data sharing in Chord-based systems was proposed in [14]. It exploits hashing mechanisms on the possible values within a given range to facilitate answering range queries. Solution for range queries problem in CAN-based systems are proposed in [30]. In this work, CAN space is partitioned to zones, in a way that allows the peers managing the zones to store information regarding the range of values that are mapped to this zone, as well as to the neighbor zones. This facilitates resolving range queries through their iterative forwarding to the zone that is managing the requested range of values.

Basically, the above approaches focus on constructing search indices enabling to perform database-like queries using operators such as selection, join, aggregation and others. These indices can help only in domains where the terminology of the *keys* names is agreed between the users, e.g., in music files, where the songs names are known. However, in domains with no well-defined naming standards, particularly in general-purpose E-Commerce applications, different users might use different terms to describe the same (or highly similar) object. Thus, in order to develop a generic infrastructure facilitating matching of similar E-Commerce ads, the ads should be preprocessed to a semi-structured form of attributes (slots) and their respective values. To achieve that, there is an emergent need for more complex type of P2P systems, built upon users that explicitly use semantic structures to describe the matters of their ads. This approach is further referred as ontology-based approach.

3   Ontology-Based Data Management

One of the basic concepts in the semantic data management is *ontology* (according to the Wikipedia, it is "the study of existence and the basic categories thereof"). Practically, it provides both human-understandable and machine-processable mechanisms, allowing enterprises and application systems to collaborate in a smart way. According to [13], ontology is a formal shared conceptualization of a particular domain. It is used to describe structurally heterogeneous and distributed information sources, such as those found on the Web, and acts as a standardized reference model, providing a stable baseline for shared understanding of the domain knowledge.

Ontological metadata facilitates a standardized access to the domain knowledge. Existing approaches of ontology-based data management assume a setting where the data sources share a single ontology allowing the access to the data. This technique of shared ontology was implemented in HyperCuP [32] that proposed a set of dynamic P2P algorithms for maintenance of ontology-based hypercube-like graph topology supporting semantic search and broadcast operations.

HyperCup developed a flexible ontology-based P2P platform generating a hypercube-like graph of users, where each user is treated as a data provider. HyperCup needs predefined domain ontology to be exploited, such that the dimensions of the hypercube will match the ontology slots, i.e., a set of attributes characterizing the domain objects. According to the above ontology, each user is categorized as a provider of particular data. This categorization determines the location of the user within the hypercube. Thus, the hypercube is virtually constructed of the connected users, whereas each user maintains a data structure of its respective neighbors. For example, in 3-dimensional hypercube, a node located in coordinates (x,y,z) will be connected to 6 logical neighbors: $(x+1,y,z)$, $(x-1,y, z)$, $(x,y+1,z)$, $(x,y-1,z)$, $(x,y,z+1)$ and $(x,y,z-1)$. The user providing multiple data objects from the same domain, or data objects from multiple domains, will maintain a set of hypercube locations, such that a separate data structure of neighbors will reflect each location.

The hypercube-like P2P structure was chosen due to its logarithmic diameter, increased fault tolerance and the symmetry that guarantees equal load of the users. The hypercube dimension d and the range of possible values in the dimensions (further referred as the *coordinates range*) k determine the maximal number of users connected to the hypercube. A complete hypercube contains at most $N_{max}=k^d$ users, where every user is connected to two logical neighbors in each dimension, resulting in $N_n=2d$ neighbors. This topology generates a symmetric structure where the load of the connected users in the system is similar, as each user holds roughly equal functionality in terms of routing load.

Any edge in the hypercube, connecting a pair of adjacent users X and Y, is assigned a numeric value, referred as *rank*. When user Y is a neighbor of user X over a dimension i, the rank of the edge, connecting X and Y, is i. Thus, the edges rank ranges from 0 to $d-1$. Any user T in the hypercube can act as an initiator of search or broadcast operation, which is performed as follows. The message, jointly with the rank of the connecting edge, is sent to all the neighbors of the initiating user T. Upon receiving a message, other users forward it only over the edges, whose ranks are higher than the rank of the edge the message was received from. This guarantees that each user in the graph will receive the message exactly once, and also that any connected user will be reached in $O(d)$ routing hops.

Consider the following example hypercube with a dimension $d=3$ and the coordinates range $k=2$ (figure 1a). Eight users, numbered from 1 to 8, are connected and form a complete hypercube. Each user is connected to exactly $d=3$ logical neighbors, and the ranks of the connecting edges are 0, 1, or 2. For example, in respect to user 8, user 1 is regarded as 0-neghbor, user 3 is 1-neighbor, and user 4 is 2-neighbor. Let

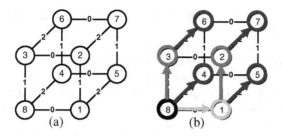

Fig. 1. HyperCuP Example (a) 3-dimensional HyperCuP structure with 8 connected users; (b) Broadcast procedure stages over the example HyperCuP structure

user 8 be the initiator of the broadcast operation. The messages are sent to the neighbors, i.e., users 1, 3 and 4. Upon receiving a message over 0-rank edge, user 1 forwards it to 1- and 2-neghbors, i.e., users 2 and 5. User 3 forwards it to 2-neighbor, user 6, and this broadcast through "higher-rank forwards" continues until all the nodes in the hypercube are covered (figure 1b). Obviously, no node receives the broadcasted message more than once, and the longest path in the hypercube is $d=3$ hops long.

HyperCuP also proposes a dynamic P2P algorithm for hypercube construction and maintenance. The algorithm is based on the idea that a user can manage not only a single node, but also a number of nodes in the hypercube graph. This is required in order to *simulate* the missing users in the topology of the next complete hypercube, which is implicitly maintained in any topology state. For example, consider node 4 simulating three missing nodes of the hypercube (figure 2a). The simulated nodes are schematically illustrated by the dashed edges 1-4, 2-4 and 3-4, as node 4 acts as a logical neighbor of nodes 1, 2 and 3.

When a new user connects the network, he takes his place (according to the data provided) in the next complete hypercube, releases the user that previously managed that node and starts functioning as a real hypercube node. For example, if a new user, which should be positioned in node 5, is connected, he is routed to one of the existing logical neighbors of node 5, i.e., either to the user maintaining node 1 or to the user maintaining node 4. As node 5 is practically simulated by the user maintaining node 4, the new user contacts the user of node 4, builds a real edge between them and takes

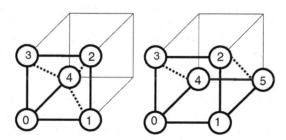

Fig. 2. (a) Implicitly preserved topology of the next complete hypercube; (b) Join of a new node

part of its functionality, i.e., builds a real edge with node *1* and starts simulating the neighbor of node *2* (fig. 2b).

When a user disconnects, one of the remaining logical neighbors takes the responsibility for the node, previously managed by the leaving user. Since the next complete hypercube is constantly maintained, previously discussed broadcast and search operations are not affected by sporadic joins and departures of users. An elaborate description of the way the HyperCuP topology is maintained, and examples of such departures and joins, can be found in [32].

As already stated, users are classified as providers of particular contents. A single predefined ontology defining the domain semantics, inherently organizes the users providing the same or similar contents, in *concept clusters* using the above construction and maintenance algorithm. Note that the similarity of users within a cluster is significantly higher that the similarity of arbitrarily chosen users. This facilitates querying the generated topology and efficiently routing the queries only to the clusters (and users) that can potentially answer it.

For example, consider the following simple ontology of cars domain, used to construct a *3*-dimensional HyperCuP (figure 1a): dimension *0* distinguishes between manual(*0*) and automatic(*1*) gearbox, dimension *1* stands for USA(*0*) or non-USA(*1*) produced cars, and dimension 2 for metallic(*0*) or non-metallic (*0*) color of the car. Clearly, a query for automatic cars produced in the USA is routed to nodes *1* and *5*, as only these nodes store the requested type of cars.

However, the predefined ontology constitutes one of the main drawbacks of HyperCuP approach. If used in a general-purpose E-Commerce application capable of supporting various types of transactions and objects, HyperCuP would require global all-inclusive ontology to be exploited. This is a severe limitation, as the state-of-the-art ontologies are usually limited to a single application domain, and even ontologies from the same domain can be highly heterogeneous due to existence of different *views* on the domain data.

Earlier research efforts, such as [16] and [12], focus on the issue of merging ontologies and generating a global ontology. To create a unified view enabling to integrate data originated by different ontologies, their semantic reconciliation is required. Merging two ontologies means creating a new ontology comprising the slots of both ontologies. Merging process is mainly based on recognizing relationships and commonalities between the slots of the ontologies. The ontology, generated as a result of merging, matches both merged ontologies.

However, the issue of constructing all-inclusive ontology is a controversial issue (see [35] for an elaborate discussion). Besides the philosophical question of creating a *universal* ontology, it leads to a setting where updates of the ontology are conducted through a central point of management, unacceptable in pure P2P networks. Moreover, existence of this global ontology forces all the users to use it, contradicting the decentralized free spirit of P2P networks.

In P2P, we rather face a situation, where individual users maintain their own views of the domain ontology. However, since data sharing is one of the primary motivations behind the state-of-the-art P2P systems, we need to find a way to distributively manage multiple dynamic ontologies escribing the domain data objects. The task of sharing heterogeneous ontological data became an important research direction in P2P community. It is referred in the literature as the *Data Integration* problem [8].

Traditional data integration approaches adapted from the distributed databases community [36], assume a central unified representation of the data objects, which contradicts the decentralized nature of P2P systems and suffers from scalability problem. In addition to the lack of central point of management, P2P data integration techniques have to cope with multiple (sometimes ambiguous and overlapping) and highly dynamic ontologies representing the data. Most of the techniques achieve the goal of sharing and integrating data through developing semantic mapping mechanisms, describing the relationships between the slots of the ontologies [19].

Automatic approaches for ontology (or schema) mapping in P2P systems do not require central ontology, but perform the mapping at one of three levels:

- Pair mapping – the mappings are performed between the relevant peers only [7]. In this setting, one of the peers involved in the mapping process, defines specific translation and coordination rules allowing to relate the slots of his ontology to the ontology of the other peer.
- Peer-mediated mapping – a generalization of pair mapping, where one of the peers defines a mapping that relates to a number of peers. This approach was implemented in [34] through machine learning technique that exploited various evidences of semantic similarity of the ontology slots. In [23], the authors used Information Retrieval techniques for extracting descriptive keywords, which were exploited later for identifying appropriate slots in the ontologies. The mappings are generated 'on-the-fly', whenever they are needed for the integration of data.
- Super-peer mediating mapping – semi-centralized approach, where the mappings are performed at the super-peers level. In this setting, super-peers is responsible for managing the mappings for the ontologies of the underlying peers, whereas super-peer to super-peer mappings facilitate data sharing between any peers. This approach was implemented in Edutella [22], RDF-based P2P platform for educational data sharing.

Most of the state-of-the-art P2P systems refer to the semantic heterogeneity between the underlying ontologies. However, they assume that the mappings between the ontologies can be constructed. Although we do not negate the possibility of constructing such mappings, we highlight an observation that the process of creating these mappings might be one of the most challenging tasks in a heterogeneous and highly dynamic P2P realm. Alternatively, in this work we propose another way to overcome the issue of semantic heterogeneity in P2P data integration. We developed the approach of Unspecified Ontologies (UNSO) that instead of providing mapping mechanisms between various ontologies, inherently supports dynamic organization of users (as providers of particular data objects) in a HyperCuP-like graph structure. The following section discusses the details of UNSO and the stages of generalizing the regular notion of ontologies to UNSO.

4   Generalization of Ontology to an Unspecified Ontology

In this work we propose a novel approach to resolve the issue of global ontology that should from one hand grow dynamically with no limited range, from other hand to be used and updated in a fully distributive way. Initially, let us characterize the structure of ontologies and their usage in semantic routing.

As a data structure, each ontology is considered as a vector, whose slots correspond to the attributes of the objects being described. As such, the range of values for each slot is the set of possible values of the respective attribute. For example, consider a simple ontology for cars domain, where the objects are described by a vector containing three slots only: [*manufacturer | engine_volume | year_of_production*]. Let us consider each slot having the following range of predefined values [*manufacturer={Ford, Mercedes, Jaguar} | engine_volume={1000-1500, 1500-2000, 2000-2500} | year_of_production={new, 2000+, 1990+}*]. Clearly, semantic P2P system based on this ontology will generate a hypercube containing at most 27 nodes, each having up to 6 logical neighbors.

A generalization of a fixed ontology to the Unspecified Ontology is performed at the following levels (referring to the above example of cars ontology):

- The set and the range of possible values is made unlimited by operating on them a fixed-length hashing instead of defining a set of predefined values. For example, in the above ontology we use hashing to a range of size three, mapping new values to their corresponding positions. For example, object [*manufacturer:BMW | engine_volume:3000 | year_of_production:1987*] is mapped to [*hash(BMW) | hash(3000) | hash(1987)*]. Therefore, the same 3-dimensional cube is now used to hold the objects, whose values were not anticipated by the slots of the predefined ontology. Moreover, the users can independently insert new objects in a fully distributed way, using the hashing above mechanism.

- More than one vector is used in the ontological description of an object, obtaining a *multi-layered* ontology that is *hierarchical* instead of using one *flat* vector. Hierarchical ontology produces a hypercube, whose nodes are recursively constructed of another hypercubes. This structure is further referred as a *multi-layered hypercube* (MLH). For example, consider a 3-layered ontology with three vectors [*attr$_{11}$ | attr$_{12}$ | attr$_{13}$*] + [*attr$_{21}$ | attr$_{22}$ | attr$_{23}$*] + [*attr$_{31}$ | attr$_{32}$ | attr$_{33}$*] (where *attr$_{ij}$* refers to slot number *j* in ontological layer number *i*) with two possible values for each slot. Such ontology generates a hypercube with 8 nodes, where each node recursively contains another hypercube (figure 3). This structure should be compared to

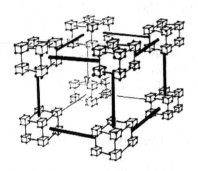

Fig. 3. Multi-Layered Hypercube (MLH)

a *512*-nodes hypercube, had we used one flat vector for the whole ontology. Obviously, hierarchical representation of the ontological vectors results in smaller and denser hypercubes, alleviating the connectivity maintenance of the hypercubes in pure decentralized P2P environment.

- The vector can dynamically grow by letting the users to add new levels to the ontology. An unspecified vector (ontology-based description) is formed by *attribute:value* pairs. Two different hashing functions are used to map the unspecified vector to the MLH. The first maps the *attributes* to the respective ontology slots, while the second maps the *values* to the numeric values of the slots. Thus, $hash_1(attribute)$ determines the dimension of the MLH, while $hash_2(value)$ determines the numeric value in this dimension. For example, consider the following description [*manufacturer:ford | engine_volume:1600*]. It is mapped to the underlying MLH by applying $hash_1(manufacturer)$ and $hash_1(engine\_volume)$ to obtain the slot numbers (MLH dimensions), and $hash_2(ford)$ and $hash_2(1600)$ to determine the numeric values in these dimensions.

- The users can specify a different number of unspecified slots. When an unspecified vector is mapped to an existing MLH, its slots are extended to the dimension of the MLH. For example, unspecified vector [*manufacturer:ford*] is extended to [*manufacturer:ford | engine_volume:1600*], when inserted to an MLH of dimension 2 from the above example. If the inserted object contains more slots than the number of dimensions in the current MLH, the vectors in the relevant hypercube are updated to accordingly contain more slots. We assume that upon long enough period of time and large enough number of object descriptions accumulated in the system, these updates will not be frequent, thus, they will be feasible. Note that exploiting two different hashing functions allows ignoring the order of the attributes in the unspecified descriptions.

- To distinguish between different objects having the same attributes (e.g., both cars and bicycles have attributes such as *color, wheels_type, number_of_gears* and so on), we require the ontological descriptions to contain so-called *universal,* or *specified slots*. A slot is referred as universal if it can be applied to as many objects as possible, and its values form a meaningful separation between the objects. For example, a universal attribute useful to separate between many objects is *size*, reflecting the size of the object comparing to a well-known standard. This allows distinguishing between the descriptions of cars and bicycles having the same attributes. It should be stated that we rely on a common sense and common patterns of thinking in specifying the values of the universal slots.

- The last $attribute_i:value_i$ pair in description must be a *discriminative attribute*, i.e., its should be unique for any given object. For example, consider an IP address of the user, or an ID number of the ad as such discriminative attributes. This allows two ads (either identical, or distinct, but accidentally mapped to the same node) to be separated according to the value of the discriminative attribute.

One of the heaviest steps in the management of the hypercube-like graph structure is the extension of the hypercube and the stored vectors as a result of a new slot mentioned in the ontological description of an object. Although these extensions are theoretically possible at any point of time, we conjecture that they mostly occur at the initial stages of graph construction. This is explained by the observation that large number of new slots will be introduced during the initial insertions of objects, while at the latter stages the probability of introducing a new slot (unless introduced maliciously) that was not encountered yet, will decrease. As a result, the hypercube-like graph will stabilize at the initial stages of objects insertions and the extensions will be infrequent. This behavior is well-known in information search studies, where "*as a user obtains more information..., the probability of soliciting information from an additional source is likely to decrease*" [18]. Our conjecture regarding the similar behavior of UNSO slots is verified in the experimental part.

The above steps of extending a fixed specified ontology to the Unspecified Ontology are illustrated in figure 4. Predefined attributes and values of a fixed ontology are mapped to the underlying hypercube graph. On the contrary, in UNSO the number of <*attribute_i:value_i*> pairs in the unspecified description is unlimited. Thus, UNSO dynamically generates a hypercube-like graph structure, where each node is recursively constructed of another hypercube.

The generated MLH acts as a convenient infrastructure for the operations proposed in HyperCuP. When an object is inserted by a user to the MLH, it is forwarded towards its proper position. There, the user connects to its logical neighbors and starts functioning as an MLH node. Disconnection of a user causes another user to take the responsibility for the node of the disconnected user. Semantic routing in the MLH consists of a series of routings to the appropriate node in the current-layer hypercube

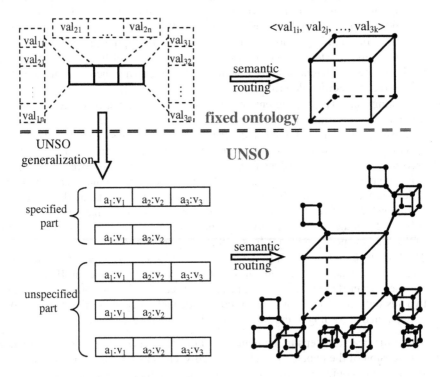

Fig. 4. Generalization of the Fixed Ontology to the Unspecified Ontology

and *deepenings* to the appropriate next-layer hypercube. Note that in the MLH the routing is performed according to Plaxton routing algorithm, i.e., every network hop corrects one digit of the address.

Important property of UNSO data structure is a property of *implicit locality* (basically, inherited from HyperCup). Both in HyperCup and in UNSO, the location of a user in the underlying MLH is determined according to the contents provided by the user. For example, consider two users providing similar (but not identical) data objects, described by the respective unspecified vectors: $<attribute_1:value_1, attribute_2:value_2, attribute_3:value_3>$ and $<attribute_1:value_1, attribute_2:value_2, attribute_3:value_4>$. Clearly, mapping of both vectors to the underlying MLH will produce identical numeric coordinates within the dimensions corresponding to $attribute_1$ and $attribute_2$, whereas the coordinates within the dimension of $attribute_3$ will be different. As a result, the distance between the above pair of data objects will be lower than the distance between arbitrarily chosen pair of data objects. This can be explained by the observation that the distance between the locations of objects, whose descriptions overlap in a subset of $<attribute_i:value_i>$ pairs, will be lower than the distance between the locations of objects with non-overlapping descriptions. We refer to this property of UNSO as implicit locality, since providers of similar contents are mapped to close locations in the underlying MLH graph.

Although the implicit locality property seems to contradict the load balancing property of hashing mechanism, this is not exactly the case. The insertion of the data objects into the MLH is performed through the mapping of $<attribute_i:value_i>$ pairs, such that $attribute_i$ is mapped to one of the MLH dimensions, and $value_i$ to the numeric value (coordinate) within the dimension. Since UNSO exploits hashing-based mapping mechanisms, the distribution of values among any given MLH dimension will be uniform, and the load of MLH nodes will be similar. Although implicit locality property might lead to high-populated regions of the MLH, the number of real (not simulated) nodes in these regions will be also higher, and they will keep proper functionality under the conditions of higher load.

Another issue deals with the mapping of values from continuous domain to the MLH dimensions' coordinates. Although hashing-based mapping is suitable for mapping the values of discrete or non-enumerable attributes (e.g., *color*, *manufacturer*, or *model*), it is inappropriate for the values of continuous attributes (e.g., *year_of_production*, *price*, or *engine_volume*) since hashing-based mapping of continuous attributes loose their original inherent order relation. To resolve this issue, we replaced the hashing-based mapping of continuous attributes with a simple *bucketing* of the values. For example, consider a mapping of *price* attribute, whose values range between *0* and *100,000* to a dimension with *10* possible numeric values. In this case, prices between *0* and *10,000* will be mapped to numeric value *0* within the coordinate, prices between *10,000* and *20,000* – to *1*, and so forth. By doing so, we facilitate answering range and approximate queries over the continuous coordinates, since close values are mapped to the same (or neighbor) buckets, and the order relation of values between the buckets is also kept.

In summary, we would like to stress the main advantages of the Unspecified Ontologies mechanism and the underlying MLH graph of UNSO over the approach proposed by HyperCuP:

- Lack of centralized ontology – the mapping of an object to its position in the MLH is performed through hashing-based mechanism, instead of using a fixed predefined ontology.
- Contents flexibility – new types of objects and attributes can be easily added to the system, not requiring any updates of the ontology.
- Unlimited range of attributes and values – the unspecified part of the ontology allows the users to mention relatively free list of attributes and values in the ontological descriptions of the objects.
- Insignificant order of attributes – the unspecified part of the ontology does not require any order of the mentioned attributes, allowing high flexibility in further search of the data objects.
- Implicit locality – similar descriptions (i.e., similar objects), are mapped to adjacent positions within the MLH. Thus, similar objects are autonomously clustered without any explicit clustering mechanism.
- Approximated search – property of implicit locality in UNSO allows employing approximated searches, finding the objects similar (but not identical) to the object being searched.
- Partial searches – a search, containing a subset of the required object attributes can be conducted, finding a wider range of relatively similar objects.
- Multi-layered structure – increases the independence of the data management, as an update a particular hypercube layer does not affect the rest of the layers.

Compared to the existing DHT-based systems, UNSO proposes functionalities that were not supported earlier. Hashing mechanism of DHT systems is based on a single key. As a result, successful search in DHT-based systems requires exact matching of the keys. This is unreasonable when the key is a natural language description of an object. Conversely, UNSO handles keys represented by a list of attributes and their respective values. Thus, UNSO facilitates partial search of a subset of object attributes, whereas the order of the specified attributes is insignificant. Hence, data management and search mechanisms of UNSO are more flexible, than the parallel mechanisms of DHT-based systems.

Comparing UNSO to HyperCuP [32] yields another important advantage of UNSO. HyperCuP is based on a fixed predefined ontology that must be explicitly used by all the users. This is a severe limitation, as the users are forced to share and use it when describing their objects. On the contrary, UNSO allows the users to provide relatively free description of objects in form of $attribute_i$:$value_i$ pairs list. As well, new objects and attributes can be easily added to UNSO, not requiring update of the ontology and the update distribution to maintain consistency. Multi-layered structure of UNSO provides an efficient mean to resolve hashing collisions, since the attributes and their values are used to distinguish between objects from different domains.

5 UNSO Implementation Details

This section discusses the details of UNSO implementation. A multi-layered UNSO model, similar to the model, described in the previous section, was implemented. The primary layer of UNSO contains the hypercube constructed by the specified part of the ontological descriptions of objects. The secondary MLHs are originated by the unspecified parts of the data objects' descriptions.

The specified part of UNSO is the subset of object attributes that should by explicitly mentioned by the users when describing the object. As the target application objects are general-purpose E-Commerce ads, the slots of the specified part should be applicable to as wide as possible range of objects. Clearly, these attributes are the *universal* attributes of the objects, such as size, weight, price, material and so forth. Note that here we refer to real-life tradable objects only, such as cars, apartments, books, tickets and others, which are the matter of E-Commerce ads.

The following set of the universal attributes was chosen to serve as the slots of the specified part of the ontology:

- *Product* – the name of the object, i.e., a noun describing the class of objects the described object belongs to. For example, car, book, telephone and so forth.
- *Relative size* – the size of the object. Since the size is a relative concept, we provide a standard size, such that the size of the described object is measured with respect to it. The standard is chosen to be an average size of a human being, and the objects are graded from 'very small' to 'very big' in comparison to it. For example, pen or mobile phone are 'very small', while house or truck are 'very big'.
- *Usage range* – the physical distance from the current location of the user, where the object is operated. As this concept is also a relative one, a standard for the possible values is provided. The usage distance is defined as 'very close', if the object is operated "at arm's reach" (i.e., in the room or indoor), and 'very far' if the distance of operation is roughly unlimited. Thus, housewares or furniture are 'very close' objects, while cars or optical equipment are 'very far'.
- *Price* – the price of the object, i.e., the sum the seller expects to get, or the sum the buyer is ready to pay for it. Price is also a universal attribute as it separates between different types of objects, such as houses and cars (although it may fail to separate books from CDs).

The *attribute:value* pairs mentioned by the user in the ontological description of an object, determine its position in the underlying MLH. The dimension of the primary hypercube equals to the number of slots in the specified part of the ontology. Thus, the above four slots generate a *4*-dimensional primary hypercube. The number of dimensions in the secondary MLHs is theoretically unlimited. Practically, a number of attributes mentioned by the users in the unspecified part of ontological descriptions is limited and quickly converges to its upper bound. Therefore, HyperCuP approach, where the connected users simulate the missing nodes, allows to maintain connectivity in the generated MLH.

In HyperCuP, the mapping of objects to the hypercube was performed according to the values of the ontology slots. On the contrary, in UNSO, the mapping is performed through a set of simple hashing functions operating with the numeric codes of the characters used in the values of ontology attributes. Although smarter hashing mechanisms could provide better distribution [28] and keep the locality and order relations between the values [17], in this implementation we chose a simple hash functions only to validate the applicability of the proposed approach.

Thus, the range of possible values (further referred as the *coordinates range*) k in the specified slots *product* and *price* is determined by the range of the hashing functions. Since for *relative size* and *usage range* slots the set of values is restricted to {*very small, small, medium, big, very big*}, the total number of nodes in the primary hypercube is practically limited by $25k^2$, where k is the coordinates range.

One of the advantages of hashing-based mapping mechanism is in a uniform distribution of ads among the MLH allowing to uniformly partition the load of the users. For example, for $k=17$, an ad [*product:car | relative_size:very big | usage_distance: very far | price:45000*] is mapped to [0 | 4 | 4 | 13] in the primary hypercube, while an ad [*product:television | relative_size:medium | usage_distance:very close | price:400*] is mapped to [15 | 2 | 0 | 2]. However, for $k=11$ the same ads are mapped to other locations, respectively [7 | 4 | 4 | 8] and [6 | 2 | 0 | 1].

As for the unspecified part of the ontology, the format is a list of *attribute:value* pairs, where neither the *attributes*, nor the *values* are limited by any predefined ontology. For example, consider the following ontological (both specified and unspecified) description of a car: [*product:car | relative_size:very big | usage_distance: very_far | price:45000*] + [*manufacturer:BMW | color:red | mileage:5000*]. The unspecified part [*manufacturer:BMW | color:red | mileage:5000*] is mapped to a position *(5, 8, 4)* if the attribute 'manufacturer' is mapped to the coordinate number *1* and the value 'BMW' is mapped to the value *5*, 'color' is mapped to coordinate *2* and 'red' to value *8*, and respectively 'mileage' is mapped to coordinate *3* and '5000' to value *4*.

Note that two different ads are mapped to the same node either if their ontological vectors are identical, or the mappings of their *attributes* and *values* completely overlap. In this case the IP address of the user inserting the ad is chosen to act as the *discriminative* attribute distinguishing between the ads. Since the IP address is not a real attribute of the described object, it acts as a discriminative attribute only and is disregarded when displaying the search results.

Every new attribute, mentioned in the ads from a particular domain, increases the total dimension of the respective MLH. For example, consider the domain of car ads with a single ad [*product:car | relative_size:very big | usage_distance: very_far | price:45000*] + [*manufacturer:BMW | color:red | mileage:5000*] from previous example. Inserting a new ad, mentioning two unspecified attributes that were not mentioned yet (e.g., *gear* and *number_of_doors*), causes the secondary hypercube to expand to a 5-dimensional hypercube. So, the original ad is remapped to *(5, 8, 4, *, *)*. However, analyzing relatively large corpus of car ads shows that the inserted ads contain in total *12* different attributes only, while most of the ads contained only *3-4* pairs of attributes and values. Thus, most of the hypercube expansions occur during the initial phases of the MLH construction. In this stage the MLH still contains relatively low number of ads and therefore the update is not expensive. Conversely, in a hypercube containing many ads, the updates are infrequent.

A possible drawback of the proposed idea is unclarity and ambiguity in supplying the values of the ontology slots. For instance, one user might define a car as *big*, while the other one might search it as *very big*. In this case the search is mapped to a different position in the hypercube, and the matching can not be identified. We conjecture that most of the users use similar *patterns of thinking* while describing the objects. If this is true, most of the ads describing the same objects are mapped to the same position in the primary hypercube, forming *clusters* of similar ads (figure 5).

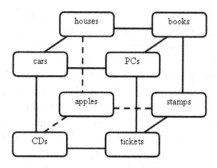

Fig. 5. Cluster of Ads in a 3-Dimensional Primary Hypercube

To resolve the issue of semantic heterogeneity, i.e., different terms with the same semantic meaning in the descriptions of objects, values of the ontological slots are standardized using WordNet [11]. In WordNet, English nouns, verbs, adjectives and adverbs are organized into *synonyms sets*, each representing a single semantic concept. For each concept, the synonyms' set is sorted according to the usage frequency. In our implementation, we employed a simple semantic standardization, replacing the original term, mentioned in object description, with its most frequent synonym. Thus, similar but not identical terms mentioned by the users, are replaced with a single representing term. For example, terms such as "automobile", "machine", or "motorcar", are replaced with their most frequent synonym "car".

Another practical issue leading to the semantic heterogeneity might be the use of hyponyms or hypernyms (respectively, terms that are more specific, or more generic than popular, standard term implied by most of the users) in the descriptions of objects. For example, a user might use *'sport car'* or *'coupe'* hyponyms or *'motor vehicle'* hypernym while describing the above mentioned red BMW *car*. Although current implementation of UNSO can not handle such standardization, it can be easily accomplished through hyponym and hypernym links of the WordNet. This will allow the standardization process to scan child and parent nodes in addition to currently scanned sibling nodes of WordNet graph of nouns, and therefore will improve the retrieval capabilities of UNSO.

To balance the communication load across the system, a modified variant of Plaxton routing algorithm [25] is implemented. Plaxton algorithm routes a message by correcting each time a single digit of the address. In the original algorithm the order of address digits corrections is known, i.e., the most significant digit of the address is corrected first, and the least significant digit is corrected last. Simultaneous routing of multiple messages to/from the same area (cluster) might lead to a communication bottleneck. To resolve this issue, we randomized the order of address digits corrections. This is further referred as a *randomized* Plaxton routing.

Over the hypercube-like graph topology (which is a subclass of expander graphs [24]), Plaxton routing algorithm corrects one digit of the address at each network hop. Since the bits of HyperCuP neighbor nodes differ in exactly one digit of the address, and each correction modifies only a single digit of the address, the order of the digit corrections can be shuffled. For example, consider correcting an address of length $logN$, where N is the maximal number of users in the hypercube. The number of possible correction orders that can be applied, i.e., the number of possible routes, is *(logN)!*. This number allows high routing flexibility in the hypercube-like expander graph topology and improves the communication load balancing.

On the first view, Plaxton routing algorithm seems to be very inefficient form of routing, since correcting a multi-dimensional address in a MLH of total dimension d with coordinates range k will require $O(kd)$ network hops. However, this observation will not hold in practical P2P systems which will be highly sparse, i.e., the number of real connected nodes will be significantly lower than the number of possible locations in the underlying MLH. Due to the sparsity of the MLH, a number of nodes will be simulated by a single user and as a result, the number of network hops required for the query routing will be significantly decreased. In any case, the above randomized Plaxton routing allows to better distribute the communication load among the connected users.

The system prototype implementation includes Graphical User Interface (GUI) enabling the users to launch search queries (figure 6). The GUI contains fields for inserting the values of the specified slots, textual fields for the unspecified attributes and values, and textual area for displaying query results.

In a typical search scenario, the user starts from filling-in the values of the specified slots of the ontology. Assuming common patterns of thinking, the system finds a node in the primary hypercube, which stores the ads from the relevant domain. For a large enough corpus of ads, the number of the matching ads might be too high. Thus,

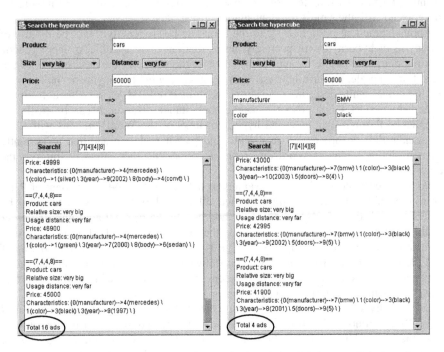

Fig. 6. Typical Search Scenario (a) Only the slots of the fixed part of the ontology are specified; (b) In addition, two unspecified slots are specified

the user needs to refine the query by mentioning the unspecified attributes and their values. As a result, the system filters out the irrelevant ads and displays to the user a shorter list of ads.

Consider the search scenario, illustrated in figure 6. In the first query (figure 6a), the specified slots [*product:car* | *relative_size:very_big* | *usage_distance:very_far* | *price:50000*] only are filled-in. The query is mapped to a node [*7* | *4* | *4* | *8*] of the primary hypercube (for *k=11*). As no unspecified attributes are mentioned, the number of returned ads is *16* (out of *34* matching ads in the corpus), which is relatively high. In the second query, the user expands the description using two unspecified attributes: *manufacturer* and *color*. The search for [*product:car* | *relative_size: very_big* | *usage_distance:very_far* | *price:50000*] + [*manufacturer:BMW* | *color:black*] is mapped to [*7* | *4* | *4* | *8*] + [*7* | *3* | *** | *** | ****]. Note that since the secondary MLH consists of a single *5*-dimensional hypercube, the system automatically expands the address through inserting wildcards instead of the attributes that are not mentioned in the search. The use of unspecified attributes filters the irrelevant ads, returning a smaller set of *4* matching ads only (figure 6b).

6   Experimental Results

To conduct the experiments, a corpus of both supply and demand E-Commerce ads was downloaded from *http://www.recycler.com*. The corpus of supply ads contains *1272* ads from *14* different categories. Before inserting the ads into the system, they were manually converted to the form of ontological descriptions. For example, the following ad "Philips 50FD995 50" plasma television, brand new, $4800" was converted to the following unspecified ontological description [*product:television* | *relative_size:medium* | *usage_distance: very_close* | *price:4800*] + [*manufacturer:Philips* | *model: 50FD995* | *size:50"* | *material:plasma* | *condition:brand new*]. The conversions were done as close as possible to the original contents of the ads, to mimic the insertions by naïve users. Corpus of *136* demand ads was automatically built by modifying a subset of the attributes and values mentioned in the supply ads.

The following experiments were conducted. Initially, we evaluate the Information Retrieval metrics of precision and recall [37] through launching queries for the objects from the demand ads. Then we validate the property of locality, namely the distance between similar and dissimilar ads in UNSO. Finally, we measure the scalability and stability of UNSO through evaluating the performance of the system for gradually increasing number of ads in the system. The results of the experiments are presented in the following sub-sections.

6.1   Information Retrieval Metrics

This experiment was designed to evaluate two traditional Information Retrieval accuracy metrics: *precision* and *recall* [37]. In context of publish-locate application, precision is computed as the number of relevant ads in a node divided by the total number of ads there. Similarly, recall is computed as the number of relevant ads in a node divided by the total number of relevant ads in the system. For example, consider *100* cars ads inserted to the system. User looking for a car launches a query, and receives

80 ads. *60* out of them are cars ads, while the rest are ads from other application domains. In this case the precision is *60/80=0.75*, and the recall is *60/100=0.6*.

An ad might be included in a query results due to two reasons: it might either be an ad that really satisfies the constraints posed by the query, i.e., mentions the terms that were searched in the query, or it might be irrelevant ad that was accidentally mapped to the same node. To accurately measure the values of precision and recall, relevance metrics should be explicitly defined. In this work, the relevance of the returned ads is automatically determined through comparing the attributes and the values mentioned in the query with attributes and values mentioned in the ads returned by the system.

The values of precision and recall are measured for different coordinate ranges *k* (hashing function range) of the UNSO slots, varying from *1* to *100*. For each value of *k* we compute the average recall and precision among launching the *136* demand queries. Recall and precision are computed through computing the number of relevant ads and the total number of ads in the nodes the queries are mapped to, and the total number of ads relevant from the given domain.

The chart in figure 7 shows the average values of precision and recall as a function of the coordinates range *k*. The dashed curves show the precision values, while the continuous curves stand for the recall. Both the precision and the recall are measured twice: for the original terms specified in the ads (the brighter curves), and after standardizing the values of the ontology slots with WordNet (the darker curves).

In general, both the probability of hashing collisions and the number of irrelevant ads, accidentally mapped to a node, decrease with the increase of *k*. Thus, the precision increases with the coordinates range *k*. It can be clearly seen from the chart that the standardized results outperform the original results. This holds for any coordinates range *k*, and the standardized precision values asymptotically converge to *1* (maximal precision,

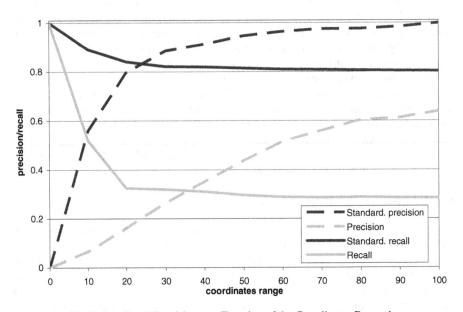

Fig. 7. Recall and Precision as a Function of the Coordinates Range *k*

if all the ads returned by a search are relevant) starting from relatively low values of k ($k>30$). The observation that the standardized precision values are higher is reasonable, since WordNet replaces similar terms mentioned in the ads with a single representing term. Thus, the number of different attributes and in particular the number of ads accidentally mapped to a node monotonically decreases with k, whereas the precision monotonically increases.

The original recall values of the system are relatively low, approximately 0.29. This is explained by the observation that without the WordNet standardization the users mention different terms to describe the same semantic concepts. Consequently, the searches succeed in finding only the ads that mentioned the appropriate term (or the ads that were accidentally mapped to the same position). Using WordNet, the recall values are significantly higher, roughly 0.8. Note that initially the recall values decrease when the coordinates range k increases. This happens due to the fact that the probability of similar ads mentioning different terms to be accidentally mapped to the same node is relatively high for low values of the coordinates range k. For example, for $k=1$ all the ads are mapped to the same location, as the MLH basically consists of a single node.

Obviously, there is a clear trade-off between the coordinates range k and the accuracy (in terms of recall and precision) of the system. From one hand the chart shows that a linear combination of recall and precision improves for higher values of k, as the recall converges starting from relatively low values of k, and the precision increases. However, practical maintenance of large enough MLHs is complicated for a low number of connected users, due to the sparsity causing the connected users to simulate high number of 'missing' nodes.

For example, let us compare two possible coordinate ranges: $k=30$ and $k=80$. The values of recall and precision for these values of k are close: the precision is respectively 0.89 and 0.97, while the recall roughly remains unchanged, 0.81. But, the estimated size of the primary hypercube only increases from $22,500$ to $160,000$ nodes. Thus, every connected user is forced to simulate about 7 times more nodes, resulting in a significantly higher communication loads and maintenance overheads of the connected users. Therefore, we conjecture that the optimal value of k for a moderate number of connected users and inserted ads is between 20 and 30. For such values of k, both precision and recall values are above 0.8, while the size of the primary hypercube remains reasonably small.

6.2 Locality

An important metric of quality of a system using semantic routing is locality, i.e., mapping of similar ads to close positions in the underlying MLH. To verify this property, a subset of 128 supply ads was randomly chosen. For each chosen ad X, we denote by X'_j a modified ad, where the values of j attributes are changed. Both X and X'_j are inserted into the system and the distance d between their positions is computed.

The distance d between the positions of two ads X and X'_j is defined as a sum of their distances (i.e., differences in the numeric coordinates) in each one of the dimensions. For example, the distance between the positions $(1, 3, 5, 7)$ and $(8, 6, 4, 2)$ in a 4-dimensional hypercube is $|(1-8)|+|(3-6)|+|(5-4)|+|(7-2)|=16$. In the MLH topology, distance between two positions is the sum of the distances in each one of the layers.

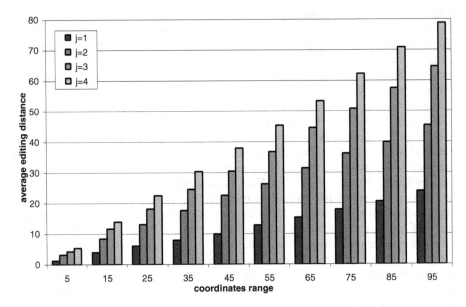

Fig. 8. Average Distance as a Function of a Number of Changes (*j*) for Different Values of the Coordinates Range *k*

The chart in figure 8 shows the average distance *d* over the chosen *128* ads as a function of *j*, computed for the coordinates range *k* varying from *1* to *100*.

Each quadruplet of bars in the chart shows the average distance between the ads for *j=1, 2, 3* and *4* (the leftmost column stands for one change, and the rightmost for four changes). It can be clearly seen that for any value of the coordinates range *k*, the distance increases with the number of changes inserted to the ads. For example, for *k=55*, the distance for one change is *12.8*, while for four changes it is *45.4*. The results show that the property of locality holds in UNSO and the average distance between two similar ads (small number of changed values) is lower than the average distance between two different ads (higher number of changed values).

The chart also shows that the distance *d* for a given *j* increases with the increase of the coordinates range *k*. The higher is the value of *k*, the wider is the range of possible coordinates the ad can be mapped to, and the higher is the distance. However, the growth of the average distance is linear with *k*. This observation holds for all the values of *j*, i.e., it is true for different magnitudes of the distance.

In the discussion on precision, we concluded that the best precision is achieved for high values of *k*. The linear growth rate of the distance shows that precision improvement will not negatively affect the distance and the property of locality will hold for different values of coordinates range *k*.

6.3 Scalability

Scalability is one of the most important properties of P2P systems, and certainly one of their biggest advantages of P2P over the Client-Server approach. We define it as an indicator of a system's ability to maintain quality performance under an increased load. In UNSO, "maintenance of quality performance" means reasonable MLH data management and efficient query routing under conditions of heavy load. The meaning of "heavy load" can be interpreted in a few ways. It can be referred as a high number of ads in the system, communication overload, high rate of users' joins and disconnections, and so on. This experiment was designed to evaluate the scalability of UNSO under conditions of high communication overload in a particular area of the MLH.

To create a high number of routing operations in a particular area, we insert into the system two sets of ads (about *120* ads in each one): housewares ads and telephones ads. These sets generate two clusters, further denoted as *P* and *Q*. We gradually increase the number of ads in each cluster and simulate the communication overload by simultaneously routing queries from *P* to *Q* and from *Q* to *P*. For each ad in *P* (and in *Q*) we randomly select an ad in *Q* (and respectively in *P*), and simulate a routing operation between the positions of the ads. In the experiments we measure the maximal number of queries routed through a single node. The measures are conducted for a number of coordinates ranges *k*, such as *k=13, 17, 23, 29*, and *37*. As the randomized Plaxton routing is not deterministic, the experiments are repeated *1000* times. The chart in figure 9 shows the average results.

The chart shows that starting from approximately *36* ads (*30%* of the maximal size of the sets) in *P* and *Q*, increasing the number of ads does not affect the maximal traffic in the system, i.e., the number of simultaneous routings increases without any significant change in the traffic load. This observation is explained by a relatively high connectivity of the underlying MLH structure (as a subclass of expander graph) and by the randomized variant of Plaxton routing algorithm that is exploited in

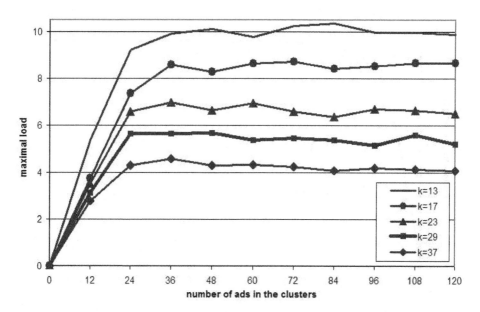

Fig. 9. Maximal Load in the Network Under Conditions of High Number of Simultaneous Routing Operations

UNSO. Note that this observation holds for different values of the coordinates range k. Moreover, the maximal load in the system decreases with the increase of k, as for high values of k the number of possible routing paths is higher and the communication overload of each node is lower.

This allows us to conclude that UNSO is scalable with respect to its functionality under conditions of communication overload resulting in a high number of concurrent routings. Thus, the proposed UNSO approach implemented over the MLH topology can work-out and function efficiently as a large-scale general-purpose E-Commerce application (e.g., launched over the Web).

6.4 Stability

In this experiment was designed to measure the "average size" of the generated structure as a function of the number of inserted ads. One of the key metrics for evaluating the size of the network is the characteristic path length. For two given nodes A and B in the MLH, a *path length* between their positions in the hypercube is defined as a minimal number of Plaxton corrections needed in order to reach B starting from A. The *characteristic path length* is defined as the average path lengths over all pairs of nodes in the system. In this experiment we gradually increase the number of ads inserted into the system and compute the characteristic path length. Since the ads inserted into the system are chosen randomly from the corpus of *1272* supply ads, for each number of ads in the system the experiment is repeated *1000* times. The average values of the characteristic path length are shown in figure 10.

The chart shows that the initial insertions of ads increase the characteristic path length by increasing the number of dimensions in the MLHs. However, starting from

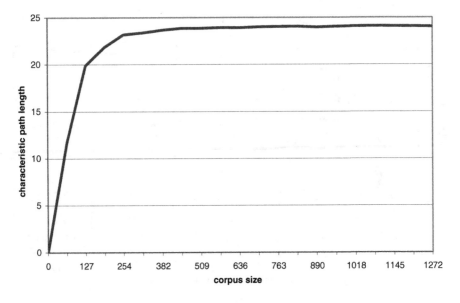

Fig. 10. Characteristic Path Length as a Function of the Corpus Size

approximately *20%* of the maximal corpus size, inserting ads has roughly no effect on the characteristic path length. This validates our assumption that the total cardinality of the set of attributes used for describing an object is final and bounded. Moreover, most of the attributes are used in the first descriptions that are inserted, while the rest of the descriptions contribute very few new attributes. Therefore, the proposed algorithm of the MLH expansion during the insertion of higher-dimensional ads does not lead to a significant overhead due to the expansion.

7 Conclusions and Future Work

In this work we proposed and evaluated a novel notion of Unspecified Ontology (UNSO). This concept refers to a non-fixed variant of ontological descriptions of the data objects. In comparison to the fixed predefined ontologies, UNSO facilitates more flexible way to describe the objects. Multi-layered hypercube graph (MLH) topology, supporting efficient semantic routing, is constructed based on UNSO. We designate the MLH to be used as an infrastructure for general-purpose E-Commerce applications over Peer-to-Peer network. This work focuses on the basic functionality of E-Commerce systems, i.e., publishing and locating the objects. It allows the users to publish their objects using ontological description, while other users are able to easily locate them.

Note, that using UNSO does not force the users to share or to use any single explicit ontology. The users can provide relatively free ontological descriptions of their data object by specifying the object attributes and their respective values. Instead of using a predefined ontological mapping, hashing-based mechanism is used to map the ads to their positions in the underlying MLH. Thus, the order of the attributes, mentioned by the user is insignificant, and if the attributes are properly recognized, they are mapped to the same hypercube coordinates.

Experimental results show that the performance of UNSO with respect to the Information Retrieval metrics is good. The precision of the system is high, and it increases with the increase of the MLH coordinates range. Although the recall values are moderate, they become very high as a result of performing a simple standardization with WordNet. Note that UNSO, unlike traditional Information Retrieval systems and search engines, demonstrates high values of both recall and precision at the same time. Smart semantic standardization tools and dynamic hashing mechanisms, uniformly distributing the ads among the MLH nodes, will assist in achieving a better performance with respect to the Information Retrieval metrics.

Performance of UNSO with respect to the P2P metrics is also good. As can be seen form the results of scalability experiments, the proposed system is highly scalable. For a relatively low number of concurrent routings, the system reaches its maximal communication load, and further routings do not increase it. This leads to a conclusion, that when implemented and launched as a large-scale data sharing P2P application, e.g., over the Web, UNSO-based systems will keep proper functioning under conditions of heavy load. Thus, we believe UNSO can serve as efficient infrastructure for real-life Web applications and it has the potential of opening Web E-Commerce activities to a larger community of P2P users.

The following directions of further research, based on the developed UNSO concepts, are of particular interest:

- Developing a statistical model for hierarchical management of the MLHs. It will simplify the maintenance of the MLH, shorten the characteristic path length, ensure semantic homogeneity in every level and inherently introduce smart error-correction mechanism. In addition, it will protect the hypercube-like graph against organized attacks, maliciously introducing new ontology slots.
- Improving the proposed simple standardization mechanism through integrating more sophisticated Natural Language Processing (NLP) tools recognizing the terms context during the semantic standardization. This will improve the Information Retrieval performance of UNSO.
- Discovering the importance (weights) of attributes and the distances between the different values of the same attribute. This will allow more accurate assessment of the distance between two nodes in the hypercube-like graph and will facilitate more accurate ranking of the results displayed to the user.
- Developing a smarter routing algorithm, dynamically generating the optimal routing path between two MLH nodes as a function of the changing workloads of the connected users.
- Adding other E-Commerce functionalities to the system. For example, real-life E-Commerce systems usually support sophisticated functionalities (e.g., public auctions and market clearings) rather then simple publish-subscribe functionality. We intend to investigate exploiting UNSO for supporting such functionalities.
- Implementing distributed P2P UNSO client, launching it over the Web and creating hypercube-like graph of real-life users, and performing large-scale experiments with large number of E-Commerce ads.

In summary, we believe that the unspecified and flexible nature of UNSO, jointly with its good data management capabilities, will facilitate UNSO usage not only for E-Commerce applications, but for any kind of publish-locate services.

References

[1] K.Aberer, M.Punceva, M.Hauswirth, R.Schmidt, *"Improving Data Access in P2P Systems"*, IEEE Internet Computing, January-February 2002.
[2] K.Aberer, P.Cudre-Mauroux, M. Hauswirth, *"The Chatty Web: Emergent Semantics Through Gossiping"*, In proceedings of the International World Wide Web Conference, Budapest, Hungary, 2003.
[3] E.Adar, B.Huberman, *"Free Riding on Gnutella"*, Technical Report, Xerox PARC, 2000.
[4] S.Androutsellis-Theotokis, D.Spinellis, *"A Survey of Peer-to-Peer Content Distribution Technologies"*, ACM Computing Survey, 36(4), pp. 335-371, 2004.
[5] S.Ayyasamy, C.Patel, Y.Lee, *"Semantic Web services and DHT-based Peer-to-Peer Networks: A New Symbiotic Relationship"*, In proceeding of the Workshop on Semantics in Peer-to-Peer and Grid Computing, Budapest, Hungary, 2003.
[6] P.Backx, T.Wauters, B.Dhoedt, P.Demeester, *"A Comparison of Peer-to-Peer applications"*, In proceedings of Eurescom Summit, Heidelberg, Germany, 2002.

[7] P.Bernstein, F.Giunchiglia, A.Kementsietsidis, J.Mylopoulos, L.Serafini, I.Zaihrayeu, *"Data Management for Peer-to-Peer Computing: A Vision"*, In proceedings of the Workshop on the Web and Databases, Madison, Wisconsin, 2002.

[8] P.A.Bernstein, S.Melnik, *"Meta Data Management"*, in Proceedings of the International Conference on Data Engineering, Boston, MA, 2004.

[9] A.Blum, T.Sandholm, M.Ziukevich, *"Online Algorithms for Market Clearing"*, In proceedings of the ACM-SIAM symposium on Discrete algorithms, San Francisco, CA, 2002.

[10] I.Clarke, O.Sandberg, B.Wiley, T.Hong, *"Freenet: a Distributed Anonymous Information Storage and Retrieval System"*, In proceeding of the ICSI Workshop on Design Issues in Anonymity and Unobservability, Berkeley, CA, 2000.

[11] C.Fellbaum, *"WordNet - An Electronic Lexical Database"*, MIT Press, 1998.

[12] N.Fridman Noy, M.A.Musen, *"PROMPT: Algorithm and Tool for Automated Ontology Merging and Alignment"*, In proceedings of the National Conference on Artificial Intelligence (AAAI'2000), Austin, TX, 2000.

[13] T.R.Gruber, *"A Translation Approach to Portable Ontology Specifications"*, Knowledge Acquisition Journal, 6(2), pp. 199–221, 1993.

[14] A.Gupta, D.Agrawal, A.Abbadi, *"Approximate Range Selection Queries in Peer-to-Peer Systems"*, In proceedings of the Conference on Innovative Data Systems Research, Asilomar, CA, 2003.

[15] M.Harren, J.M.Hellerstein, R.Huebsch, B.T.Loo, S.Shenker, I.Stoica, *"Complex Queries in DHT-based Peer-to-Peer Networks"*, In proceedings of the International Workshop on Peer-to-Peer Systems, Cambridge, MA, 2002.

[16] E.Hovy, *"Combining and Standardizing Large-Scale, Practical Ontologies for Machine Translation and Other Uses"*, In proceedings of the International Conference on Language Resources and Evaluation, Granada, Spain, 1998.

[17] P.Indyk, R.Motwani, P.Raghavan, S.Vempala, *"Locality-Preserving Hashing in Multidimensional Spaces"*, In proceedings of the Symposium on Theory of Computing, El Paso, TX, 1997.

[18] E.J.Johnson, W.Moe, P.S.Fader, S.Bellman, J.Lohse ,*"On the Depth and Dynamics of Online Search Behavior"*, Management Science, 50 (3), pp. 299-308, 2004.

[19] J.Madhavan, A.Y.Halevy, *"Composing Mappings Among Data Sources"*, In proceedings of the Conference on Very Large Databases, Berlin, Germany, 2003.

[20] P.Maes, R.H.Guttman, A.G.Moukas, *"Agents that Buy and Sell: Transforming Commerce as we Know it"*, Communications of the ACM, 42(3), pp. 81-91, March 1999.

[21] D.S.Milojicic, V.Kalogeraki, R.Lukose, K.Nagaraja, J.Pruyne, B.Richard, S.Rollins, Z.Xu, *"Peer-to-Peer Computing"*, Technical Report HPL-2002-57, HP Labs, 2002.

[22] W.Nejdl, B.Wolf, *"Edutella: A P2P Networking Infrastructure Based on RDF"*, In proceedings of the World Wide Web Conference, Honolulu, HI, 2002.

[23] W.S.Ng, B.C.Ooi, K.L.Tan, A.Zhou, *"PeerDB: A P2P-Based System for Distributed Data Sharing"*, In proceedings of the International Conferene on Data Engineering, Bangalore, India, 2003.

[24] D.Peleg, E.Upfal, *"Constructing Disjoint Paths on Expander Graphs"*, in International Journal on Combinatorics and the Theory of Computing, 9, pp.289-313, 1989.

[25] C.Plaxton, R.Rajaraman, A.Richa, *"Accessing Nearby Copies of Replicated Objects in a Distributed Environment"*, In proceedings of ACM SPAA, Newport, RI, 1997.

[26] S.Ratnasamy, P.Francis, M.Handley, R.Karp, S.Shenker, *"A Scalable Content-Addressable Network"*, In proceedings of ACM SIGCOMM, San Diego, CA, 2001.

[27] S.Ratnasamy, S.Shenker, I.Stoica, *"Routing Algorithms for DHTs: Some Open Questions"*, In proceedings for the International Workshop on Peer-to-Peer Systems, Cambridge, MA, 2002.

[28] R.L.Rivest, *"The MD5 Message-Digest Algorithm"*, Request for Comments 1321, IETF Network Working Group, 1992.

[29] A.Rowstron, P.Druschel, *"Pastry: Scalable, Distributed Object Location and Routing for Large-Scale Peer-to-Peer Systems"*, In proceeding of the International Conference on Distributed Systems Platforms (Middleware), Heidelberg, Germany, 2001.

[30] O.D.Sahin, A.Gupta, D.Agrawal, A.Abbadi, *"A Peer-to-Peer Framework for Caching Range Queries"*, In proceedings of the International Conference on Data Engineering, Boston, MA, 2004.

[31] S.Saroiu, K.P.Gummadi, S.D.Gribble, *"Measuring and Analyzing the Characteristics of Napster and Gnutella Hosts"*, Multimedia Systems, 9, pp. 170-184, 2003.

[32] M.Schlosser, M.Sintek, S.Decker, W.Nejdl, *"A Scalable and Ontology-Based P2P Infrastructure for Semantic Web Services"*, In proceeding of the IEEE International Conference on Peer-to-Peer Computing, Linkoping, Sweden, 2002.

[33] I.Stoica, R.Morris, D.Karger, M.F.Kaashoek, H.Balakrishan, *"Chord: A Scalable Peer-to-Peer Lookup Service for Internet Applications"*, In proceedings of ACM SIGCOMM, San Diego, CA, 2001.

[34] I.Tatarinov, Z.G,Ives, J.Madhavan, A.Halevy, D.Suciu, N.N.Dalvi, X.Dong, Y.Kadiyaska, G.Miklau, P.Mork, *"The Piazza Peer-to-Peer Data Management Project"*, ACM SIGMOD Record, 32(3), pp.47-52, 2003.

[35] M.Uschold, *"Creating, Integrating and Maintaining Local and Global Ontologies"*, In proceedings of the European Conference on Artificial Intelligence, Berlin, Germany, 2000.

[36] G.Wiederhold, *"Mediators in the Architecture of Future Information Systems"*, in "Readings in Agents", pp. 185-196, Morgan Kaufmann Pubs., 1997.

[37] I.H.Witten, A.Moffat, T.C.Bell, *"Managing Gigabytes: Compressing and Indexing Documents and Images"*, Morgan Kaufmann Publishers, 1999.

[38] B.Yang, H.Garcia-Molina, *"Designing a Super-Peer Network"*, In proceedings of the International Conference on Data Engineering, Los Alamitos, CA, 2003.

Interoperability Through Emergent Semantics
A Semiotic Dynamics Approach

Luc Steels[1,2] and Peter Hanappe[1]

[1]Sony Computer Science Laboratory, Paris, France
[2]Vrije Universiteit Brussel, Brussels, Belgium
`steels@arti.vub.ac.be, hanappe@csl.sony.fr`

Abstract. We study the exchange of information in collective information systems mediated by information agents, focusing specifically on
the problem of semantic interoperability. We advocate the use of mechanisms inspired from natural language, that enable each agent to develop
a repertoire of grounded categories and labels for these categories and
negotiate their use with other agents. The communication system as well
as its semantics is hence emergent and adaptive instead of predefined.
It is the result of a self-organised semiotic dynamics where relations between data, labels for the data, and the categories associated with the
labels undergo constant evolution.

1 Introduction

Many interactive information systems such as web browsers typically allow a
user to taxonomically structure data and associate tags with this taxonomy.
In the case of web browsers, the data consists of URLs to web pages, the taxonomy is the hierarchy of bookmark folders, and tags are names that users associate with folders and sub-folders. We call the taxonomy created and maintained by a user the "owner taxonomy" and its tags the "owner tags". The
taxonomy implies a particular way of categorising the data so that there is in
fact a semiotic relation between data, tags, and categories, forming a semiotic
triad (see figure 1). The semantics of the tags (i.e. the meaning of the categories) is usually not explicitly defined. We could either do this by defining
the logical dependencies between categories (formal semantics), or by defining
classifiers, i.e. computable functions capable of deciding whether the category
applies to a data item or not (grounded semantics).

Categorisations and tagging by users is based on cognitive processes which are
not accessible to information systems, and may not even be consciously known
by the users themselves. For example, a user may decide to put all the songs he
likes in one folder and the ones he does not like in another. This categorisation is
completely subjective and can never be automated nor emulated by a machine.
Similarly user tags often use natural language words but this is only suggestive
and not necessarily accurate nor rational. For example, a user may have a folder
tagged 'New York' but it could contain pictures of New York, pictures taken in
New York, pictures taken while living in New York, etc.

S. Spaccapietra et al. (Eds.): Journal on Data Semantics VI, LNCS 4090, pp. 143–167, 2006.
© Springer-Verlag Berlin Heidelberg 2006

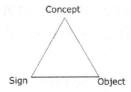

Fig. 1. Data, tags, and categories associated with tags form a semiotic relation. The paper proposes a system whereby agents autonomously establish such relations and coordinate them with others.

The taxonomies and tags of a user are usually local and private and this is unproblematic as long as there is no exchange between them. But there is now a rapidly growing number of collective information systems where users want to exchange data with each other, and they are therefore necessarily confronted with the problem that the taxonomy and tags imposed by one user are not necessarily the same as those of another. Moreover the information systems may be heterogeneous in the sense that the conceptual schemata used by one information system for storing data and meta-data may be quite different from those used by another information system.

One type of collective information system are peer-to-peer systems which allow direct information exchange between peers without the need to go through a central server. Well-known examples for music file sharing are systems like Gnutella, Kazaa, or eMule that are used by millions of people today. Similar sharing networks are growing for movies or game software. Also in the domain of scientific data or educational materials, there are growing networks of peer-to-peer shared systems [8]. Another type of collective information systems form websites which encourage social sharing of data by allowing users to upload data and introduce tags for these data. Examples include www.flickr.com for exchanging pictures, www.citeulike.com for exchanging scientific papers, and del.icio.us for exchanging information about websites. Although these systems are not peer-to-peer in the strict sense, because they are managed from central servers, they nevertheless are highly distributed and the taxonomy is not imposed in a top-down manner. Users can at any time add or delete data, introduce or change their own tags, and thus impose taxonomies on their data.

The distributed creation of taxonomies and tags and the multiplicity of conceptual schemata generate the well known problem of *semantic interoperability*. One solution is to standardise. The different users of a collective information system could all agree a priori to use the same taxonomies to structure their data and to use the same conceptual schemata for their data and meta-data. The tags in the owner taxonomies can then act as a shared communication protocol between peers. For example, all users of web browsers could agree to use the taxonomies of Yahoo for organising their data, and adopt the labels used by Yahoo (possibly with translations into different languages). Unfortunately such a standardisation approach is unlikely to work for truly open-ended collective information systems in rapidly changing domains like music file sharing, picture exchange, medical imaging, scientific papers, etc. New topics and new kinds of data come up all the time, styles shift, and interests of users diverge, so it is very hard to capture all this once and for all in a static taxonomy. Another issue is that taxonomies and conceptual schemata may be linked to specific proprietary software that others may not want to use.

Alternatively, it is possible that each peer has its own local taxonomy, but that these are translated into a (more) global taxonomy which is used for querying and information exchange and thus acts as an interlingua between peers. The translation to conceptual schemata of each peer could be aided by mediators [19] and achieved through automated schema matching based on finding structural similarities between schemas (see the survey in [9]). A promising recent variant of automated schema matching is based on ostensive interactions, in which agents send each other examples of the instances of schema elements so that the mapping can be made [16]. The difficulty with this approach is that a one-to-one mapping of taxonomies or conceptual schemata is not always possible. In these cases data semantics must be taken into account.

The first approach which is trying to do this is currently being explored by the Semantic Web initiative [4] and by advocates of CYC or Wordnet [7]. The data is associated with descriptions with a formal semantics, defined in terms of ontologies [5]. This approach is clearly highly valuable for closed domains, but there are known limitations when applied to open-ended information systems [1], [12], [11]. The ontologies do not capture the grounded semantics, they only constrain inference. Moreover the semantic web requires standardisation based on universal (or at least domain-wide) ontologies. But it is hard to imagine that a world-wide consensus is reachable and enforceable in every domain of human activity for which information systems are currently in use. Even in restricted domains this is hard because of an increasingly interconnected global world. Human activity and the information systems built for them are open systems. They cannot be defined once and for all but must be adaptable to new needs.

In this paper, we also take a semantics approach but pursue grounded as opposed to formal semantics. We view semantic interoperability as a coordination problem between the world, information systems, and human users, and propose to set up a semiotic dynamics that achieves this coordination. Rather than trying to map owner taxonomies or conceptual schemata directly onto each other, we propose that each information system has an associated agent. The agents self-organise an interlingua with labels whose underlying categories are grounded in the actual data and meta-data. The interlingua is not universal but coordinated among those agents that need to cooperate. The semiotic dynamics is user-driven in the sense that users continuously stimulate the formation of new labels and categories and steer the grounding of the categories by giving examples and counter examples.

Our proposal has two components. On the one hand we try to orchestrate the same sort of semiotic dynamics that we see happening in natural languages or in social exchange websites like www.flickr.com, namely there is an emergent system of labels whose use is coordinated among the agents without central coordination. Second we try to achieve grounded semantics by programming the agents so that they can develop operational classifiers grounding these labels.

The semantics is emergent in the sense that it is derived by the system itself and it is dynamic because it continuously tracks the re-categorisations that users inevitably carry out as they organise and reorganise their data.

Our proposals are strongly related to other approaches for achieving 'emergent semantics', notably [2], which also emphasises user orientation, and [10], which explores grounded semantics. Similar to [3] we focus on orchestrating a user-driven semiotic dynamics in information agents.

The work reported here relies on a decade of research into the origins and evolution of communication systems for robot-robot and robot-human communication [12], [14]. We have applied these ideas to the semantic interoperability problem and performed a case study in the domain of music file sharing. The development of classifiers can be done in many different ways but for this case study we have relied on recent work in the automatic construction of classifiers inspired by methods from genetic programming [18]. In the present paper, we use however a simpler example to explain the proposed mechanisms and study their behaviour.

We are well aware of important limitations of the proposals discussed in this paper, and therefore see it as a first exploration rather than the final solution to semantic interoperability (if that ever could be found). More specifically, grounded semantics is only possible in domains where the meaning of a taxonomy *can* be grounded, which is only the case in well-delineated domains. For example, although it would be straightforward to develop a classifier for the tag 'black-and-white' (which would also work for 'bw', 'noir-et-blanc', etc.), it is quite impossible to develop a grounded semantics for 'New York' as the range of images where this tag might be applicable is vast and strongly varied. However it is only by defining and exploring the kinds of systems discussed in this paper that progress on the issues can be made.

The first part of the paper defines some of the terminology that we will use later. Then we describe the behaviours of the information agents, particularly as they pertain to the negotiation of a shared repertoire of labels and classifiers that constitute the meaning of the labels. Next we give example interactions from our implementation in the music domain.

2   Definitions

We assume that the information systems handle sets of *data*. The data can be files (text, music, movie, or image files) or any data stored by other means. For simplification, only one type of data is assumed (for example, only music files). Furthermore, we assume that every datum has a unique identifier that can be communicated between peers. The identifiers can be a URL that indicates where the data (or meta-data) can be found, or it can be an index into a database that is accessible to everyone[1]. In the exchanges between agents, the identifiers are

---

[1] For music files, the MusicBrainz database could be used (http://www. musicbrainz.org); for movies, the Internet Movie Database (http://www.imdb.com); for scientific papers, Citeseer (http://citeseer.ist.psu.edu).

sent instead of the data. In the worst case, when no identifiers are available, the data itself will be transmitted. We will use $\mathcal{D}$ to indicate the set of all data.

We will use also *tags* and *labels*. Both are character strings. The tags are used by the owners in their taxonomy. The labels are used by the information agents. The set of all labels will be denoted by $\mathcal{L}$, and the set of all tags $\mathcal{N}$. Agents have also access to classifiers which are computable functions over data items. They are used to give grounded semantics to the labels.

2.1   Classifiers

Definition 1. *Classifier*
A classifier is a function, $c : \mathcal{D} \rightarrow \{0,1\}$, that, given a data element d, returns 1 or 0, depending on whether d belongs to a particular class (category) c or not. The set of classifiers is denoted by C.

For example, there might be a classifier that is able to detect whether a song sample contains a female voice or not, or whether a song was performed by The Beatles. Classifiers use data and meta-data to decide what data belongs to the category and what not (see also Section 4.6)

Agents need the ability to discriminate a data set D_1 from another set D_2. For example, songs which have a female voice and those which do not. For this purpose, we introduce two functions, the *scope* and the *discriminative success* of a classifier.

Definition 2. *Scope of a classifier*
The scope of a classifier c for a set of data D, $\sigma(D,c)$, is the fraction of elements in D for which c returns 1:

$$\sigma(D,c) = \frac{\sum_{d \in D} c(d)}{|D|}$$

Definition 3. *Discriminative success of a classifier*
The discriminative success of a classifier c measures how well c can discriminate between two data sets D_1 and D_2:

$$\delta(D_1, D_2, c) = \sigma(D_1, c) - \sigma(D_2, c)$$

The categorisation process consists of finding the classifier with the highest discriminative success, given two data sets D_1 and D_2.

Definition 4. *Categorise*
Let D_1 and D_2 be two sets of data and C a set of classifiers. We can order the classifiers $c \in C$ in descending order based on their discriminative success: $[\langle c_1, p_1 \rangle, ..., \langle c_m, p_m \rangle]$ with $c_i \in C$, and $p_i = \delta(D_1, D_2, c_i)$, and $p_i, p_{i+1} \rightarrow p_i \geq p_{i+1}$. Clearly the better c_i distinguishes the elements in D_1 from the elements in D_2, the greater $\delta(D_1, D_2, c_i)$ will be and hence by taking the first element of the sequence above, we find the most discriminating category: $categorise(C, D_1, D_2) = first([\langle c_1, p_1 \rangle, ..., \langle c_m, p_m \rangle]).$

In the case where several classifiers c_i, ..., c_n have a maximum discriminative success, additional heuristics could be used in choosing the best classifier. For example, one may choose the classifier that has been used most successfully in previous exchanges with other agents. Classifiers will not only be used to distinguish between two sets but also to filter an existing data set, based on the following definition:

Definition 5. *Filter*

$$filter(D, c) = \{d \mid d \in D \text{ and } c(d) = 1\}$$

2.2   Dictionaries

The association of labels with classifiers and vice versa is stored in a *dictionary*.

Definition 6. *Dictionary*
A dictionary W is a two-way mapping from a set of labels L to a set of classifiers C. Each association between a classifier and a label has a certain strength $\gamma \in [0.0, 1.0]$. More formally: $W \subset \mathcal{L} \times \mathcal{C} \times [0.0, 1.0]$.

For example, there could be a label 'female-voice' which is associated with the classifier able to decide whether a song contains a female voice or not.

Given a classifier c and a dictionary W, we can construct the list of possible labels for a classifier c as an ordered set based on the strength γ of the relation between c and a label l:

$$labels(c, W) = ((l_1, \gamma_1), ..., (l_n, \gamma_n)) \text{ with } (c, l_i, \gamma_i) \in W \text{ and } \gamma_i \geq \gamma_{i+1}$$

Definition 7. *Coding of a classifier*
The label coding a classifier c is the first label from this set: $code(c, W) = first(labels(c, W))$.

The inverse operation, *decode*, is defined similarly. Given a label l and a dictionary W, we construct the list of possible classifiers as an ordered set based on the strength γ of the relation between l and a classifier c:

$$cats(l, W) = ((c_1, \gamma_1), ..., (c_n, \gamma_n)) \text{ with } (c_i, l, \gamma_i) \in W \text{ and } \gamma_i \geq \gamma_{i+1}$$

Definition 8. *Decoding of a label*
The decoded classifier is the first classifier from the ordered set: $decode(l, W) = first(cats(l, W))$.

This process can be easily extended to coding or decoding conjunctions (i.e. sets) of classifiers. Coding should seek the minimal number of words that cover the set of classifiers resulting from discrimination and decoding should reconstruct the minimal set of classifiers that are associated with each of the words.

2.3   Peer Information System

Definition 9. *Peer information system*
A peer information system a, at time t, is defined as $PI_{a,t} = \langle IS_{a,t}, O, IA_{a,t} \rangle$, with:

- $IS_{a,t} = \langle D_{a,t}, N_{a,t}, M_{a,t}, MD \rangle$ *an information system which consists of a set of data D, a set of tags N and a mapping $M : N \rightarrow \mathcal{P}(D)$ mapping tags to subsets of D by an extensional definition, and a set of meta-data MD.*
- *O a (human) owner.*
- $IA_{a,t} = \langle L_{a,t}, C_{a,t}, W_{a,t} \rangle$ *an information agent with a set of labels L, a set of classifiers C and a dictionary W.*

Definition 10. *Collective information network A collective information system IN consists of a set of information systems: $IN = \{PI_1, ... PI_n\}$.*

When the owner of one information system queries another information system, we call the information system of the querying peer the caller (or client) and the system providing information the callee (or server).

3 Agent Behaviours

3.1 Interaction

We assume that the (human) owner of the caller initiates a query by identifying a set $G_c \subseteq D_c$ of data elements that are considered to be good examples of the kind of elements the owner is requesting from the callee. The owner can do this by using the tags of the owner taxonomy that remains fully under his control, or by explicitly identifying in some other way a subset of the examples in the information system's data set. We assume furthermore that the

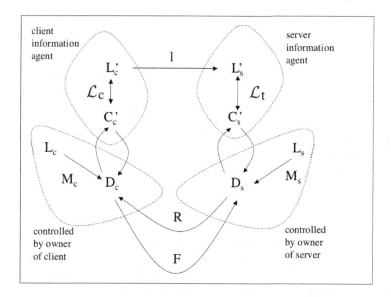

Fig. 2. The different entities and relations involved in collective information exchange and the items that are exchanged between the two. To the left are components of a caller and to the right those of a callee.

query is formulated within a specific context $K_c \subseteq D_c$, which consists of other data elements against which G_c is to be distinguished (counter-examples). The counter-examples should not overlap with the examples, i.e. $G_c \cap K_c = \emptyset$.

For example, the owner could choose a number of tags (like 'jazz', 'female-voice', 'piano') yielding a set of possible data elements based on the tagging system. If this is the user's first interaction, these data elements are viewed against the set of all other music files in his information system. We expect the information agent to come up with the best classifier for distinguishing the data elements against the context and then querying other peers to find the data that are the most compatible. Agents do not exchange the music files themselves, neither the classifiers directly (as different peers may use different libraries or programming languages for their classifiers), but rather labels that are progressively negotiated.

Five types of situations may occur and they are defined in the following subsections. In section 5, we give specific examples for each of these situations in the context of a music application.

3.2   Successful Interaction

The following script gives an overview of the interaction in case of a successful query. The left side details the actions on the caller side and the right side the actions on the callee side. In the middle we show the items that are exchanged between caller and callee.

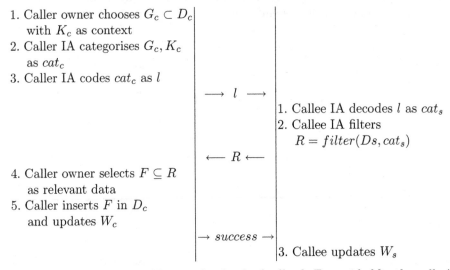

1. Caller owner chooses $G_c \subset D_c$
   with K_c as context
2. Caller IA categorises G_c, K_c
   as cat_c
3. Caller IA codes cat_c as l

$\longrightarrow l \longrightarrow$

1. Callee IA decodes l as cat_s
2. Callee IA filters
   $R = filter(Ds, cat_s)$

$\longleftarrow R \longleftarrow$

4. Caller owner selects $F \subseteq R$
   as relevant data
5. Caller inserts F in D_c
   and updates W_c

$\longrightarrow success \longrightarrow$

3. Callee updates W_s

If the interaction succeeds completely, the feedback F provided by the caller's owner is positive, in other words he received mainly good examples. This implies that the label l naming cat_c, as used by the caller, was compatible with the interpretation of this label by the callee as cat_s and compatible with the desires of the user. In this case, both caller and callee update their mappings from labels to categories so that the use of the label l for the categories cat_c and cat_s is re-enforced in the future. This is done by increasing the relation between the used label and the used classifier with a quantity Δ_{inc}, and diminishing competing relations. Competitors are relations that either use another label for the same classifier, in which case they are decreased with Δ_{n-inh}, or that have associated another classifier with the same label, in which they are decreased with Δ_{o-inh}. More formally, $UpdateCaller(W_{c,t}, l, cat_c)$ is defined as:

$$
\begin{aligned}
W_{c,t+1} = & \{r_i | r_i = (c_i, l_i, \gamma_i) \in W_{c,t} \text{ with } c_i \neq cat_c \text{ and } l_i \neq l\} \quad \cup \\
& \{(cat_c, l, \gamma_i + \Delta_{inc}) \text{ for } w_c = (cat_c, l, \gamma_i) \in W_{c,t}\} \quad \cup \\
& \{r_j | r_j = (cat_c, l_j, \gamma_i + \Delta_{n-inh}) \text{ with } l_j \neq l\} \quad \cup \\
& \{r_j | r_j = (cat_j, l, \gamma_i + \Delta_{o-inh}) \text{ with } cat_j \neq cat_c\}
\end{aligned}
$$

Similarly, $UpdateCallee(W_{s,t}, l, cat_s)$ is defined as:

$$
\begin{aligned}
W_{s,t+1} = & \{r_i | r_i = (c_i, l_i, \gamma_i) \in W_{s,t} \text{ with } c_i \neq cat_s \text{ and } l_i \neq l\} \quad \cup \\
& \{(cat_s, l, \gamma_i + \Delta_{inc}) \text{ for } w_s = (cat_s, l, \gamma_i) \in W_{s,t}\} \quad \cup \\
& \{r_j | r_j = (cat_s, l_j, \gamma_i + \Delta_{n-inh}) \text{ with } l_j \neq l\} \quad \cup \\
& \{r_j | r_j = (cat_j, l, \gamma_i + \Delta_{o-inh}) \text{ with } cat_j \neq cat_s\}
\end{aligned}
$$

3.3   The Information Agent Fails to Categorise

Consider next the situation in which the caller does not have a classifier to discriminate G_c from K_c (caller step 2 fails). In that case, the caller performs two steps:

1. The caller constructs a new classifier cat_n that distinguishes the elements in G_c from those in K_c.
2. The caller invents a new label l_n (a random string drawn from a sufficiently large alphabet) and extends W with a new relation between l_n and cat_n with an initial value for the strength being γ_{init}: $W'_c = W_c \cup \{(l_n, cat_n, \gamma_{init})\}$.

The interaction between caller and callee can now continue as before with the transmission of l_n as new label.

An important issue arises when the random string was already used by another agent for another classifier. This issue (known as homonymy: one label having different meanings) is dealt with by the dynamics of the system as presented here, but it can be minimised by using a technique that guarantees unique symbols even if generated in a distributed fashion, such as the universally unique identifiers (UUID) [6].

3.4   The Callee Does Not Know the Label

The callee does not have the label l that was transmitted by the caller (callee step 1 fails). In that case, the callee signals failure to the caller. It then receives G_c and K_c as examples of what the caller is looking for and then goes through the following steps:

1. Callee IA categorises G_c as distinctive from the context K_c with the classifier cat_s. When this fails, the callee IA creates a new classifier (further called cat_s) and adds it to its categorial repertoire.

2. Callee IA extends W_s with a relation between cat_s, the label l, and an initial strength γ_{init}: $W'_s = W_s \cup \{(l, cat_s, \gamma_{init})\}$.

Then the callee continues the game as before. The interaction is summarised as follows:

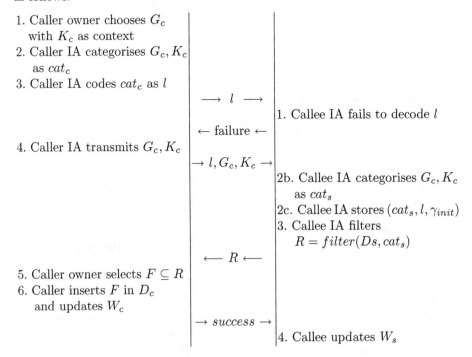

1. Caller owner chooses G_c
   with K_c as context
2. Caller IA categorises G_c, K_c
   as cat_c
3. Caller IA codes cat_c as l

$\longrightarrow l \longrightarrow$

1. Callee IA fails to decode l

$\longleftarrow$ failure $\longleftarrow$

4. Caller IA transmits G_c, K_c

$\rightarrow l, G_c, K_c \rightarrow$

2b. Callee IA categorises G_c, K_c
   as cat_s
2c. Callee IA stores $(cat_s, l, \gamma_{init})$
3. Callee IA filters
   $R = filter(Ds, cat_s)$

$\longleftarrow R \longleftarrow$

5. Caller owner selects $F \subseteq R$
6. Caller inserts F in D_c
   and updates W_c

$\longrightarrow success \longrightarrow$

4. Callee updates W_s

3.5   Handling Partial Success

The next case occurs when the results given by the callee to the caller is deemed to be partly irrelevant by the (owner of the) caller. A score can be computed which is simply the percentage of elements that was deemed appropriate by the owner. A percentage below θ_{fail} signals the failure. There are two causes for this problem: (1) The classifier used by the caller is not precise enough to capture the distinction that was intended by the user, or (2) the classifier associated with the transmitted label by the caller is different from the classifier associated with the same label by the callee.

The distinction between the two cases is done as follows. After the evaluation of the results by the owner, the calling agent is in possession of two sets of good examples (G_c and F) and two sets of counter-examples (K_c and B). With the extra information available, the agent can now try to find a classifier that has a higher discriminative success than the initially chosen classifier. If such a classifier can be found, the agent concludes that it has misinterpreted the intentions of its owner. If such a classifier cannot be found, it signal a communication failure, indicating that the callee has a different interpretation of the label that does not match with its own. The next two sections detail the interactions in both cases.

3.6   The Caller Has Misinterpreted the Owner's Request

In case the calling agent can find a new classifier cat'_c with a higher discriminative success between the new sets $G_c \cup F$ and $K_c \cup B$, the interaction proceeds as before using cat'_c instead of cat_c. The classifier cat'_c can either be an existing classifier or it can be a classifier that is newly created. The classifier cat'_c is coded as label l'.

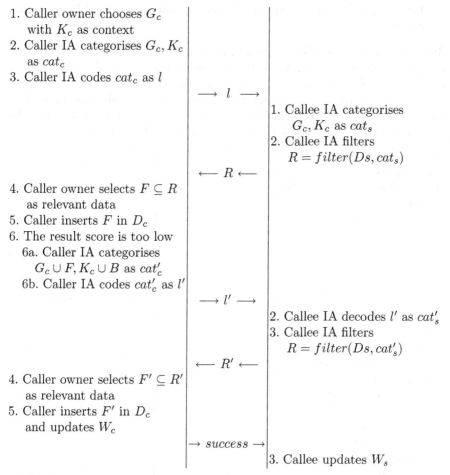

1. Caller owner chooses G_c
   with K_c as context
2. Caller IA categorises G_c, K_c
   as cat_c
3. Caller IA codes cat_c as l

$\longrightarrow l \longrightarrow$

1. Callee IA categorises
   G_c, K_c as cat_s
2. Callee IA filters
   $R = filter(Ds, cat_s)$

$\longleftarrow R \longleftarrow$

4. Caller owner selects $F \subseteq R$
   as relevant data
5. Caller inserts F in D_c
6. The result score is too low
   6a. Caller IA categorises
       $G_c \cup F, K_c \cup B$ as cat'_c
   6b. Caller IA codes cat'_c as l'

$\longrightarrow l' \longrightarrow$

2. Callee IA decodes l' as cat'_s
3. Callee IA filters
   $R = filter(Ds, cat'_s)$

$\longleftarrow R' \longleftarrow$

4. Caller owner selects $F' \subseteq R'$
   as relevant data
5. Caller inserts F' in D_c
   and updates W_c

$\rightarrow success \rightarrow$

3. Callee updates W_s

The second query can fail for the same reasons as the first invocation. For example, the callee may not know the label l' and signal a failure. In that particular case, the interaction falls back to the situation discussed in section 3.4.

3.7   The Caller and Callee Interpret the Label Differently

In this case caller and callee should try to coordinate their categories and labels so that exchange becomes possible or fruitful in the future. Actions are necessary both on the side of the caller and of the callee. First of all the strength of the labels they used in the failed communication are to be diminished:

1. Caller IA diminishes the association strength between cat_c and l in W_c by a factor Δ_{dec}. This will decrease the chance that the relation is coded in the future with this particular label.
2. Callee IA diminishes the association strength between cat_s and l in W_s by a factor Δ_{dec}. This will decrease the chance that l is decoded in the future with this relation.

If the caller was not able to come up with a better classifier than the one used in the first transaction, the caller IA can send examples of the objects of interest $G_c \cup F$ and the context $K_c \cup B$ so that the callee can attempt to acquire the right meaning by finding a distinctive classifier and by adding an association between this classifier and the label l. This case then becomes identical to the one discussed earlier (section 3.4, "the callee does not know the label").

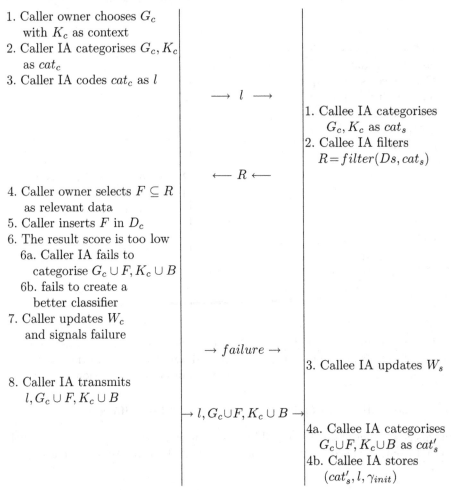

1. Caller owner chooses G_c
    with K_c as context
2. Caller IA categorises G_c, K_c
    as cat_c
3. Caller IA codes cat_c as l

$\longrightarrow l \longrightarrow$

1. Callee IA categorises
    G_c, K_c as cat_s
2. Callee IA filters
    $R = filter(Ds, cat_s)$

$\longleftarrow R \longleftarrow$

4. Caller owner selects $F \subseteq R$
    as relevant data
5. Caller inserts F in D_c
6. The result score is too low
    6a. Caller IA fails to
        categorise $G_c \cup F, K_c \cup B$
    6b. fails to create a
        better classifier
7. Caller updates W_c
    and signals failure

$\longrightarrow failure \longrightarrow$

3. Callee IA updates W_s

8. Caller IA transmits
    $l, G_c \cup F, K_c \cup B$

$\longrightarrow l, G_c \cup F, K_c \cup B \longrightarrow$

4a. Callee IA categorises
    $G_c \cup F, K_c \cup B$ as cat'_s
4b. Callee IA stores
    $(cat'_s, l, \gamma_{init})$

3.8   Parameters

In summary, we find the following main parameters for the agent's adaptive mechanisms. Each time we give values for these parameters that have proven to yield adequate performance in large-scale tests of the system.

1. γ_{init} is the initial strength with which a new relation enters into the dictionary $\mathcal{L}$ of the agents. $\gamma_{init} = 0.5$.
2. Δ_{inc} is the increase of γ in the relation used, in case there is success. $\Delta_{inc} = 0.1$. [ENFORCEMENT]
3. Δ_{n-inh} is the decrease of relations with the same label (but different categories) in case of success. $\Delta_{n-inh} = -0.2$.
4. Δ_{o-inh} is the decrease of relations with the same classifier (but different labels) in case of success. $\Delta_{o-inh} = -0.1$. [LATERAL INHIBITION]
5. Δ_{dec} is the decrease of γ in the relation used, in case when there is failure. $\Delta_{dec} = -0.1$. [DAMPING]
6. θ_{disc} is the threshold used in the categorisation. $\theta_{disc} = 0.5$
7. θ_{fail} is the threshold used to signal a failed exchange. $\theta_{fail} = 0.5$

There is some leeway with the exact value of these parameters. It is even possible to make all of them 0 (accept γ_{init}) but then all labels ever invented by any agent will propagate in the population and so we get a very large dictionary. If they are non-zero, then obviously $\Delta_{inc} > 0$ and $\Delta_{n-inh} < 0$, $\Delta_{o-inh} < 0$. Also $\Delta_{dec} < 0$ because otherwise a relation that is not successful would increase in strength. The importance of the parameters is summarised in figure 3, taken from simulation experiments. Adoption means that new labels propagate, enforcement

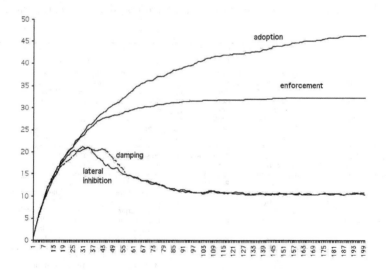

Fig. 3. The evolution in average dictionary size for labelling 10 objects in a population of 10 agents. Enforcement combined with lateral inhibition and damping leads to the most efficient dictionary, in which only 10 labels are used for 10 objects.

means that the strength is increased in case of success, damping means that the strength is decreased in case of failure, and lateral inhibition means that the strength of competitors is decreased in case of success.

4   An Example: Music Sharing

We now illustrate the interactions described in the previous sections for the case of music sharing. The example is drawn from our experimental implementation. We introduce three users and their respective information agents. Each peer has local meta-data, displayed in Fig. 4. We make the assumption that all songs have a unique identification number that is common to all agents. In practice, this ID can be a URL or an index of a public database. However, to make the examples more readable we will use the title of the songs instead of their ID's.

All agents know the name of the artists, but, as can be seen in the tables below, these names are formatted differently for every agent. The other meta-data are specific to every agent. $Agent_0$'s database contains a genre and a BPM (beats per minute) column. $Agent_1$ stores the year in which the recording was released and $Agent_2$ has information on the global energy of the songs. The peers thus have different meta-data and different databases schemas.

We also assume that owners have imposed a taxonomy on their data in the form of a directory structure, as shown in Fig. 5. These taxonomies are mainly used to facilitate the organisation and selection of a set of music files by the users.

The example details four interactions. The agents start from a zero state in which their dictionaries are still empty and have no labels nor categories.

Songs		Meta-data of Agent 0			Meta-data of Agent 1		Meta-data of Agent 2	
ID	Title	Artist	Genre	BPM	Nom	Année	Band	Energy
15	Let's Spend The Night ...	The Rolling Stones	Rock	141	Rolling Stones, The	1967	stones	0.612
14	Ruby Tuesday	The Rolling Stones	Rock	102	Rolling Stones, The	1967	stones	0.322
13	Paint It Black	The Rolling Stones	Rock	160	Rolling Stones, The	1966	stones	0.571
12	And I Love Her	The Beatles	Rock 'n Roll	115	Beatles, The	1964	beatles	0.431
11	Another Girl	The Beatles	Rock 'n Roll	180	Beatles, The	1965	beatles	0.607
10	Twist and Shout	The Beatles	Rock 'n Roll	128	Beatles, The	1963	beatles	0.745
09	I'm Down	The Beatles	Rock 'n Roll	164	Beatles, The	1965	beatles	0.623
08	A Hard Day's Night	The Beatles	Rock 'n Roll	141	Beatles, The	1964	beatles	0.619
07	Norwegian Wood	The Beatles	Pop	61	Beatles, The	1965	beatles	0.494
27	Amazing Grace	Elvis Presley	Rock 'n Roll	63	Presley, Elvis	1972	the_king	0.38
06	Eleanor Rigby	The Beatles	Pop	138	Beatles, The	1966	beatles	0.51
26	Are You Lonesome ...	Elvis Presley	Rock 'n Roll	75	Presley, Elvis	1956	the_king	0.0
05	I Feel Fine	The Beatles	Rock 'n Roll	180	Beatles, The	1964	beatles	0.523
25	Love Me Tender	Elvis Presley	Rock 'n Roll	81	Presley, Elvis	1957	the_king	0.128
04	You Know My Name	The Beatles	Pop	96	Beatles, The	1969	beatles	0.502
24	Smoke on the Water	Deep Purple	Rock	120	Deep Purple	1972	deep_purple	0.53
03	Across The Universe	The Beatles	Pop	82	Beatles, The	1970	beatles	0.55
02	Helter Skelter	The Beatles	Rock	155	Beatles, The	1968	beatles	0.642
01	Blackbird	The Beatles	Pop	94	Beatles, The	1968	beatles	0.191
21	Billie Jean	Michael Jackson	Pop	119	Jackson, Michael	1983	michael_jackson	0.533
00	Sie Liebt Dich	The Beatles	Rock 'n Roll	153	Beatles, The	1964	beatles	0.663
20	True Blue	Madonna	Pop	119	Madonna	1986	madonna	0.619

Fig. 4. On the left, the list of available music files. On the right, the meta-data of all the files available to each information agent.

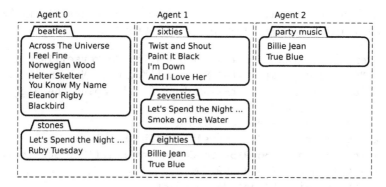

Fig. 5. The user-defined taxonomies for the three agents

4.1   Query 1: Agent 0 Asks Agent 1 for More "Beatles"

In the first query, $user_0$ selects the folder "beatles" and asks its agent to seek similar songs. Since the user explicitly selects "beatles" and not "stones", the agent interprets the request as: "find more beatles, not stones". The search query then proceeds as follows.

$Agent_0$ start by categorising the owner's request. It checks whether it has a category in its dictionary that discriminates between the set of examples and the set of counter-examples. Because the dictionary is empty, $agent_0$ fails to find a classifier and, therefore, constructs the new one, defined as: `Artist(The Beatles)`. The new category does not have any label associated with it. $Agent_0$ constructs a new label randomly[2] (in this case, the label is 6365915a) and binds it to the classifier with a default strength of $\gamma_{init} = 0.5$. This corresponds to the situation described in Sec. 3.3, "The information agent fails to categorise".

$Agent_0$ then queries $agent_1$ using the label 6365915a. $Agent_1$ fails to decode the label because its dictionary is empty and returns a failure message to $agent_0$ to indicate this fact. In response, $Agent_0$ transmits the examples and counter-examples of 6365915a: the identifiers of "beatles" songs on the one hand, and the "stones" songs on the other. With these two sets of data, $agent_1$ can now create a new classifier, `Nom(Beatles, The)`, and associate it to the label 6365915a with a default strength of 0.5 (see Sec. 3.4, "The callee does not know the label").

$Agent_0$ sends the query again and $agent_1$ now successfully decodes the label 6365915a. It uses the associated category `Nom(Beatles, The)` to filter its data collection which results in the following list of songs: [And I Love Her], [Twist And Shout], [I'm Down].

When $agent_0$'s owner evaluates the results, all songs are considered good and the query is a success. Both $agent_0$ and $agent_1$ updates their dictionaries and increase the strength of the binding between the label 6365915a and their respective categories with $\Delta_{inc} = 0.1$. This corresponds to the *UpdateCaller* and *UpdateCallee* functions described in Sec. 3.2.

---

[2] We use randomly generated labels based on the UUID algorithm.

The following listing shows the same query in a more compact form. We will use this form of presentation in the remainder of the text.

- [0, Agent0]: search examples: [Across The Universe] [I Feel Fine] [Norwegian Wood] [Helter Skelter] [You Know My Name] [Eleanor Rigby] [Blackbird], counter-examples: [Let's Spend the Night Together] [Ruby Tuesday]
- [1, Agent0]: categorisation failed
- [2, Agent0]: creates Category<Artist(The Beatles)>
- [3, Agent0]: binds 6365915a to Category<Artist(The Beatles)>
- [4, Agent1]: query for 6365915a
- [5, Agent1]: fails to decode 6365915a
- [6, Agent0]: transmits examples and count-examples of 6365915a
- [7, Agent1]: categorisation failed
- [8, Agent1]: creates Category<Nom(Beatles, The)>
- [9, Agent1]: binds 6365915a to Category<Nom(Beatles, The)>
- [10, Agent1]: query for 6365915a
- [11, Agent1]: decodes 6365915a as Category<Nom(Beatles, The)>
- [12, Agent1]: filter data: results: [I'm Down] [And I Love Her] [Twist And Shout]
- [13, Agent0]: owner evaluation: good (3 out of 3): [Twist And Shout] [I'm Down] [And I Love Her]
- [14, Agent0]: search sucessful
- [15, Agent0]: update dictionary
- [16, Agent1]: update dictionary

The first query shows how both $agent_0$ and $agent_1$ boostrap their dictionaries. $Agent_0$ creates a new category and label to describe the owner's request and $agent_1$ learns the new label from $agent_0$. Once the new categories and labels are introduced, the interaction proceeds successfully.

The dictionaries of the two agents after the first query are displayed in Fig. 6. The succession of operations that form the core of the exchange are depicted in Fig. 7.

Fig. 6. The dictionaries of agent 0 & 1 after the first query

4.2 Query 2: Agent 1 Asks Agent 0 for More "Sixties"

In the second query, $user_1$ select the folder "sixties" and requests for more songs like these. $Agent_1$ interprets the request as "find more sixties, not seventies nor eighties" and chooses to ask $agent_0$ whether it has more music files.

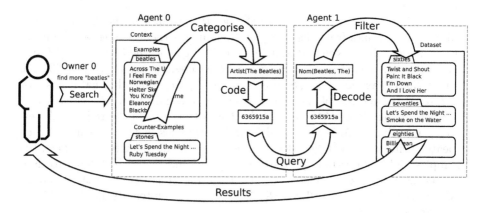

Fig. 7. The figure shows the main operations that form a successful interaction. It uses query 1 as an example.

The query start as follows. In step 1, $agent_1$ categorises the set of examples and counter-examples as Nom(Beatles, The). This is a reasonable choice because three out of four of the examples are indeed Beatles songs. It uses the existing label, 6365915a, to describe this category and query $agent_0$. This last one knows the label from the previous interaction. Because there is only one category associated with this label, namely Artist(The Beatles), the decoding of the label is unambiguous and $agent_0$ returns all the identifiers of the Beatles songs owned by its user. The beginning of the interaction is shown below:

- [0, Agent1]: search examples: [Twist And Shout][Paint It Black]
  [I'm Down][And I Love Her], counter-examples: [Billie Jean]
  [Smoke on the Water][True Blue][Let's Spend the Night Together]
- [1, Agent1]: uses Category<Nom(Beatles, The)>
- [2, Agent1]: codes Category<Nom(Beatles, The)> as 6365915a
- [3, Agent0]: query for 6365915a
- [4, Agent0]: decodes 6365915a as Category<Artist(The Beatles)>
- [5, Agent0]: filter data: results: [Blackbird][Eleanor Rigby]
  [Norwegian Wood][Across The Universe][You Know My Name][And
  I Love Her][Helter Skelter][I Feel Fine][Twist And Shout]
  [I'm Down]
- [6, Agent1]: owner evaluation: good (4 out of 10): [Twist And
  Shout][I Feel Fine][I'm Down][And I Love Her], bad (6 out
  of 10): [Across The Universe][Norwegian Wood][Helter Skelter]
  [You Know My Name][Eleanor Rigby][Blackbird]

When $owner_1$ evaluates the results in step 6, only four out of ten songs are retained. The other Beatles songs are not considered "sixties" by the user (even though, strictly speaking, they are recorded at the end of the sixties). We are in the case described in Sec. 3.6: either $agent_1$ misinterpreted its owner's request, or $agent_0$ misunderstood the label 6365915a. To distinguish between the two cases, $agent_1$ takes the set of all the positive examples (the "sixties" songs and the good results from the query) and compares them against all the negative examples (the "seventies" and "eighties" songs and the bad results). Using those two sets, it is clear that the category selected by $agent_1$ to describe the request, Nom(Beatles, The), does not satisfy. $Agent_1$ concludes that it has misinterpreted the request of the owner. It corrects its mistake and creates a new classifier, Année(from 1963 to 1966), that better reflects the request. A new label is introduced (5f6a1a0c) and bound to the classifier. The search is then repeated using the new label. Because $agent_0$ does not know the new label, the examples and counter-examples are transmitted along with the label to indicate its meaning. $Agent_0$ categorises these examples as Genre(Rock 'n Roll) and uses the new category, Genre(Rock 'n Roll), to filters its data set. This is summarised below:

- [7, Agent1]: owner request misinterpreted, uses new
  Category<Annee(from 1963.0 to 1966.0)> instead.
- [8, Agent1]: binds 5f6a1a0c to Category<Annee(from 1963.0
  to 1966.0)>
- [9, Agent1]: transmits examples and count-examples of 5f6a1a0c
- [10, Agent0]: categorisation failed
- [11, Agent0]: creates Category<Genre(Rock 'n Roll)>
- [12, Agent0]: binds 5f6a1a0c to Category<Genre(Rock 'n Roll)>
- [13, Agent0]: query for 5f6a1a0c
- [14, Agent0]: decodes 5f6a1a0c as Category<Genre(Rock 'n Roll)>
- [15, Agent0]: filter data: results: [And I Love Her][I Feel
  Fine][I'm Down][Twist And Shout]
- [16, Agent1]: owner evaluation: good (4 out of 4): [Twist And
  Shout][I Feel Fine][I'm Down][And I Love Her]
- [17, Agent1]: search sucessful
- [18, Agent1]: update dictionary
- [19, Agent0]: update dictionary

The results of the query are all considered useful by $owner_1$ and the interaction ends successfully. Note that the agents were able to have an effective communication although they use different categories and meta-data. The updated dictionaries of agents 0 and 1 are displayed in Fig. 8.

Fig. 8. The dictionary of agent 0 and 1 after the second query

4.3   Query 3: Agent 2 Asks Agent 0 for More "Party Music"

In the third query, $owner_2$ is looking for more "party music". The request will be directed to $agent_0$. This is $agent_2$'s first query and it's dictionary is still empty. To describe the request it introduces a new category, Band(beatles), and a new label, 8b85235d (see Sec. 3.3, "The information agent fails to categorise"). In this query, there are no counter-examples for the selected "party music" because the owner has no folders from which to distinguish them. The summary of the interaction starts as follows:

- [0, Agent2]: search examples: [Twist And Shout][I'm Down],
  counter-examples: none
- [1, Agent2]: categorisation failed
- [2, Agent2]: creates Category<Band(beatles)>
- [3, Agent2]: binds 8b85235d to Category<Band(beatles)>

Because $agent_0$ does not know the new label, it signal a failure to $agent_2$ which, in turn, sends over the identifiers of the examples to explain the meaning of the label. $Agent_0$ reuses the existing category Category<Artist(The Beatles)> to describe the songs and binds the new label to it (cfr. Sec. 3.4, "The callee does not know the label"). It then uses this category to filter its data set and return the results of the query. This is shown below:

- [4, Agent0]: query for 8b85235d
- [5, Agent0]: fails to decode 8b85235d
- [6, Agent2]: transmits examples and count-examples of 8b85235d
- [7, Agent0]: uses Category<Artist(The Beatles)>
- [8, Agent0]: binds 8b85235d to Category<Artist(The Beatles)>
- [9, Agent0]: query for 8b85235d
- [10, Agent0]: decodes 8b85235d as Category<Artist(The Beatles)>
- [11, Agent0]: filter data: results: [Twist And Shout][And I Love
  Her][Norwegian Wood][Helter Skelter][I'm Down][Blackbird][You
  Know My Name][Across The Universe][I Feel Fine][Eleanor Rigby]

$Agent_2$ presents the results to the user for evaluation. The user selects only 4 out of 10 results, which is deemed too low to be successful. As in the previous query, the information agent re-analyses all the positive examples and negative examples in its possession and concludes it has misinterpreted the selection of the owner. It tries to create a better category than the one used and introduces the classifier Energy(from 0.523 to 0.745) together with the label f5af0ee6. The label and the examples and counter-examples are transmitted to its peer. $Agent_0$ finds that the existing classifier Genre(Rock 'n Roll) fits the description well and binds the new label to it. This is summarised below:

- [12, Agent2]: owner evaluation: good (4 out of 10): [Twist And
  Shout][I Feel Fine][Helter Skelter][I'm Down], bad (6 out of
  10): [Across The Universe][Norwegian Wood][You Know My Name]
  [Eleanor Rigby][Blackbird][And I Love Her]

- [13, Agent2]: owner request misinterpreted, uses new
  Category<Energy(from 0.523 to 0.745)> instead.
- [14, Agent2]: binds f5af0ee6 to Category<Energy(from 0.523
  to 0.745)>
- [15, Agent2]: transmits examples and count-examples of f5af0ee6
- [16, Agent0]: uses Category<Genre(Rock 'n Roll)>
- [17, Agent0]: binds f5af0ee6 to Category<Genre(Rock 'n Roll)>

$Agent_2$ queries $agent_0$ again. Both agents are able to code/decode the label
and the songs that fit the classifier Genre(Rock 'n Roll) are sent to $agent_2$.
Three out of four results are deemed relevant to $owner_2$ and the query is considered a success.

- [18, Agent0]: query for f5af0ee6
- [19, Agent0]: decodes f5af0ee6 as Category<Genre(Rock 'n Roll)>
- [20, Agent0]: filter data: results: [And I Love Her][I'm Down]
  [Twist And Shout][I Feel Fine]
- [21, Agent2]: owner evaluation: good (3 out of 4): [Twist And
  Shout][I Feel Fine][I'm Down], bad (1 out of 4):
  [And I Love Her]
- [22, Agent2]: search sucessful
- [23, Agent2]: update dictionary
- [24, Agent0]: update dictionary

When $agent_0$ updates its dictionary, it strengthens the tie between the label
f5af0ee6 and the category Genre(Rock 'n Roll) and reduces those of competing bindings. In this case, one other label is associated with the category, specifically, the label 5f6a1a0c. The weight of this binding is reduced by Δ_{n-inh} from
0.6 to 0.5 ($\Delta_{n-inh} = 0.1$). The states of the dictionaries after the third query
are shown in Fig. 9.

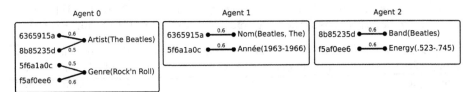

Fig. 9. The dictionaries of the agents after the third query

4.4   Owner 0 Makes Changes to His Taxonomy

After the third query, $owner_0$ edits his data set. The owners of the information
systems can intervene at any moment in the organisation of the music files, as it
is under their control, and the information agents must be able to cope with these
changes gracefully. In this example, $owner_0$ adds a new folder, named "elvis".
The new directory structure is shown in Fig. 10.

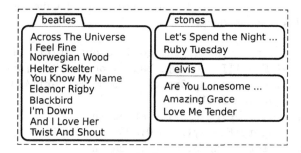

Fig. 10. $Owner_0$ adds the directory "elvis" to its data organisation. The folders also contains the music files obtained in query 1.

4.5   Query 4: Agent 2 Asks Agent 0 for More "Party Music"

The last query start similarly as the previous one. This time again, $agent_2$ is seeking more "party music" from $agent_0$. The initial request of the owner is suitably categorised as Energy(from 0.523 to 0.745) and the same label as in query 3 is reused. $Agent_0$ decodes the label as Genre(Rock 'n Roll) and uses this classifier to filter its data set:

- [0, Agent2]: search examples: [Billie Jean][Twist And Shout]
  [I Feel Fine][Helter Skelter][True Blue][I'm Down],
  counter-examples: none
- [1, Agent2]: uses Category<Energy(from 0.523 to 0.745)>
- [2, Agent2]: codes Category<Energy(from 0.523 to 0.745)> as
  f5af0ee6
- [3, Agent0]: query for f5af0ee6
- [4, Agent0]: decodes f5af0ee6 as Category<Genre(Rock 'n Roll)>
- [5, Agent0]: filter data: results: [And I Love Her][I Feel
  Fine][Amazing Grace][Twist And Shout][I'm Down][Are You Lonesome
  Tonight][Love Me Tender]

Unlike the previous query, a large number of the result are considered unrelevant to the owner. The Elvis' songs that were added since the previous query are not retained by $owner_2$ and the query is deemed unsuccessful. When $agent_2$ evaluates the set of all the positive example (all the "party music" songs plus all the good results) and the set of all the negative example (in this case, the bad results), it finds that the category chosen to code the request was valid. $Agent_2$ concludes that the failing communication is due to a misinterpretation of the label by $agent_0$. We are in the situation described in Sec. 3.7, "The caller and callee interpret the label differently".

The label is therefore considered unreliable and the strength of its binding to the selected classifier is decreased by both agents. $Agent_2$ then explains the use of the label by pointing $agent_0$ to the set of examples and counter-examples. $Agent_0$ concludes that the classifier Genre(Rock 'n Roll) unsufficiently discriminates

between both sets and, as a result, introduced a new classifier BPM(from 119.0
to 180.0). This is shown next:

- [6, Agent2]: owner evaluation: good (3 out of 7): [Twist And
  Shout][I Feel Fine][I'm Down], bad (4 out of 7): [Are You
  Lonesome Tonight][Amazing Grace][Love Me Tender][And I Love Her]
- [7, Agent2]: search failed
- [8, Agent2]: decreasing binding strength
  [f5af0ee6,Category<Energy(from 0.523 to 0.745)>,0.5]
- [9, Agent0]: decreasing binding strength
  [f5af0ee6,Category<Genre(Rock 'n Roll)>,0.4]
- [10, Agent2]: transmits examples and count-examples of f5af0ee6
- [11, Agent0]: categorisation failed
- [12, Agent0]: creates Category<BPM(from 119.0 to 180.0)>
- [13, Agent0]: binds f5af0ee6 to Category<BPM(from 119.0
  to 180.0)>

Now that the confusion over the label is reduced, the query can proceed and
ends successfully. Note that, once again, the categories used by both agents is different using different meta-data (BPM versus Energy). The query ends as follows:

- [14, Agent0]: query for f5af0ee6
- [15, Agent0]: decodes f5af0ee6 as Category<BPM(from 119.0
  to 180.0)>
- [16, Agent0]: filter data: results: [I'm Down][I Feel Fine]
  [Let's Spend the Night Together][Eleanor Rigby][Twist And Shout]
  [Helter Skelter]
- [17, Agent2]: owner evaluation: good (5 out of 6): [Twist And
  Shout][I Feel Fine][Helter Skelter][Let's Spend the Night
  Together][I'm Down], bad (1 out of 6): [Eleanor Rigby]
- [18, Agent2]: search sucessful
- [19, Agent2]: update dictionary
- [20, Agent0]: update dictionary

The states of the dictionaries at the end of the four queries are shown in
Fig. 11.

This example is limited to only four queries. In subsequent interactions the
dictionaries will continue to evolve. As a results of successful and failed queries,

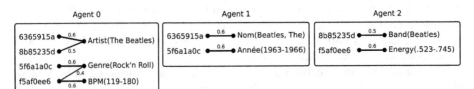

Fig. 11. The dictionaries of the agents after the fourth query

the weights of the bindings between labels and categories will be adapted, and new words will be introduced to disambiguate existing ones. The environments of the agents also changes as the owners make modify the folder structures, new music files are inserted into the system, and the user's tastes evolve. The dynamics of such open-ended communication systems have been studied before [12,14] but more simulations are required that take into account the specificities of the current proposition.

4.6   Categorisation

In the example, the agents introduce new categories to discriminate between sets of data. We assumed that each agent has a table of meta-data and that the categories are described as a predicate over this meta-data. The construction of classifiers is a well-documented problem in the field of Machine Learning and is not the topic of this paper. From the point of view of the agent, the component that constructs the categories is a black box that can be called upon when needed.

Although the algorithms discussed in this paper are independent of the implementation of the classifiers, the discriminative qualities of the latter have an impact on the success of the communication between the agents and, thus, of the evolution of the dictionaries. The influence of the precision of the categories, the threshold used in the categorisation (θ_{disc}), and the threshold used in the owner evaluation (θ_{fail}) on the convergence and size of the dictionaries remains to be studied, however.

5   Conclusions

This paper considered the question of semantic interoperability in collective information exchange. We advocated the creation of a semiotic dynamics whereby information agents coordinate the use of labels, similar to the way this is now done by human users in social exchange websites, and they develop an emergent grounded semantics for these labels in terms of classifiers that are functions over data or meta-data. We illustrated this for the domain of electronic music distribution.

On the positive side, the examples in section 5 show how the agents "bootstrap" their dictionaries. The only data exchanged between the agents are the unique identifiers of the data and the labels of the query. No meta-data is exchanged nor any indication of the owner's data organisation. This makes it possible for the taxonomies and the meta-data to be completely local to each information system. We have seen cases of successful communication but also how failure is handled in two situations: when the calling agent misunderstands the request of its owner, and when the called agent misinterprets the label of the query. Agents are not using the tags of the folders in the interpretation of the owner's request. So there is no attempt to do taxonomy or schema matching. In fact, the owner's taxonomy plays only a marginal role, it was mainly used to define the initial set and the context for the query. The definitions of classifiers does not depend on them.

The idea of bootstrapping semantic interoperability from local interactions in a bottom-up fashion is not new (see in particular [2]). The novelty of the presented work resides in the fact that the peers do not exchange the organisation of their meta-data (or database schema's) and that no direct mapping is built between these schema's. Instead, the peers locally maintain a bi-directional mapping between classifiers and tags. In addition, the classifiers nor the mapping are established by human experts but are introduced by the agents through the exchange of examples and counter-examples. The system is continuously adapting based on the validity of the results. This validation is not done automatically, as has been proposed in the literature, but by the user. The input from the end user, not necessarily an expert, remains a key element of the system.

Although we believe that the approach advocated in this paper provides an interesting alternative to information exchange without semantics or the semantic web, we want to stress the limits of the approach. It will not always be possible to have a grounded semantics, partly because user behaviour may be too erratic and subjective to construct classifiers, and partly because the building blocks available for grounding (such as the signal processing primitives in the case of music) or the machine learning methods (in this case genetic programming) may not be effective enough to achieve an adequate grounded semantics. We therefore see the grounding and negotiation of labels for classifiers as one of the building blocks to achieve emergent semantics. Other building blocks consist of exploiting the co-occurrence of tags (as displayed by tag clouds), which establish associative relations that narrow down the set of data elements corresponding to a tag, or the query path of a user that establishes additional context [10].

References

1. Aberer, K.,et.al. (2003) Emergent Semantics. Principles and Issues. To appear in Proc. of the International Conference on Semantics of a Networked World. www.ipsi.fraunhofer.de/~risse/pub/P2004-01.pdf
2. Aberer, K.,et.al. (2003) The Chatty Web: Emergent Semantics through Gossiping. In: Proceedings of the 12th World Wide Web Conference. citeseer.ist.psu.edu/aberer03chatty.html
3. Agostini, A. and P. Avesani (2003) A Peer-to-Peer Advertising game.. July 2003, 15 pages. In: Proceedings of the First International Conference on Service Oriented Computing (ICSOC-03), Springer-Verlag LNCS 2910, pp. 28-42
4. Berners-Lee, T., J. Hendler, and O. Lassila. (2001) The Semantic Web. Scientific American. May 2001.
5. Davies, J., Fensel, D., & Harmelen, F. van. (2003). Towards the semantic web: Ontology driven knowledge management. Chicester, UK: John Wiley & Sons
6. Leach, P., Mealling, M., and R. Salz (2004) A UUID URN Namespace. The Internet Engineering Task Force. Internet drafts. http://www.ietf.org/internet-drafts/draft-mealling-uuid-urn-03.txt
7. Lenat, D., George A. Miller and T. Yokoi. "CYC, WordNet and EDR — critiques and responses — discussion." In:Communications of the ACM 38 (11), November 1995, pp. 45-48. http://www.acm.org/pubs/articles/journals/cacm/1995-38-11/p24-lenat/p45-lenat.pdf

8. Nejdl, W. et.al. (2003) RDF-based Peer-to-Peer-Networks for Distributed (Learning) Repositories. VLDB journal www.kbs.uni-hannover.de/Arbeiten/ Publikationen/2002/

9. Rahm, E., and Philip A. Bernstein (2001) A Survey of Approaches to Automatic Schema Matching VLDB Journal: Very Large Data Bases. 10: 334-350 http://citeseer.ist.psu.edu/rahm01survey.html

10. Santini, S., A. Gupta and R. Jain (2001) Emergent Semantics Through Interaction in Image Databases IEEE Transaction of Knowledge and Data Engineering, summer 2001. www.sdsc.edu/~gupta/publications/kde-sp-01.pdf

11. Staab, S. (2002) Emergent Semantics. IEEE Intelligent Systems. pp. 78-86. www.cwi.nl/~media/publications/nack-ieee-intsys-2002.pdf

12. L. Steels, "The Origins of Ontologies and Communication Conventions in Multi-Agent Systems," Autonomous Agents and Multi-Agent Systems, vol. 1, no. 1, Oct. 1998, pp. 169-194. http://www3.isrl.uiuc.edu/~junwang4/langev/localcopy/ pdf/steels98theOrigins.pdf

13. Steels, L. (2002) Emergent Semantics. IEEE Intelligent Systems. Trends and Controversies. p. 83-85. www.cwi.nl/~media/publications/nack-ieee-intsys-2002.pdf

14. Steels, L. (2003) Evolving grounded communication for robots. Trends in Cognitive Science. Volume 7, Issue 7, July 2003, pp. 308-312. www.csl.sony.fr/downloads/ papers/2003/steels-03c.pdf

15. Steels, L. and Kaplan, F. Collective learning and semiotic dynamics. In Floreano, D. and Nicoud, J-D and Mondada, F., editor, Advances in Artificial Life (ECAL 99), Lecture Notes in Artificial Intelligence 1674, pages 679-688, Berlin, 1999. Springer-Verlag.

16. Tzitzikas, Y. and Meghini, C. (2003) Ostensive Automatic Schema Mapping for Taxonomy-based Peer-to-Peer Systems. Proc. of CIA-2003, the Seventh International Workshop on Cooperative Information Agents - Intelligent Agents for the Internet and Web. Lecture Notes in Artificial Intelligence n. 2782, pages 78-92. August 2003 http://www.csi.forth.gr/~tzitzik/publications/Tzitzikas_CIA_2003.pdf

17. Zhang, H., B. Croft, B. Levine, V. Lesse (2004) A Multi-agent Approach for Peer-to-Peer based Information Retrieval System In Proceedings of the 2004 Multi-Agent Conference, AAMAS. New York. http://www.aamas2004.org/ proceedings/057_zhangh-p2pir.pdf

18. Zils, A. and Pachet, F. (2004) Automatic Extraction of Music Descriptors from Acoustic Signals using EDS. In Proceedings of the 116th AES Convention, May 2004. http://www/downloads/papers/uploads/zils-04a.pdf

19. Wiederhold, G. (1992) Mediators in the Architecture of Future Information Systems In: IEEE Computer, March 1992, pages 38-49. http://www-db. stanford.edu/pub/gio/1991/afis.ps

Emergent Semantics from Folksonomies: A Quantitative Study

Lei Zhang, Xian Wu, and Yong Yu

APEX Data and Knowledge Management Lab,
Department of Computer Science and Engineering,
Shanghai JiaoTong University, Shanghai, 200030, China
{zhanglei, wuxian, yyu}@apex.sjtu.edu.cn

Abstract. Defining and using ontology to annotate web resources with semantic markups is generally perceived as the primary way to implement the vision of the Semantic Web. The ontology provides a shared and machine understandable semantics for web resources that agents and applications can utilize. This top-down approach (in the sense that an ontology is defined first on top of existing web resources and then used later to markup them), however, has a high barrier to entry and is difficult to scale up. In this paper, we investigate using a bottom-up approach for semantically annotating web resources as supported by the now widely popular social bookmarks services on the web where users can annotate and categorize web resources using "tags" freely choosen by the user without any pre-existing global semantic model. This kind of informal social categories is coined as "folksonomies". We show how global semantics can be statistically inferred from the folksonomies to semantically annotate the web resources. The global semantic model also disambiguate the tags and group synonymous tags together. Finally, we show that there indeed are hierarchical relations among the emerged concepts in the folksonomy and it is plausible to further identify them if we use more advanced probabilistic models.

1 Introduction

Semantic Web is a vision that web resources are made not only for humans to read but also for machines to understand and automatically process [1]. This requires that web resources be annotated with machine understandable metadata. Currently, the primary approach to achieve this is to firstly define an ontology and then use the ontology to add semantic markups for web resources. These semantic markups are written in standard languages such as RDF [2] and OWL [3] and the semantics is provided by the ontology that is shared among different web agents and applications. We refer to this approach as the top-down approach because an global semantic model (i.e., the ontology) is defined and imposed on top of web resources before we actually use the semantic model to annotate these resources.

The top-down approach has several drawbacks. Firstly, establishing an ontology as a semantic backbone for a large number of distributed web resources is

S. Spaccapietra et al. (Eds.): Journal on Data Semantics VI, LNCS 4090, pp. 168–186, 2006.

not easy. Different people/applications may have different views on what exists in these web resources and this leads to the difficulty of the establishment of and commitment to a common ontology. Even if the consensus of a common ontology can be achieved, it may not be able to catch the fast pace of change of the targeted web resources. A lot of work has been done on developing ontology engineering tools to help people create ontologies, such as Protégé [4], OilEd [5], WebODE [6], ORIENT [7] and SWOOP [8]. While these tools facilitate the actual construction of ontologies, they generally do not help much in forming the required consensus for ontolgy building in a distributed environment. Using these tools also requires some level of expertise in ontology engineering or knowledge engineering, which put a high barrier to entry for the mass developers and users. Studies on ontology evolution, such as [9,10], focus on how changes of ontologies are tracked [11,12], versioned [13,14] and managed [15] but does not provide mechanisms to automatically and actively change the ontology according to the changes of web resources it intends to cover. Secondly, even if we have successfully built an ontology, using it to make semantic annotations in an automatic and scalable manner is still a challenging task. Usually, the semantic annotations are made manually [16,17] or semi-automatically [18,19,20,21]. Although this helps create high quality semantic annotations, it is hard to scale up. Till now, only very little work has been done on large-scale fully automatic semantic annotations of web reseources [22,23,24].

The above shortcomings of the top-down approach have actually already been identified in the "emergent semantics" research [25,26] in which semantics is treated as an agreement that is achieved in a bottom-up and incremental manner without relying on pre-existing global semantic models. In this paper, we investigate whether and how the semantic annotation problem can be attacked in this bottom-up emergent semantics way. Our work is enabled and supported by the now widely popular social bookmarks services on the web, like Delicious[1], Furl[2] and Yahoo My Web 2.0[3]. These services allow web users to annotate and categorize web resources using "tags" that are freely chosen by the user without any "a-priori" dictionary, taxonomy, or ontology to conform to. Thus, the tags can be any strings that the user deems appropriate for the web resource. The name "folksonomy" has been coined for this kind of informal social categorization of web resources. In our view, this is also a massive bottom-up annotation of web resources that directly complements the traditional top-down approach of semantic annotation. If emergent semantics can be derived from these free-style bottom-up annotations, it will remedy the headache of top-down approach to semantic annotations. It removes the high barrier to entry because web users can annotate web resources easily and freely without using or even knowing taxonomies or ontologies. It directly reflects the dynamics of the vocabularies of the users and thus evolves with the users. It also decomposes the burden of annotating the entire web to the annotating of interested web resources by each individual web users.

---

[1] http://del.icio.us
[2] http://www.furl.net
[3] http://myweb2.search.yahoo.com

Apparently, without a shared taxonomy or ontology, the folksonomy suffers the usual problem of ambiguity of semantics. The same tag may mean different things for different people and two seemingly different tags may bear the same meaning. Without a clear semantics, these bottom-up annotations won't be much useful for web agents and applications on the Semantic Web. In this paper, we propose to use a probabilistic generative model to model the user's annotation behavior and to automatically derive the emergent semantics of the tags. Synonymous tags are grouped together and highly ambiguous tags are identified and separated. Finally, we show that we can use more advanced probabilistic models to discover the hierarchical relations among the emerged concepts in the folksonomy.

2   Folksonomy

The idea of a bottom-up approach to the semantic annotation is enlightened and enabled by the now widely popular social bookmarks services on the web. These services provide easy-to-use user interfaces for web users to annotate and categorize web resources, and furthermore, enable them to share the annotations and categories on the web. For example, the Delicious (`http://del.icio.us`) service allows you to easily add sites you like to your personal collection of links, to categorize those sites with keywords, and to share your collection not only between your own browsers and machines, but also with others. There are many bookmarks manager tools available [27,28]. What's special about the social bookmarks services like Delicious is their use of keywords called "tags" as a fundamental construct for users to annotate and categorize web resources. These tags are freely chosen by the user without a pre-defined taxonomy or ontology. Some example tags are "blog", "mp3", "photography", "todo" etc. The tags page[4] of the Delicious web site lists most popular tags among the users and their relative frequency of use. These user-created categories using unlimited tags and vocabularies was coined a name "folksonomy" by Thomas Vander Wal in a discussion on information architecture[5]. The name is a combination of "folk" and "taxonomy".

As pointed out in [29], folksonomy is a kind of user creation of metadata which is very different from the professional creation of metadata (e.g. created by librarians) and author creation of metadata (e.g. created by a web page author). Without a tight control on the tags to use and some expertise in taxonomy building, the system soon runs into problems caused by ambiguity and synonymy. [29] cited some examples of ambiguous tags and synonymous tags in Delicious. For example, the tag "ANT" is used by many users to annotate web resources about Apache Ant, a building tool for Java. One user, however, uses it to tag web resources about "Actor Network Theory". Synonymous tags, like "mac" and "macintosh", "blog" and "weblog" are also widely used. What's more important about folksonomies is that the tags are all in a flat namespace without hierarchy or any parent-child relationships.

---

[4] `http://del.icio.us/tag/`, accessed at November 2005.

[5] `http://atomiq.org/archives/2004/08/folksonomy_social_classification.html`, accessed at November 2005.

Despite of the seemingly chaos of unrestricted use of tags, social bookmarks services still attract a lot of web users and provide a viable and effective mechanism for them to organize web resources. [29] contributes the success to the following reasons.

— Low barriers to entry
— Feedback and asymmetric communications
— Individual and community aspects

Unlike the professional creation of metadata or the top-down approach of the semantic annotation, folksonomy does not need sophisticated knowledge about taxonomy or ontology to do annotation and categorization. This significantly lowers the barrier to entry. In addition, because these annotations are shared among all users in a social bookmark service, there is an immediate feedback when a user tags a web resource. The user can immediately see other web resources tagged by other users using the same tag. These web resources may not be what the user expected. In that case, the user can adapt to the group norm, keep the tag in a bid to influence the group norm, or both [30]. Thus, the users of folksonomy are negotiating the meaning of the terms in an implicit asymmetric communication. This local negotiation, from the emergent semantics perspective, is the basis that leads to the incremental establishment of a common global semantic model. [31] made a good analogy with the "desire lines". Desire lines are the foot-worn paths that sometimes appear in a landscape over time. The emergent semantics is like the desire lines. It emerges from the actual use of the tags and web resources and directly reflects the user's vocabulary and can be used back immediately to serve the users that created them. In the following of the paper, we quantitatively analyze the folksonomy and show that emergent semantics indeed can be inferred statistically from it.

3   The Data of Social Bookmarks

Social bookmark services can provide many functionalities for end users. Different services may have different functions. Some allow users to give a short description of each bookmark. Some allow users to rate each bookmark for its quality. These different functions acquire different kind of data from end users for web bookmarks. In this paper, we focus on the most important data that are common to most social bookmarks. The core function of a social bookmark service is to let users bookmark URLs and assign tags to URLs. Tags are words or phrases that are freely chosen by users. This core function is common to most social bookmark services. Hence, in this paper, we focus on this core function and the data asscoicated with it, namely the user, the URL and the tag.

3.1   Co-occurrence Data Model

We abstract the data in social bookmarks services as a set of quadruples

$$(user, URL, tag, time)$$

which means that a user tags a URL with a specific tag at a specific time. In this paper, we focus more on what URL gets what tags and ignore the user and time information in the quadruple. What interests us is thus the co-occurrence of tags and URLs. Let's denote the set $X = \{x_1, x_2, \ldots, x_N\}$ and $Y = \{y_1, y_2, \ldots, y_M\}$ to be the set of URLs and the set of tags in the collected folksonomy data respectively. Each quadruple then translates to a co-occurence of a URL and a tag. The set of quadruples then translates to the co-occurrence set $S = \{(x_{i(r)}, y_{j(r)}, r) : 1 \leq r \leq L\}$. L is the total number of co-occurrences/pairs in S. $x_{i(r)}$ corresponds to the URL in X which appears in the rth pair. $y_{j(r)}$ corresponds to the tag in Y which appears in the rth pair. $n_{ij} = |\{(x_i, y_j, r) \in S\}|$ measures the frequency of co-occurrence of URL x_i and tag y_j.

We have collected a sample of Delicious data by crawling its web site during March 2005. The data set consists of 2,879,614 taggings made by 10,109 different users on 690,482 different URLs with 126,304 different tags. The co-occurrence data can be easily computed from the raw dataset. The following paper will use the dataset for experiments.

3.2 Social Aspects: The Power Law

The biggest difference between a set of personal bookmarks and a social bookmarks service is the implicit social interactions enabled by the latter. Typically, users of a socical bookmarks service can see other users' public bookmarks and tags. For a given tag (or a set of tags), users can see what URLs other users have tagged using the same tag(s). This function is very valuable for the users because it enables them to discover potentially high-quality web resources collected by other users of the same topic. When the user bookmarks a URL, tags used by other users for the same URL can also be seen. This may influence the user on what tag(s) to use for bookmarking the URL. Because these functions of the social bookmarks service are both very valuable and interesting, users of the service frequently use these functions, which is actually implicit social interactions. As we have analyzed in section 2, through these implicit social interactions, users are negotiating the meanings and uses of tags on URLs. These local negotiations, from the emergent semantics perspective, enable the incremental establishment of a common global semantic model.

When a lot of users are involved in the implicit social interactions, interesting phenomenons emerge. If an URL is bookmarked by many users, it has more chance to be seen by other users. The more chance to be seen by other users, the more the URL may be bookmarked. This positive loop will lead to an exponential growth of the number of the times an URL being bookmarked. Tags have the similar situation. If a common tag is used by many people for tagging many URLs, it has more chance to be seen by other users. The more chance for the tag to be seen, the more it may be used by users to tag more URLs. This is also a self-rewarding positive loop. Similar situations also occur on the web. If a web page is linked by many other pages, it has more chance to be seen by users. The more chance to be seen by users, the more chance it may be linked by more web pages. On the web, this phenomenon is reflected in the distribution

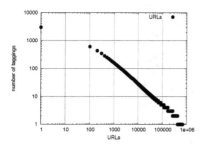
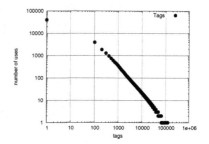

Fig. 1. The distribution of the taggins of URLs

Fig. 2. The distribution of the uses of tags

of the in-bound links of web pages. Only very few pages have very large amount of in-bound links and most web pages only have a few in-bound links. Study showes that the growth of the web follows the Power Law [32], meaning that the probability of attaining a certain size x is proportional to $1/x$ to a power β, where β is greater than or equal to 1.

We expect that the social bookmarks data also has the Power Law distribution. To verify this, using the Delicious data set we collected, we computed the distribution of the number of taggings of URLs and the number of uses of tags. More precisely, for every URL $x_i \in X$, we computed the number of taggings users have made on it: $n_{x_i} = |\{(x_i, y, r) \in S\}|$. For every tag $y_j \in Y$, we computed the number of uses of the tag by all the users: $n_{y_j} = |\{(x, y_j, r) \in S\}|$. Fig.1 and Fig.2 show the results of the two computed distributions respectively[6]. Since both the axes of the figures are in log-scale, the figures clearly show Power Law distributions. This reflects the implicit social interactions inherent in the social bookmarks service.

4 Deriving Emergent Semantics

4.1 Probabilistic Generative Model

The co-occurrences of URLs and tags is not a random phenomenon. It reflects the underlying semantics that users has assigned to these URLs and tags. We propose use the following probabilistic generative model to model the user's behavior in assigning a tag to a URL. The model assumes the exist of a set of concepts $C = \{c_1, c_2, \ldots, c_K\}$.

1. User randomly encounters a URL x_i on the web with probability p_i .
2. The URL makes the user thinking of a concept c_α with probability $p_{\alpha|i}$.
3. The concept c_α trigers the user to use tag y_j with probability $p_{j|\alpha}$.

Here, both $p_{\alpha|i}$ and $p_{j|\alpha}$ are conditional probabilities. $p_{\alpha|i}$ is the probability of thinking of concept c_α given the URL x_i. $p_{j|\alpha}$ is the probability of using tag y_j given the concept c_α. This probabilistic generative model can be visually

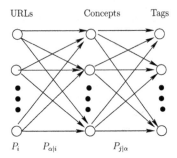

Fig. 3. Probabilistic generative model

depicted as Fig.3 The model makes a simplified independence assumption that once a concept is thought by a user, the tag to use is only determined by the concept and is indenpendent of the URL that trigers the concept. Note that the set of concepts is actually the underlying semantics that controls the co-occurrences of URLs and tags. The problem is then how to get the set of concepts and their probability relations with the tags and URLs. Directly estimates the probabilities is very difficult. The set of URLs X is potentially very large because of the overwhelming size of the web . The set of tags Y could also be very large because folksonomy has no control on the use of tags. Any string could be a tag. Thus, the frequency of a pair (x_i, y_j) may be very very low and this creates the data sparseness problem for model parameter estimation. However, the introduce of the concept set C remedies the problem. Hofmann and Puzicha [33] proposed a EM algorithm for estimating the parameters. The above model corresponds to the asymmetric SMM model for co-occurrence data in [33].

Hofmann and Puzicha showed [33] that the asymmetric SMM model is equivalent to its symmetric version: the SMM model which is easier to compute and can handle larger dataset. In our case, the SMM model can be explained as the following probabilistic model:

1. The user randomly thought of a concept c_α with probability π_α .
2. A URL x_i is selected by the user for the concept c_α with probability $p_{i|\alpha}$.
3. A tag y_j is selected by the user for the concept c_α with probability $q_{j|\alpha}$

The x_i and y_j are conditionally independent given the concept c_α and the joint probability distribution of the SMM is a mixture of separable component distributions (hence the name, Separable Mixture Model) which can be parameterized by

$$p_{ij} = P(x_i, y_j) = \sum_{\alpha=1}^{K} \pi_\alpha P(x_i, y_j | c_\alpha) = \sum_{\alpha=1}^{K} \pi_\alpha p_{i|\alpha} q_{j|\alpha}$$

Following the EM approach, to optimally fit the SMM model to the observation of co-occurrences set S, and estimate the parameters, the log-likelihood of each pair co-occurrences probability $\left(p_{ij}^{n_{ij}} \right)$ for all pairs

---

6 In order to reduce the size of the figures' EPS file, only 1/100 data points are drawn.

$$L = \sum_{i=1}^{N} \sum_{j=1}^{M} n_{ij} log \left(\sum_{\alpha=1}^{K} \pi_\alpha p_{i|\alpha} q_{j|\alpha} \right)$$

should be maximized. As a standard method for EM algorithm for mixture models, a hidden variable $R_{r\alpha}$ is introduced which denotes the probability that the observation $(x_{i(r)}, y_{j(r)}, r)$ is generated from the concept c_α. The EM method leads to the

E-Step

$$\langle R_{r\alpha} \rangle^{(t+1)} = \frac{\hat{\pi}_\alpha^{(t)} \hat{p}_{i(r)|\alpha}^{(t)} \hat{q}_{j(r)|\alpha}^{(t)}}{\sum_{v=1}^{K} \hat{\pi}_v^{(t)} \hat{p}_{i(r)|v}^{(t)} \hat{q}_{j(r)|v}^{(t)}}$$

M-Step

$$\hat{\pi}_\alpha^{(t)} = \frac{1}{L} \sum_{r=1}^{L} \langle R_{r\alpha} \rangle^{(t)}$$

$$\hat{p}_{i|\alpha}^{(t)} = \frac{1}{L\hat{\pi}_\alpha^{(t)}} \sum_{r:i(r)=i}^{L} \langle R_{r\alpha} \rangle^{(t)}$$

$$\hat{q}_{j|\alpha}^{(t)} = \frac{1}{L\hat{\pi}_\alpha^{(t)}} \sum_{r:j(r)=j}^{L} \langle R_{r\alpha} \rangle^{(t)}$$

Iterating the E-Step and M-Step, the parameters converge to a maximum of the likelihood. Our collected raw Delicious data is very large for the EM algorithm. We made a random sample of the collected Delicious data. The sample has 17,707 URLs, 7,238 tags and 300,869 co-occurrences in total. We set the number of concepts to 50 and run through the EM algorithm of the SMM model. After computation, the parameter $q_{j|\alpha}$ gives the conditional distribution of tags over the 50 concepts. We selected the top 10 concepts and for each concept the first five tags that have the highest $q_{j|\alpha}$ value. The result is shown in Table 1. We can see that tags that have the same semantics are effectively grouped together in one concept. The concepts thus can be seen as a "classes" in an ontolgy or "synsets" in WordNet [34].

4.2   Emergent Semantics

Using the results obtained by the probability generative model, we can derive and represent the emergent semantics of URLs and tags. For a given URL, its semantics should be represented by the concepts the URL is related to. Let's use $p_{\alpha|i}$ to denote the conditional probability that a concept c_α is thought of by the user given an URL x_i. For a given URL x_i, the $p_{\alpha|i}$ values for all concepts c_α actually represents a discrete probability distribution on all the concepts. This distribution describes in detail the concepts that the URL relates to and the strength of the relatedness. We thus use this distribution as the representation

Table 1. Concepts and Tags

Concept	Top 5 tags in the concept
1	technology Google Search Internet future
2	Php PHP webdev mysql code
3	programming development Programming cs toread
4	del.icio.us delicioius bookmarks tags folksonomy
5	humor fun humour Funny ukquake
6	software windows tools Software freeware
7	books book library literature copyright
8	bittorrent p2p torrents BitTorrent P2P
9	comics comic humor webcomic Comics
10	security wordpress hack wifi Security

of the semantics of the URL. Since it is a discrete distribution, we can represent it as a vector. The semantics of a URL x_i is thus represented as

$$\overrightarrow{semantics(x_i)} = \big\langle\, p_{\alpha|i} \mid \alpha = 1, 2, \ldots, K \big\rangle$$

where $p_{\alpha|i}$ can be computed as follows using Bayesian theorem:

$$p_{\alpha|i} = \frac{p_{i|\alpha}\pi_\alpha}{p(x_i)} = \frac{p_{i|\alpha}\pi_\alpha}{\sum_{\alpha=1}^{K} p_{i|\alpha}\pi_\alpha}$$

π_α and $p_{\alpha|i}$ have been obtained via the EM algorithm in the probabilistic generative model. Therefore, the representation of the semantics of a URL can be computed.

Using the previous experiment data, we calculated the semantic representations of all URLs in the data. Fig.4 to Fig.7 show the concept distributions of four URLs. URL-1 is a special URL used by the Delicious service for replacing all ill-formated URLs users have bookmarked. Since there is a great variety of different ill-formated URLs and their tags, this special URL has no prominent concepts associated with it. This is also reflected in its concept distribution in Fig.4 where the URL is related to almost all concepts in very low strength (< 0.07). In contrast, the other three URLs all have prominent concepts. URL-2 to URL-4 are http://www.yahoo.com, http://jakarta.apache.org and http://www.filelist.org respectively. Their concept distributions all have spikes that have strong relatedness to the URL (> 0.6).

Similar to the representation of the semantics of an URL, we can define the representation of the semantics of a tag y_j as:

$$\overrightarrow{semantics(y_j)} = \big\langle\, q_{\alpha|j} \mid \alpha = 1, 2, \ldots, K \big\rangle$$

where $q_{\alpha|j}$ is the conditional probability that a concept c_α is generated given the tag y_j. This probability can be computed as

$$q_{\alpha|j} = \frac{q_{j|\alpha}\pi_\alpha}{p(y_j)} = \frac{q_{j|\alpha}\pi_\alpha}{\sum_{\alpha=1}^{K} q_{j|\alpha}\pi_\alpha}$$

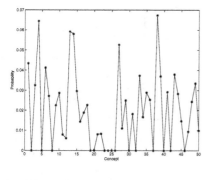

Fig. 4. Distributions of URL-1

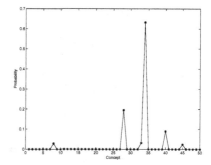

Fig. 5. Distributions of URL-2

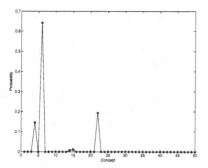

Fig. 6. Distributions of URL-3

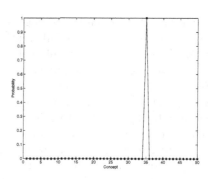

Fig. 7. Distributions of URL-4

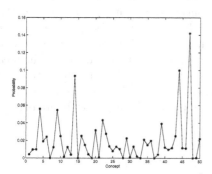

Fig. 8. Distribution of "todo"

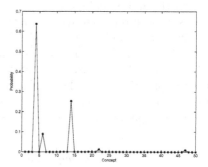

Fig. 9. Distribution of "xp"

where both $q_{j|\alpha}$ and π_α have been obtained in the probabilistic generative model. Therefore we can also compute the semantic representation of a tag. Using the previous experiment data, we calculated four tags' semantic representations. The result is shown in Fig.8 to Fig.11.

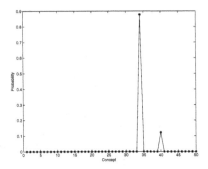 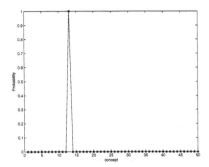

Fig. 10. Distribution of "google"   **Fig. 11.** Distribution of "cooking"

The tags "todo" and "cooking" are two extreme cases. Because what to do next is vastly different for different people, the tag "todo" is used to mark a lot of different URLs for different meanings of what to do next. This makes the "todo" tag very ambiguous. This is reflected in its concept distribution in Fig.8. On the contrary, the tag "cooking" is used very unambiguously in our experiment data set. Thus, its concept distribution as shown in Fig.11 only has one very big spike. The other two tags, "xp" and "google", are between the two extreme cases. For tag "xp", it is mainly used for the meanings of "windows xp" or "extrem programming". Likewise, the tag "google" is mostly used together with "search" or "gmail" for the meaning of internet search or google gmail. The two tags' concept distributions (as in Fig.9 and Fig.10) therefore has two or more spikes.

The above examples have shown the clear difference between ambiguous tags/URLs and unambiguous ones. Their concept distributions (or equivalently, their semantic representations) have very different characteristics. The concept distributions of ambiguous tags/URLs are more evenly distributed while those of unambiguous ones usually have very prominent spikes. This leads us to the idea of quantitatively measure the ambiguousness of a tag/URL using the entropy of its concept distribution. The ambiguousness of a tag/URL thus can be seen as a function of its semantic representation. More precisely, we define the ambiguity of a URL x_i and/or a tag y_j as follows:

$$ ambiguity(x_i) = -\sum_{\alpha=1}^{K} p_{\alpha|i} \log p_{\alpha|i} $$

$$ ambiguity(y_j) = -\sum_{\alpha=1}^{K} q_{\alpha|j} \log q_{\alpha|j} $$

where $p_{\alpha|i}$ and $q_{\alpha|j}$ are exactly the dimension value within the vectors $\overrightarrow{semantics(x_i)}$ and $\overrightarrow{semantics(y_j)}$. Using this definition, we calculated the ambiguity of all tags in the experiment data set and the result is shown in Table 2. The table shows the top 10 tags with the largest and smallest ambiguity

Table 2. Tags and their entropy

NO.	Tags	Ambiguity	Tags	Ambiguity
1	todo	3.24	cooking	0
2	viapopular	3.19	webmail	0
3	.imported	3.18	Deutsch	0
4	temp	3.08	netlabel	0
5	linklog	3.07	OWL	0
6	new	3.05	ttf	0
7	resources	3.04	vegetarian	0
8	from/furl	3.03	Sudan	0
9	resource	3.02	dictionary	0
10	[en]	3.00	rgb	0

values in column two and four respectively. In addition to "todo", we noticed that the tags "viapopular", ".imported", and "from/furl" are also very ambiguous. These tags are used to mark URLs imported from other bookmarks, which basically does not restrict the meaning of the tags to any specific concept. General tags, like "new", "resource" and "[en]" also appears ambiguous because they are too general to mean any particular concept. Note that the ambiguous word "OWL" appears very unambiguously in the list because the Delicious community is mostly concerned with IT technology. Thus, "OWL" in Delicious does not mean the bird of night but the web ontology language OWL. Hence, this tag appears very unambiguously.

In this subsection, we have defined the representation of the semantics of a tag/URL as a concept vector that corresponds to a discrete concept distribution of the tag/URL. We'd like to emphasize that this semantic representation is very different from the ontology-based top-down approach to semantic annotation. In the top-down approach, ontology is built beforehand whereas in our bottom-up approach the set of concepts is dynamically determined from the data set via a probabilistic model. Traditional semantic annotation is basically a binary judgement. An object is either an instance of a concept or not. However, in our model, the semantics of a tag/URL is not a binary classification but a discrete probability distribution over all the concepts. Compared with binary classification, this representation can better accommodate the inaccuracy, fuzziness and ambiguity of semantics. We have shown how ambiguity can be computed from the semantic representation. This semantic representation is also a computational result of the data set, that is, it is emerged rather than assigned. In the above example, the "OWL" tag is currently unambiguous in the data. When users are going to use "OWL" to mean more and more about other things, e.g. the night bird, its computed semantic representation from the data will change accordingly to accommodate new meanings. This is the real power of the emergent semantics. It dynamically reflects the current state of the system and evolves with it.

Compared to the top-down approach of semantics, what we currently lacking is a hierarchy structure of the emerged concepts. Well-organized hierarchy structures of concepts is a strong point of the top-down approach. In the following subsection, using a more refined probabilistical model, we show that there indeed **are** hierarchical relations among the emerged concepts.

4.3   Hierarchical Concept Relations

In order to find a hierarchy of all the concepts hidden in the tags, we utilized the HACM model in [33]. HACM is a hierarchy clustering model. Fig.12 from [33] shows the schema for data generation in HACM model. The rectangle at the

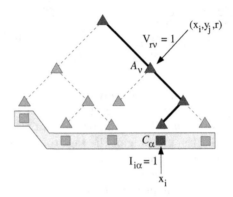

Fig. 12. Schema for data generation in HACM

bottom represents the concepts like in the SMM model. Triangle nodes denote inner nodes of a hierarchy. In the folksonomy scenario, the users' tagging behavior can be explained using the HACM model as follows:

1. The user encounters some URL x_i with probability p_i.
2. The URL makes the user think of one concept c_α in the bottom of the hierarchy. A hidden binary variable $I_{i\alpha}$ is used to denote which concept is chosen for the URL.
3. The user selects a generalization level v for the concept. This generalization level determines an inner node in the path from the concept c_α at the bottom to the root node at the top. A hidden binary variable V_{rv} is introduced to encode the resolution level A_v for the rth co-occurrence observation.
4. A tag y_j is chosen given the inner node A_v with probability $q_{j|\alpha}$.

Note that the major difference with previous generative models is that the user has to select a generalization level before generate the tag from the assigned concept. Here, we omit the mathematical details and the EM algorithm of the HACM model. Interested readers are referred to [33] for further reading.

We experimented using HACM model to automatically generate hierarchy structures from the Delicious data we collected. In the experiment, we assumed a complete binary tree structure. We are well aware that this is a radical simplification and bold assumption because concept hierarchies need not to be so. The concept hierarchy can even not be a tree but be a lattice. The purpose

Height 0

programming	0.5616
technology	0.0491
software	0.0246
tutorial	0.0242
Java	0.0226

Height 1

software	0.0943		software	0.1117
images	0.0917		reference	0.0638
reference	0.0875		browsers	0.0557
coffee	0.0710		database	0.0544
gallery	0.0554		sql	0.0530

Height 2

software	0.5659	tv	0.1659	reference	0.2770	delicious	0.1175
OSX	0.0397	torrents	0.1145	tutorial	0.1072	atom	0.0931
extension	0.0315	humour	0.1093	programming	0.0775	xml	0.0722
desktop	0.0263	television	0.0404	xhtml	0.0505	feed	0.0464
Windows	0.0173	TV	0.0380	HTML	0.0465	presentation	0.0446

Height 3

linux	0.5088	books	0.2987	gtd	0.4860	wiki	0.5319	security	0.3797	reference	0.4429	delicious	0.4745	python	0.7184
maps	0.0846	programming	0.0815	lifehacks	0.1272	software	0.0722	passwords	0.0556	wiki	0.1802	bookmarks	0.0911	calendar	0.0599
math	0.0775	ssh	0.0763	Python	0.0401	wikipedia	0.0400	Security	0.0522	wikipedia	0.0462	software	0.0468	software	0.0388
Linux	0.0727	scheme	0.0544	reference	0.0213	interview	0.0301	iraq	0.0384	learning	0.0349	tutorial	0.0367	linux	0.0152
london	0.0226	reference	0.0449	read	0.0190	python	0.0290	Xml	0.0359	useful	0.0276	Delicious	0.0323	.net	0.0148

Height 4a

reference	0.2397	technology	0.1771	programming	0.1088	programming	0.1036	software	0.2356	writing	0.4911	p2p	0.2679	dhtml	0.2027
film	0.0857	gadgets	0.1060	microsoft	0.0794	regex	0.1012	palm	0.1869	books	0.0403	Music	0.1465	comic	0.1074
useful	0.0787	science	0.0659	software	0.0640	linux	0.0898	management	0.1421	Writing	0.0323	torrents	0.0723	webcomic	0.0595
debian	0.0454	Shopping	0.0482	books	0.0243	reference	0.0766	3d	0.0727	science	0.0231	software	0.0615	Comics	0.0558
Travel	0.0362	Tech	0.0452	cs	0.0219	regexp	0.0670	gtd	0.0593	scifi	0.0215	P2P	0.0372	tags	0.0348

Height 4b

science	0.1500	xhtml	0.1617	books	0.2722	reference	0.3097	usability	0.3194	images	0.2423	Funny_Stuff,	0.0881	xml	0.3724
software	0.0796	apache	0.1522	Google	0.1720	language	0.2605	1A	0.2605	photoshop	0.1117	Mountains:Rainier, 0.0881		programming	0.0707
backup	0.0760	standards	0.1411	crypto	0.0702	writing	0.0962	folksonomy	0.0916	Family	0.1040	International:Vietnam:Saigon 0.0881		XML	0.0676
linux	0.0664	Ascii	0.0616	security	0.0627	rhetoric	0.0339	taxonomy	0.0478	tutorial	0.0425	Thru-Hiking,	0.0881	cooking	0.0553
technology	0.0456	inspiration	0.0317	reference	0.0416	dictionaries	0.0291	gui	0.0380	illustration	0.0279	Skiing:Rockies,	0.0881	webservices	0.0475

Fig. 13. Automatically generated taxonomy

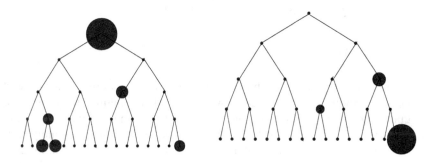

Fig. 14. The distribution of the tag "programming"

Fig. 15. The distribution of the tag "xml"

of this experiment, thus, is not to prove the correctness or robustness of the method to derive concept hierarchies but to quantitatively study whether there are narrower-broader relationships among the emerged concepts. We randomly sampled the raw data to get a small test data with 1642 URLs and 1121 tags co-occurred for 37,124 times to speed up this experiment. Fig.13 shows one of the results of the experiments. The depth of the taxonomy is set to 5. The last two rows of Fig.13 are actually at the same height 4 but are wrapped to fit the page size. The numbers at the right size of the tags is the probability of the tag generated at that generalization level. In order to assess the generated structure and demonstrate the ability of the HACM model to identify abstraction levels in the hierarchy, we have visualized the probabilisty distribution involving the tag "programming" and "xml" in Fig.14 and Fig.15 respectively. We can see that the "programming" tag is mostly used as a very general term. Hence the root node contains the majority of its probability mass. The tag is also used with "microsoft" and "regex" for its narrower sense of MS programming and programming with regular expressions. This is reflected in the lower-left corner of the Fig.14. On the contrary, the tag "xml" is used mostly as a very specific sense as in "xml programming". It thus appears large at the bottom of the hierarchy. It, however, also used in a more general sense as a data format as in discussion with "atom" and "feed" in height 2. These examples are only spotlights, but they showes that there indeed **are** hierarchical relations among the emerged concepts and it is possible to discover them using more refined probabilistic models. The discovered hierarchy can be used as a basis for further manual refinement for a taxonomy.

The advantage of such a generated taxonomy is that it is dynamically generated from free-style bottom-up annotations and it directly reflects the users' vocabularies. The taxonomy thus can be effectively understood and utilized by the community users. This avoids the drawbacks of the top-down approach to semantic annotation in which the ontology is built before its actual use and therefore may have missmatch with the requirements of its applications and may out-of-sync with the resources the ontology intends to cover. Needless to say, the bottom-up annotation removes the high barrier to entry in top-down semantic annotations because the users need not to have sophiscated knowledge about taxonomy or ontology to make the annotation.

5   Related Work

Semantic annotation is a key problem in the Semantic Web area. A lot of work has been done about the topic. Early work like [16,17] mainly uses an ontology engineering tool to build an ontology first and then manually annotate web resources in the tool. In order to help automate the manual process, many techniques has been proposed and evaluated. [22] learns from a small amount of training examples and then automatically tags concept instances on the web. The work has been tested on a very large-scale basis and achieves impressive precision. [20] helps users annotate documents by automatically generate natural language sentences according to the ontology and let users interact with these sentences to incrementally formalize them. Annother interesting approach is proposed by [21] that utilizes the web itself as a disambiguation source. Most annotations can be disambiguated purely by the number of hits returned by web search engines on the web. [24] improves the method using more sophisticated statistical analysis. Given that many web pages nowadays are generated from a backend database, [19] proposes to automatically produce semantic annotations from the database for the web pages. Information extraction techniques are employed by [23] to automatically extract instances of concepts of a given ontology from web pages. However, these work on semantic annotation follows the traditional top-down approach to semantic annotation which assumes that an ontology is built before the annotation process.

Our work of automatic taxonomy generation from folksonomy can be seen as a method for ontology learning [35] which has lot of related work. [36] gives a comprehensive review of the state-of-the-art ontology learning methods and places them in a framework for comparision. Most ontology learning methods learn ontology from structured data (e.g. database schema), semi-structured data on the web (e.g. HTML, XML and DTDs) and unstructured data (i.e. text). Very few work exploits the social bookmarks for ontology learning. [37] learns ontology from bookmarks, but the bookmarks used are those personal bookmarks stored on personal PCs that are not shared. Our work learns a taxonomy from the shared social bookmarks.

Much work has been done to help users manage their bookmarks on the (semantic) web such as [27]. [28] gives a good review of the social bookmarks tools available. These tools help make the social bookmarking easy to use but lacks capabilities to derive emergent semantics from the social bookmarks.

Work on emergent semantics [25,26] has appeared recently, for example [38,39,40]. [39] proposes an emergent semantics framework for large scale distributed systems and gives a good example of the framework. It shows how the spreading of simple ontology mappings among adjacent peers can be utilized to incrementally achieve a global consensus of the ontology mapping. [40] described how to incrementally obtain a unified data schema from the users of a large collection of heterogeneous data sources. [38] is more related to our work. It proposes that the semantics of a web page should not and can not be decided alone by the author. The semantics of a web page is also determined by how the users use the web page. This idea is similar to our thought. In our work, a URL's semantics is determined from the users' tags. However, our method of achieving emergent semantics is different from [38]. We use a probabilistic generative model to analyze user tags while [38] uses common sub-paths of users' web navigation path.

6   Conclusion and Future Work

Traditional top-down approach to semantic annotation in the Semantic Web area has a high barrier to entry and is difficult to scale up. In this paper, we propose a bottom-up approach to semantic annotation of the web resources by exploiting the now popular social bookmarking efforts on the web. The informal social tags and categories in these social bookmarks is coined a name "folksonomy". We quantitatively studied a data set of the Delicious folksonomy and found that power law distributions exist in the data set. This serves as one possible evidence of the implicit social interactions embeded in the folksonomies. Using a probabilistic generative model to interpret the data set, we derived emergent semantics from the folksonomy data. The semantics of URLs and tags can be represented using discrete probability distributions on derived concepts. The ambiguity of the semantics can be quantitatively measured using entropy values of the distributions. Finally, we show that there indeed are hierarchical relations among the emergent concepts and it is plausible to further identify them if we use more refined probabilistic models. In summary, compared to the top-down approach, the bottom-up approach does not depend on a pre-defined semantic model to assign semantics to resources but rather derives them from the real usage data. This entitles the approach several advantages such as the low barrier to entry and the tight connection to user vacabularies.

As our work done in this paper is mainly quantitative, future work needs be done more theoretically. We have several topics in our mind that need further exploration. The first one is how the top-down approach and the bottom-up approach may be combined together to leverage both advantages to solve the challenging problem of semantic annotation. This requires innovative thinking and deep insights. An accompanying question about what is the relationship between the representations of semantics in the bottom-up approach and the formal representations in the top-down approach and how we may link them together is also intriguing. Comparing the bottom-up approach in this paper with other probabilistic methods such as LSI [41] and conducting a formal rigorous evaluation is another future topic. Finally, automatically obtaining concept hierarchies from folksonomies is an open, difficult and challenging problem that worth a great effort to attack.

References

1. Berners-Lee, T., Hendler, J., Lassila, O.: The Semantic Web. Scientific American **284** (2001) 34–43
2. Manola, F., Miller, E.: RDF Primer. W3C Recommendation (2004)
3. McGuinness, D.L., van Harmelen, F.: OWL Web ontology language overview. W3C Recommendation (2004)
4. H.Gennari, J., A.Musen, M., W.Fergerson, R., E.Grosso, W., Crubézy, M., Eriksson, H., F.Noy, N., W.Tu, S.: The evolution of Protégé: An environment for knowledge-based systems development. Technical Report SMI-2002-0943, Stanford Medical Informatics (2002)
5. Bechhofer, S., Horrocks, I., Goble, C., Stevens, R.: OilEd: a reason-able ontology editor for the semantic web. In: Proceedings of the Joint German/Austrian Conference on AI. LNCS 2174 (2001) 396–408
6. Corcho, O., López, M.F., Pérez, A.G., Vicente, O.: WebODE: An integrated workbench for ontology representation, reasoning, and exchange. In: Proceedings of EKAW 2002. LNCS 2473 (2002) 138–153
7. Zhang, L., Yu, Y., Lu, J., Lin, C., Tu, K., Guo, M., Zhang, Z., Xie, G., Su, Z., Pan, Y.: ORIENT: Integrate ontology engineering into industry tooling environment. In: Proc. of the 3rd Intl. Semantic Web Conference (ISWC2004). (2004)
8. Kalyanpur, A., Sirin, E., Parsia, B., Hendler, J.: Hypermedia inspired ontology engineering environment: SWOOP. In: Proc. of the 3rd Intl. Semantic Web Conference (ISWC2004). (2004)
9. Heflin, J., Hendler, J.: Dynamic ontologies on the web. In: Proceedings of the Seventeenth National Conference on Artificial Intelligence (AAAI-2000), Menlo Park, CA, USA, AAAI/MIT Press (2000) 443–449
10. F.Noy, N., Klein, M.: Ontology evolution: Not the same as schema evolution. Knowledge and Information Systems **5** (2003)
11. Kiryakov, A., Ognyanov, D.: Tracking changes in RDF(S) repositories. In: Proceedings of the EKAW 2002, Siguenza, Spain, Springer (2002) 373–378

12. Noy, N.F., Kunnatur, S., Klein, M., Musen, M.A.: Tracking changes during ontology evolution. In: Proc. of the 3rd Intl. Semantic Web Conference (ISWC2004). (2004)
13. Klein, M., Fensel, D.: Ontology versioning for the semantic web. In: Proceedings of the 1st International Semantic Web Working Symposium (SWWS'01), Stanford University (2001) 75–91
14. Klein, M., Fensel, D., Kiryakov, A., Ognyanov, D.: Ontology versioning and change detection on the web. In: Proceedings of the EKAW 2002, Siguenza, Spain, Springer (2002) 197–212
15. Stojanovic, L., Maedche, A., Motik, B., Stojanovic, N.: User-driven ontology evolution management. In: Proceedings of the EKAW 2002, Siguenza, Spain, Springer (2002) 285–300
16. N.F.Noy, M.Sintek, S.Decker, M.Crubezy, R.W.Fergerson, M.A.Musen: Creating semantic web contents with Protege-2000. IEEE Intelligent Systems **2** (2001) 60–71
17. S.Handschuh, S.Staab: Authoring and annotation of web pages in CREAM. In: Proc. of the 11th Intl. World Wide Web Conference (WWW2002). (2002)
18. Kiryakov, A., Popov, B., Ognyanoff, D., Manov, D., Kirilov, A., Goranov, M.: Semantic annotation, indexing, and retrieval. In: Proc. of the 2nd Intl. Semantic Web Conference (ISWC2003). (2003)
19. Handschuh, S., Staab, S., Volz, R.: On deep annotation. In: Proc. of the 12th Intl. World Wide Web Conference (WWW2003). (2003) 431–438
20. Blythe, J., Gil, Y.: Incremental formalization of document annotations through ontology-based paraphrasing. In: Proc. of the 13th conference on World Wide Web (WWW2004), ACM Press (2004) 455–461
21. Cimiano, P., Handschuh, S., Staab, S.: Towards the self-annotating web. In: Proc. of the 13th Intl. World Wide Web Conference (WWW2004). (2004)
22. Dill, S., Eiron, N., Gibson, D., Gruhl, D., R.Guha, Jhingran, A., Kanungo, T., Rajagopalan, S., Tomkins, A., A.Tomlin, J., Y.Zien, J.: SemTag and Seeker: Bootstrapping the semantic web via automated semantic annotation. In: Proc. of the 12th Intl. World Wide Web Conference (WWW2003). (2003) 178–186
23. Etzioni, O., Cafarella, M., Downey, D., Kok, S., Popescu, A.M., Shaked, T., Soderland, S., S.Weld, D., Yates, A.: Web-scale information extraction in KnowItAll (preliminary results). In: Proc. of the 13th Intl. World Wide Web Conf.(WWW2004). (2004)
24. Cimiano, P., Ladwig, G., Staab, S.: Gimme the context: Context-driven automatic semantic annotation with C-PANKOW. In: Proc. of the 14th Intl. World Wide Web Conference (WWW2005). (2005)
25. Maedche, A.: Emergent semantics for ontologies. IEEE Intelligent Systems **17** (2002)
26. Aberer, K., et.al: Emergent semantics principles and issues. In: Proc. of Database Systems for Advanced Applications. LNCS 2973 (2004)
27. Kahan, J., Koivunen, M.R., Prud'Hommeaux, E., Swick, R.R.: Annotea: An open RDF infrastructure for shared web annotations. In: Proc. of the 10th Intl. World Wide Web Conference. (2001)
28. Hammond, T., Hannay, T., Lund, B., Scott, J.: Social bookmarking tools (i) - a general review. D-Lib Magazine **11** (2005)
29. Mathes, A.: Folksonomies - cooperative classification and communication through shared metadata. Computer Mediated Communication, LIS590CMC (Doctoral Seminar), Graduate School of Library and Information Science, University of Illinois Urbana-Champaign (2004)

30. Udell, J.: Collaborative knowledge gardening. InfoWorld, August 20 (2004)
31. Merholz, P.: Metadata for the masses. http://www.adaptivepath.com/publications/essays/archives/000361.php, accessed at May, 2005. (2004)
32. Adamic, L.A., Huberman, B.A.: The web's hidden order. Communications of the ACM **44** (2001)
33. Hofmann, T., Puzicha, J.: Statistical models for co-occurrence data. Technical report, A.I.Memo 1635, MIT (1998)
34. G.A.Miller: WordNet: A lexical database for english. Communications of the ACM **2** (1995)
35. A.Maedche, S.Staab: Ontology learning for the semantic web. IEEE Intelligent Systems **16** (2001)
36. M.Shamsfard M, A.: The state of the art in ontology learning: a framework for comparison. Knowledge Engineering Review **18** (2003)
37. J.J.Jung, Y.H.Yu, S.S.Jo: Collaborative web browsing based on ontology learning from bookmarks. In: Proc. of the Intl. Conference of Computational Science (ICCS2004). (2004)
38. W.I.Grosky, D.V.Sreenath, F.Fotouhi: Emergent semantics and the multimedia semantic web. SIGMOD Record **31** (2002)
39. Aberer, K., Cudre-Mauroux, P., Hauswirth, M.: The chatty web: Emergent semantics through gossiping. In: Proc. of 12th Intl. Conf. on World Wide Web (WWW2003). (2003)
40. Howe, B., Tanna, K., Turner, P., Maier, D.: Emergent semantics: Towards self-organizing scientific metadata. In: Proc. of the 1st Intl. IFIP Conference on Semantics of a Networked World: Semantics for Grid Databases (ICSNW 2004). LNCS 3226 (2004)
41. W.Furnas, G., Deerwester, S., T.Dumais, S., K.Landauer, T., A.Harshman, R., A.Streeter, L., E.Lochbaum, K.: Information retrieval using a singular value decomposition model of latent semantic structure. In: Proc. of the ACM SIGIR'88, Grenoble, France (1988) 465–480

Emergent Semantics in Knowledge Sifter: An Evolutionary Search Agent Based on Semantic Web Services

Larry Kerschberg[1], Hanjo Jeong[1], and Wooju Kim[2]

[1] E-Center for E-Business, Department of Information and Software Engineering,
George Mason University, MSN 4A4, Fairfax, Virginia, 22030-4444
{kersch, hjeong}@gmu.edu
http://eceb.gmu.edu/
[2] Yonsei University, Sinchon-dong, Seodaemun-gu, Seoul Korea 120-749, Korea
{wkim@yonsei.ac.kr}

Abstract. This paper addresses the various facets of emergent semantics in content retrieval systems such as Knowledge Sifter, an architecture and system based on the use of specialized agents to coordinate the search for knowledge in heterogeneous sources, including the Web, semi-structured data, relational data and the Semantic Web. The goal is to provide just-in-time knowledge to users based on their decision-making needs. There are three important factors that can assist in focusing the search: 1) the user's *profile*, consisting user preferences, biases, and query history, 2) the user's *context* to focus on the current activity, and 3) the user's *information space*, in which he may receive the information on specialized hardware with limited bandwidth, implying that the knowledge must be filtered and tailored to the presentation medium.

Emergent semantics in the context of Knowledge Sifter allow for evolutionary adaptive behavior. We present a meta-model that captures the agent operation and interactions, as well as the artifacts that are created and consumed during system operation. These are stored in a repository, and a collection of emergence agents are presented that perform emergence functions such as: data mining for patterns; concept discovery and evolution; user preferences tracking; collaborative filtering of user profiles; results ranking; and data source reputation and trust.

1 Introduction

The emergence of the Internet and World Wide Web have made it possible to represent semantics about people, places and events via the Web. The evolving Semantic Web allows the Web to be treated as a distributed data-, information- and knowledge space.

The advent of Internet Protocol Version 6 will allow virtually every object to have a fixed IP-address, thereby making it available on the Internet. New technologies such as RFID allow objects to be tracked through complex supply chains. Hand-held devices now incorporate digital cameras, phones, e-mail, Web browsers, PDAs, GPS, smart cards, and other capabilities to allow users to conduct business transactions using these devices. We are literally immersed in a ubiquitous information space, and the key to managing the *infoglut* is to have effective tools to find, filter, aggregate and

S. Spaccapietra et al. (Eds.): Journal on Data Semantics VI, LNCS 4090, pp. 187–209, 2006.

present information in a timely fashion for humans, and their proxies, to make informed decisions. This paper addresses the problem of intelligent search services to provide timely, focused and precise knowledge to users *just in time*. We also show how *emergent semantics and emergent behavior* play an important role in supporting the evolution of knowledge to improve the intelligent search agent, which we call Knowledge Sifter.

The concept of just-in-time knowledge management (JIT-KM) [17, 26] is appealing in that the goal is to provide the *right information*, to the *right people*, at the *right time* – just in time – so they can take action based on that information. While the just-in-time concept originated with Toyota in its drive to improve its manufacturing processes, the concept can also be applied to the timely delivery of information. There are a number of inter-related current trends that impact our study of JIT-KM. They are: On Demand Computing, On Demand Business, On Demand Retail, and On Demand Organizations.

On Demand Computing allows users to treat the computing infrastructure as an *information utility*, which can marshal the required resources (computers, storage,etc.) and charge based on usage. Users do not have to be aware of where the computers and storage facilities reside – they are virtual. On Demand Organizations, or Virtual Organizations, can be configured on the fly from existing Web services offered by vendors. The goal is to dynamically configure a collection of Web services by searching for candidates, negotiating with service providers for quality-of-service agreements, vetting the selected services, composing them, orchestrating their workflow and managing the virtual organization life-cycle [10, 11].

Both On Demand Computing and On Demand Organizations are based on the *virtualization* of resources and services that are then managed on behalf of users to deliver the desired functions. They are both related to the notions of GRID computing [7] and Semantic Web Services [23, 32]. The amount of meta-data [15, 34] required to manage these virtual environments is considerable.

On Demand Business integrates the enterprise with its suppliers by optimizing business processes and the supply chain to reduce inventories. On Demand Retail treats stores shelves as space to be managed by suppliers who are paid when customers actually purchase the merchandise. The main concept is the *integration and interoperation of information* among business partners and suppliers to achieve a high degree of transparency and efficiency among their business processes.

In a recent *New York Times* article [8], Wal-Mart, the world's largest retailer, was using its 460-terrabyte data warehouse to monitor worldwide operations in near real-time. They have created an extranet called Retail Link that allows suppliers to see how well their products are selling. Eventually, Wal-Mart will have the capability the conduct *scan-based trading* in which the supplier will own the product until it is scanned for purchase. This will reduce inventory costs for Wal-Mart. Wal-Mart will be requiring its major suppliers to use RFID tags on its shipments, in order to keep track of inventory as it enters the warehouses.

This example indicates that Wal-Mart is providing virtual shelf space for its suppliers; they are responsible for stocking those shelves and maintaining their inventories in a just-in-time fashion. Wal-Mart collects and uses massive amounts of data to obtain an up-to-the-minute picture of world-wide operations and can make command decisions based on their analysis of the data.

The above trends inform the concept of Just-in-Time Knowledge Management, which might also be called On Demand Knowledge Management. The sheer volume of data and information available to us make it imperative that we be able to sift and winnow through the mountains of data to find those *knowledge nuggets* so crucial to effective decision-making. The Wal-Mart case study motivates another aspect of the *data/knowledge space*, namely that large collections of data can be mined for patterns, rules and constraints. Clearly, these mined patterns are examples of emergent semantics that can be used to improve the knowledge delivered to users. In this paper we wish to explore the notions of just-in-time knowledge management and emergent semantics in the context of a meta-search agent called Knowledge Sifter (KS).

Our goal is to combine the notions of just-in-time knowledge management with emergent semantics [1-3] so as to: 1) improve the semantic formulation of queries posed to KS; 2) retrieve more precise information from heterogeneous sources; 3) store KS artifacts in a knowledge repository that can be mined for emergent concepts and patterns; 4) use collaborative filtering and machine learning techniques to look for community-wide emergence for recommendation during query formulation and results rating; and 5) compose patterns into larger fragments that can be used to tailor KS performance for certain types of queries.

This paper is organized as follows. Section 2 deals with issues associated with requirements and technologies for JIT-KM. Section 3 presents Knowledge Sifter, which is an agent-based search tool based on Semantic Web Services. Section 4 presents a meta-model for Knowledge Sifter that can be used to populate a repository with artifacts such as user preferences, user queries, associated results and user feedback. We also introduce the concept of data-DNA as a metaphor for emergent-, learned- or compiled fragments. Emergence Agents mine emergent concepts and patterns from the repository of Knowledge Sifter artifacts. Also presented are some results related to collaborative filtering and user preference tracking. Section 5 presents our conclusions.

2 Just-in-Time Knowledge Management

The notion of Just-in-Time Knowledge Management (JIT-KM) is that the right information should be available to decision-makers at the right time and in the right place, just in time. This simple concept has very widespread implications for the systems needed to support it. First, how do we determine what is the right information? How do we know who should receive that information? What is the right format of the information based on the decision-maker's location, context, and type of presentation device? How can we capture and represent the user's preferences, bias, context, and most importantly, his or her information requirements?

We explore these issues within the context of a research project called Knowledge Sifter, which is being conducted at George Mason University's E-Center for E-Business. We show how the Knowledge Sifter architecture can be used for JIT-KM.

2.1   Requirements for JIT-Knowledge Management

In order to deliver JIT-information, we must ensure that the information is timely, authentic, trusted and tailored to the decision-maker's needs. These *knowledge nuggets* are pieces of information that make a quantifiable difference in the decision-making process.   Timeliness is important in that out-of-date (stale) information can be irrelevant to the current context and task.   Authenticity and trust are related in that the decision-maker should have confidence in the information and the sources that provided it. Finally, there are the issues of *data lineage* and *data provenance*, that is, how was the data processed to derive the information? What is the quality of the original and derived data, and how reliable is the source of the data? These issues are all crucial for the decision-makers to have confidence in the information products, how they were derived, and the assessment of the quality and reliability of the data provider.

The technical requirements for JIT-Knowledge Management (JIT-KM) involve the customization of JIT-KM delivery to users based on a User Profile that captures a user's preferences, context, bias, goals and decision-making rules.   In addition, the user query, posed to existing search engines and sources, should be semantically enhanced to incorporate elements of the User Profile so as to obtain more precise and relevant results.   These results may be ranked by Knowledge Sifter and presented to the user for feedback as to their relevance to the decision problem. This addresses the notion of a *pull scenario* in which information is pulled from multiple heterogeneous sources; this is what Knowledge Sifter has been designed for.

Another type of scenario, a push-scenario, receives massive amounts of data from these sources and must filter the data to find information and knowledge relevant to the user's task. In order to deal with this information, it would be ideal if it were tagged appropriately using Semantic Web ontologies.

2.2   Technologies for JIT-Knowledge Management

The JIT-information requirements suggest that active technologies are needed to support the timely delivery of JIT services.   These include *pull scenarios* in which ad-hoc and standing queries are posed to heterogeneous sources — both internal to the enterprise and external — such as the Internet and World Wide Web.   These queries represent items of interest to the decision-maker and evidence substantiating an existing decision scenario would help him to take action.

Alternatively, *push scenarios* deliver content to users via *active* subscription services. These services may include: a) standing queries; b) just-in-time alerts (rule-based monitoring of events); c) real-time filtered media news feeds; d) dynamic scenario (hypothesis) specification, tracking and revision (reasoning about evolving evidence); e) ranking and integrating search results (information integration from multiple heterogeneous sources); f) collaborative filtering (viewing the work of other users related to common tasks) and g) collaborating with other analysts in creating and annotating knowledge products that can be stored in a knowledge base.

An important component of JIT-KM is the use of *meta-data* — data about data — to model and manage the JIT services.   Metadata is important in capturing data lineage as information objects are processed throughout the various phases of the activity life cycle.   This may include the evolution of user preferences; historical information regarding the results of standing- and ad-hoc queries; the ranking of search results; the authoritativeness of data sources; and the user's perceptions regarding the quality and timeliness of information provided. We now address these issues in the context of the Knowledge Sifter research.

3 The Knowledge Sifter Architecture

The Knowledge Sifter project, underway at George Mason University (Mason), has as its primary goals: 1) to allow users to perform ontology-guided semantic searches for relevant information, both in-house and open-source, 2) to refine searches based on user feedback, and 3) to access heterogeneous data sources via agent-based knowledge services. Increasingly, users seek information outside of their own communities to open sources such as the Web, XML-databases, and the emerging Semantic Web.

The Knowledge Sifter project also wishes to use open standards for both ontology construction and for searching heterogeneous data sources. For this reason we have chosen to implement our specifications and data interchange using the Web Ontology Language (OWL) [5, 37], and Web Services [4] for communication among agents and information sources. Each Knowledge Sifter agent is implemented as a Web service, and some data sources provide a Web service interface (API) to retrieve data.

3.1 Knowledge Sifter Agent-Based Web Services Framework

The rationale for using agents to implement intelligent search and retrieval systems is that agents can be viewed as autonomous and proactive. Each agent is endowed with certain responsibilities and communicates using an Agent Communication Language [6]. Recently, Huhns [12] has noted that agents can be thought of a Web services, and this is the approach we have taken to implement the agent community comprising Knowledge Sifter. The family of agents presented here is a subset of those incorporated into the large vision for Knowledge Sifter. This work is motivated by earlier research into Knowledge Rovers [13, 14] performed at Mason. This research is also informed by our previous work on WebSifter, [18-20] a meta-search engine that gathers information from traditional search engines, and ranks the results based on user-specified preferences and a multi-faceted ranking criterion involving static, semantic, categorical and popularity measures.

The Knowledge Sifter architecture [15, 16] may be considered a service-oriented architecture consisting of a collection of cooperating agents. The application domain we are considering is that of Image Analysis. The Knowledge Sifter conceptual architecture is depicted in Figure 1. The architecture has three layers: User Layer, Knowledge Management Layer and Data Layer. Specialized agents reside at the various layers and perform well-defined functions. This collection of cooperating agents supports interactive query specification and refinement, query decomposition, query processing, as well as result ranking and presentation. The Knowledge Sifter architecture is general and modular so that new ontologies and new information resources can be easily incorporated [27]. The various agents and services are described below.

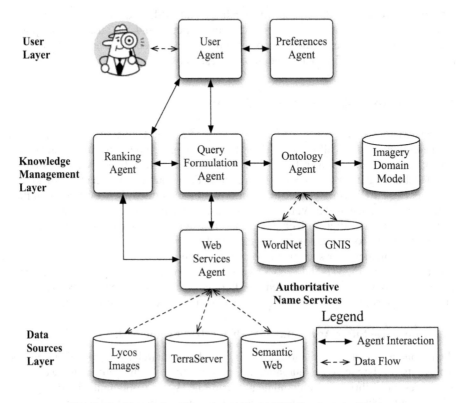

Fig. 1. The Knowledge Sifter Agent-Based Web Services Architecture

3.1.1 User and Preferences Agents

The User Agent interacts with the user to elicit user preferences that are managed by the Preferences Agent. These preferences include the relative importance attributed to terms used to pose queries, the perceived authoritativeness of Web search engine results, and other preferences to be used by the Ranking Agent. The Preferences Agent can also learn the user's preference based on experience and feedback related to previous queries.

3.1.2 Ontology Agent

The Ontology Agent accesses an imagery domain model, which is specified in the Web Ontology Language (OWL). In addition, there are two authoritative name services: Princeton University's WordNet [25] and the US Geological Survey's GNIS [35]. They allow the Ontology Agent to use terms provided by the name services to suggest query enhancements such as generalization, specialization and synonyms.

For example, WordNet can provide a collection of synonyms for a term, while GNIS translates a physical place in the US into latitude and longitude coordinates that are required by a data source such as TerraServer. Other appropriate name and translation services can be added in a modular fashion, and the domain model could

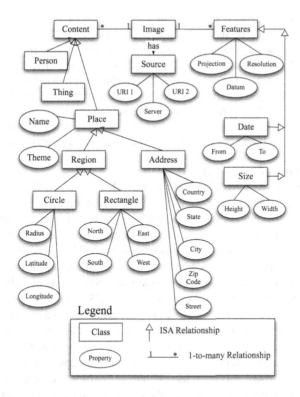

Fig. 2. Ontology Schema in the Unified Modeling Language Notation

be updated to accommodate new concepts and relationships. We now discuss the various sources used by the Ontology Agent.

Ontologies play a major role in Knowledge Sifter in that they represent semantic concepts that can be used to identify persons, places, things, and events of interest to a user. Users may have their own ontologies, in addition to ones supplied by a system such as Knowledge Sifter. Wouters et al [38, 39] present techniques to extract a user-oriented sub-ontology from a base ontology while preserving consistency and independence. Volz et al [36] argue that data independence principles can be applied to heterogeneous ontologies by creating ontological views which are constructed using RDF graphs and queried using the RQL language.

3.1.3 Imagery Domain Model and Schema
The principal ontology used by Knowledge Sifter is the Imagery Domain Model, specified using the Web Ontology Language, OWL. A UML-like diagram of the ontology is provided in Figure 2.

The class Image is defined as having *source*, *content*, and file descriptive *features*. Subcategories of content are *person*, *thing*, and *place*. Since we are primarily interested in satellite and geographic images, the class *place* has two general attributes, *name* and *theme*, together with the subclasses *region* and *address*. The Region is meant to uniquely identify the portion of the Earth's surface where the place is located, either by a *rectangle* or a *circle*. In the case of a rectangle we need two latitude values (*north* and *south*) and two longitude values (*east* and *west*), while to specify a circle we need the *latitude* and *longitude* of its center point, and a *radius*. The *address* of our location is identified by *country*, *state*, *city*, *zip code* and *street*. Each image belongs to a specific online source, the *server*, and has *URI-1* as a unique identifier, together with a secondary *URI-2* for a thumbnail (if any). Some qualitative and quantitative attributes are also modeled as subclasses of the general class *features*, namely *resolution* (in square meters per pixel), *projection* and *datum* (for future GIS utilizations), a *date* range, and image *size* (with *height* and *width* expressed in pixels).

3.1.4   Authoritative Name Services

The two name services are WordNet, developed at Princeton University, which is a lexical database for the English language. When the initial query instance, specifying a person, place, or thing, is sent to the Ontology Agent, it then consults WordNet to retrieve synonyms. The synonyms are provided to the Query Formulation Agent to request that the user select one or more synonyms. The decision is communicated to the Ontology Agent which then updates the appropriate attribute in the instantiated version of the OWL schema. If the attribute value is the name of a class of type *place* then the Ontology Agent passes the instance to the USGS GNIS.

The second name service is the USGS Geographic Names Information System (GNIS) which is a database of geographic names within the United States and its territories [35]. GNIS was developed by the USGS and the U.S. Board on Geographic Names to meet major national needs regarding geographic names and their stan-dardization and dissemination. It is an integration of three separate databases, the National Geographic Names Data Base, the USGS Topographic Map Names Data Base, and the Reference Data Base. Records within the database contain feature name, state, county, geographic coordinates, USGS Geographic Map name, and others. Other specialized name and translation services can be integrated into Knowledge Sifter and linked to the Domain Model.

3.1.5   Query Formulation Agent

The User Agent poses an initial query to the Query Formulation Agent. This agent, in turn, consults the Ontology Agent to refine or generalize the query based on the semantic mediation provided by the available ontology services. Once a query has been specified by means of interactions among the User Agent and the Ontology Agent, the Query Formulation Agent decomposes the query into subqueries targeted for the appropriate data sources. This involves semantic mediation of terminology used in the domain model ontology and name services with those used by the local sources. Also, query translation is needed to retrieve data from the intended heterogeneous sources.

For example, if the user specifies the domain of his search as *place*, Lycos and TerraServer will be chosen. In cases of *person* and *thing*, only Lycos will be chosen. In the case of person and thing, the user is asked to choose a specific meaning from the list retrieved from WordNet, and then the synonym set and hypernym set regarding that particular meaning are retrieved. Synonyms can be chosen as alternate names. Hypernyms can be used to generalize the user's concept. The terms chosen by the user are used to query Lycos. For example, if the user specifies the concept 'Rushmore' the following synonym set is returned by WordNet:

Rushmore, Mount Rushmore, Mt. Rushmore – (a mountain in the Black Hills of South Dakota; the likenesses of Washington and Jefferson and Lincoln and Roosevelt are carved on it)

In this case, the synonym set {Rushmore, Mount Rushmore, Mt. Rushmore} and the hypernym set {Mountain Peak} are retrieved from WordNet. If user chooses "Mount Rushmore" and "Mountain Peak", two different queries, "Mount AND Rushmore" and "Mountain AND Peak" are posed to Lycos, because the Lycos image search doesn't support the logical connector "OR" in search terms.

In the case of place, the user-selected synonym set and hypernym set are requested from the GNIS server using a similar approach, that is, the queries ("Mount AND Rushmore" and "Mountain AND Peak") are posed to the GNIS server in order to collect a list of locations from which the user can choose. The user can specify a state to restrict the GNIS results. After the user chooses one specific location, the name of the location is also used to submit queries to the Lycos server. Concurrently, a query is sent to TerraServer Web service with the appropriate latitude and longitude for the selected place.

In our future research, we will endow the Query Formulation Agent with more rules and policies to help it to make more intelligent decisions about query specification and query optimization. For example, in the case of image databases, a strategy might be to query the image metadata, retrieve and view thumbnails, and then request the collection of selected images. In addition, Knowledge Sifter will have a repository of processed queries, instantiated and annotated according to the OWL schema. This information will be used by the Query Formulation Agent as a Case Base that can be searched and the results reused. For example, a user query might be specified in stages, and the Case Base could be used to retrieve a relevant query processing strategy, send a request to the Web Services Agent and the results returned for user consideration. If needed, the Ontology Agent could assist in query enhancement as described above.

3.1.6 Web Services Agent

The main role of the Web Services Agent is to accept a user query that has been refined by consulting the Ontology Agent, and decomposed by the Query Formulation Agent. The Web Service Agent is responsible for the choreography and dispatch of subqueries to appropriate data sources, taking into consideration such facets as: user preference of sites; site authoritativeness and reputation; service-level agreements; size estimates of subquery responses; and quality-of-service measures of network traffic and dynamic site workload [24].

The Web Services Agent transforms the subqueries to XML Protocol (SOAP) requests to the respective local databases and open Web sources (TerraServer or Lycos) that have Web Service published interfaces; this is the case for the TerraServer, while Lycos provides an HTTP interface.

3.1.7 Ranking Agent

The Ranking Agent is responsible for compiling the sub-query results from the various sources, ranking them according to user preferences, as supplied by the Preferences Agent, for such attributes as: 1) the authoritativeness of a source which is indicated by a weight – a number between 0 and 10 – assigned to that source, or 2) the weight associated with a term comprising a query.

3.1.8 Data Sources and Web Services

At present, Knowledge Sifter consults two data sources: Lycos Images and the TerraServer. The Lycos server supports keyword-based image search via the web page http://multimedia.lycos.com. It makes use of both an image server and external data sources such as web pages for the image search. For a Lycos image search, no advanced search is supported and only conjunctions of terms are used. Therefore, the user cannot specify the image metadata such as *size* or *resolution*, so the results of search are limited. To address these problems the Query Formulation Agent generates a collection of conjunctive and disjunctive queries, while the evaluation and ranking process is left to the Ranking Agent.

The TerraServer is a technology demonstration for Microsoft. There is a Web Service API for TerraServer. TerraServer is an online database of digital aerial photographs (DOQs – Digital Orthophoto Quadrangles) and topographic maps (DRGs – Digital Raster Graphics). Both data products are supplied by the U.S. Geological Survey (USGS). The images are supplied as small tiles and these can be made into a larger image by creating a mosaic of tiles. The demonstrator at terraserver-usa.com uses a mosaic of 2x3 tiles.

Our purpose is to take the ontology-enhanced query and generate specific sub-queries for the TerraServer metadata. The resulting image identifiers and their metadata are wrapped into an instance of our image ontology. And an array of these is returned to the Web Service Agent to compile with other results.

3.2 Knowledge Sifter End-to-End Scenario

Consider the following scenario in which a user wishes to search for the term 'Rushmore'. This scenario shows how the various agents, name services, and data sources interact in handling a user query.

1. The user provides the User Agent with a keyword query: 'Rushmore'.
2. The user identifies the term as being a person, place or thing via radio buttons in the query form. The user has chosen 'Place'.
3. The User Agent passes the query to Query Formulation Agent.
4. The Query Formulation Agent invokes the Ontology Agent to instantiate an OWL schema for the 'Place' with Name = 'Rushmore'.
5. The Ontology Agent chooses a service agent based on the initial query. In this case, it requests from WordNet a list of concepts for 'Rushmore'. WordNet then passes the results back to the Ontology Agent which then passes the results to the User Agent via the Query Formulation Agent for the user decision.
6. The user chooses the 'Mount Rushmore' concept, which has three synonyms ('Rushmore', 'Mt. Rushmore', and 'Mount Rushmore').

7. The Ontology Agent then submits the synonym set to the USGS Geographic Name Information Server and receives a list of candidate geographic coordinates.
8. The list of candidate coordinates is sent to the Query Formulation Agent and the user chooses the desired location.
9. The Ontology Agent then updates the OWL schema instance with the chosen latitude and longitude.
10. The Query Formulation Agent then passes the fully-specified query to the Web Service Agent.
11. The Web Services Agent forwards appropriate sub-queries to both Lycos and TerraServer. The TerraServer and Lycos data sources are queried, and the results are sent back to the Web Services Agent. The results are compiled into new OWL instances that describe image metadata.
12. All results are combined and sent to the Query Formulation Agent.
13. The Query Formulation Agent sends the result sets and the original query to the Ranking Agent for ranking.
14. Within the Ranking Agent the image metadata for each returned item is ranked using the weights and preferences provided by the Preferences Agent. The Preferences Agent maintains the user preferences.
15. The Ranking Agent generates a score for each image result, and returns the scored list to the User Agent.
16. The User Agent then sorts the results by ranking and presents them to the user.
17. The user can then select an item from the list to download and view the image.

We have implemented a proof-of-concept prototype of Knowledge Sifter and this was reported in [15, 16].

4   Emergent Semantics in Knowledge Sifter

Our approach to Emergent Semantics (ES) in Knowledge Sifter (KS) is to collect, organize and store significant artifacts created during the end-to-end scenarios for KS such as in Section 3.2. In addition, it is important to collect lineage and provenance information regarding agent interactions among themselves and with external sources. We specify a meta-model for Knowledge Sifter, KSMM, represented in UML and as a Protégé ontology that can be exported to the Web Ontology Language (OWL). Sections 4.1 through 4.2 present this material in detail.

Emergent semantics processing is performed by agents specializing in different types of semantics associated with Knowledge Sifter. They access the KS Repository that contains *data-DNA fragments* and create *emergent artifacts* that are also stored in the KS Repository. This is discussed in Sections 4.3 and 4.4.

4.1   Knowledge Sifter Meta-model

The previous sections have described how the cooperative agents and web services support the search for relevant knowledge from both local and open-source data sources. The end-to-end scenario shows how the various agents and sources interact. The OWL schema is instantiated with information regarding a query and its various

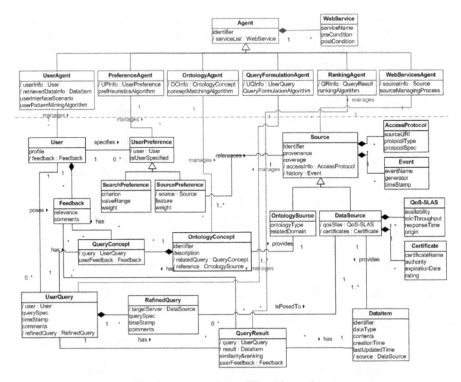

Fig. 3. The Knowledge Sifter Meta-schema

transformations into the final ranked results. In this section we elaborate on this concept by presenting a meta-model of the Knowledge Sifter framework so that relevant information can be captured regarding the *lineage* and *provenance* of all aspects of the search process, from query specification, to query reformulation, web service decomposition, results ranking and recommendation presentation. This includes information on the various Knowledge Sifter activities (managed by agents), the outcomes of those activities, the quality of the ranked results, measures of Web service performance, and the authoritativeness and reliability of data sources.

This meta-model is then used to capture and store both KS data and metadata for future analysis, filtering and mining for emergent properties related to the use of Knowledge Sifter resources. By stepping back and abstracting the agents, classes, their relationships and properties, we can construct the Knowledge Sifter Meta-Model (KSMM) [30]. Figure 3 depicts the UML Static Model for the KSMM. At the top is the Class Agent, which is specialized to those agents in the KS framework, specifically the UserAgent, PreferencesAgent, OntologyAgent, QueryFormulationAgent, RankingAgent and WebServicesAgent. These agents manage their respective object classes, process specifications, and WebServices. For example, the UserAgent manages the User Class, the UserInterfaceScenario, the User PatternMiningAlgorithm, and the WebServices. The User specifies User Preferences that can be specialized to Search Preferences and Source Preferences. The User poses UserQuery that has several QueryConcept, which in turn

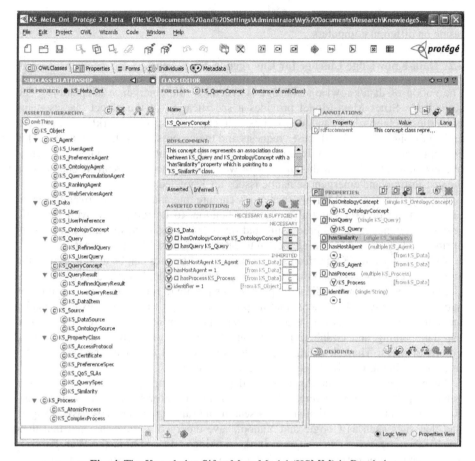

Fig. 4. The Knowledge Sifter Meta-Model (KSMM) in Protégé

relates to an OntologyConcept. The Ontology Agent manages both the UserQuery and the OntologyConcept that is provided by an OntologySource. Both OntologySource and DataSource are specializations of Source. Source is managed by the WebServicesAgent and has attributes such as provenance, coverage, access protocol and history. DataSource has attributes such as Quality-of-Service Service-Level-Agreements (QoS-SLAS) and Certificate.

A UserQuery consists of several RefinedQuery, each of which is posed to several DataSource. DataSource provides one-or-more DataItem in response to a RefinedQuery as the QueryResult. Based on the returned QueryResult, the User may provide Feedback as to the result relevance and other comments. These may impact the evolution of metadata associated with UserPreference, query formulation, data source usage and result ranking. A KSMM has been specified by a Protégé ontology [28] and a screen shot of the main panel is shown in Figure 4.

The KS meta-classes correspond to those of the UML diagram in Figure 3. The Protégé KSMM can also be exported to a Web Ontology Language (OWL) specification. This specification can be consulted via a namespace hyper-link, thus making the agents, which are implemented as Web Services, portable and able to reside on different computers.

4.2 Data/Knowledge Lineage for Emergence Adaptation

The notion of data/knowledge lineage is crucial to the emergence adaptation. The Knowledge Sifter Meta-Model provides a specification of the object classes, their properties, relationships and constraints. It can also specify workflow processes among the agents that handle user requests and the processing of those requests. This concept can be extended to dynamically configure semantic web services for virtual organizations [10, 11]. In this discussion we focus on how the KSMM can address the just-in-time and emergent semantic issues for Knowledge Sifter.

By creating the KSMM we can now capture metadata for the overall search process, from the user's initial query specification, to its refinement with semantic ontological concepts, to its processing and ranking. In addition, we can capture agent attributes, measures of agent interaction to determine overall KS performance.

User feedback and KS performance measures and metrics can be used to evolve the system in several ways that affect emergence. For example, User feedback allows the User Preference Agent to adjust the preferences profile to reflect evolving preferences and biases, to adjust the sources that he prefers and deems to be both of high quality and authoritative. Moreover, as user profiles and preferences are aggregated, we can use data mining and collaborative filtering techniques to discover patterns among groups of users. These learning approaches can be used to make Knowledge Sifter more active in taking advantage of emergent semantics.

Each Knowledge Sifter Agent can adapt to changing query and web services behavior patterns. For example the User Agent can inform the Web Services and Ranking Agents that a particular user's search and ranking preferences have changed, and that sites such as Google and Yahoo! have emerged as favorites and that their results should receive extra support in the rankings. In addition, the Web Services Agent can monitor network traffic and the response times of data sources to determine whether certain sites will not be able to deliver their results in a timely fashion, in which case partial results would be provided in JIT-fashion to the user, until the full results could be assembled. In order to refine these concepts, the following section introduces the notion of data-DNA; these are fragments or snippets of data/knowledge that can be composed into larger fragments.

The notions of lineage, provenance and trust are important components of our emergence research. Consider for example the case of an intelligence analyst who has developed an hypothesis, represented as an and-or goal tree in which each node represents a subtask for which evidence is needed to verify that task. Knowledge Sifter can be used to search for the required evidence. The analyst can create a data-DNA fragment from the relevant evidence, annotate the fragment, associate it with the subtask it supports, and store it for later use. The lineage and provenance of this fragment provide time stamps as to when the evidence was collected, from which sources, and an assessment of the analyst's trust in that evidence. The data-DNA fragments can also be shared with others for collaborative intelligence assessment. One could also model the analyst's preferred work style and process model, store it in the User Profile and use it to guide Knowledge Sifter's search process. A goal of our research is to have Knowledge Sifter learn this model using emergent semantic and Semantic Web Services techniques.

4.3 Data-DNA and Emergent Behavior

The concept of *data-DNA* provides for self-describing meta-data for objects in the context of emergent semantics in Knowledge Sifter. The idea is to capture, store and annotate with lineage metadata about every artifact, created or used during the course of Knowledge Sifter's operation, so as to be able to recreate and analyze the end-to-end processing of a user's query.

The KSMM provides the domain model, i.e., the meta-model, by which tagging and indexing can be accomplished. Thus, individual artifacts such as a user query, a semantically enhanced query, results obtained by Web services, and the ranking of results can all be stored, indexed, and annotated. The artifacts, or *data-DNA fragments*, can be composed into larger fragments representing scenarios. The scenarios could be developed off-line and stored in the KS repository, or alternatively, they could be obtained by mining the collection artifacts stored during Knowledge Sifter's normal operation for a collection of users and their queries.

For example, a user might be driving in South Dakota on a family outing (vacation) and would like to visit Mount Rushmore, as per our previous example in section 3.2. He uses his advanced PDA to start the Knowledge Sifter search service. The first request is to find images of Mount Rushmore, and then view a topographical map of the area. Then KS retrieves data-DNA fragments corresponding to the user's context which is family outing (vacation) and proposes one of the following actions according to the workflow contained in the fragments: 1) Driving instructions with autoload into the car's GPS, 2) hotel reservations within a 15 mile radius at a Hilton Hotel chain (15 mile radius and Hilton Hotels in the user's preferences), reservations for dinner for four (from a list of restaurants in the preferences), and tickets for tonight's Rushmore Sound-and-Light Show.

The collection and assembly of relevant data-DNA fragments, and their associated scenarios, would be managed by the Ontology Agent using the KSMM Ontology. The Ontology Agent would handle both the Imagery Domain Model and the data-DNA fragments stored in the KS repository. The user model, consisting of intent, preferences and context information, would be used to retrieve, assemble and mange the fragments. The Ontology Agent cooperates with the Query Formulation Agent to instantiate the data-DNA fragments with user-specific data for presentation to the Web Services Agent for processing. The Web Services Agent then dispatches the instantiated fragments to appropriate Web services. The Web Services Agent also coordinates the workflow involved in processing the requests. Given the decentralized and distributed nature of these services, we envision that agents will search for external data-DNA fragments via a negotiation process. For example, a task might involve a business process whose provider subscribes to an ebXML protocol [29]. In that case the agent would negotiate the fragment, instantiate it with user data and add it to that user's instantiated data-DNA.

In our family outing example, there are opportunities for parallel execution of transaction fragments. For example, the GPS coordinates of the family can be determined from the cell phone GPS and then loaded into the car's GPS. Concurrently,

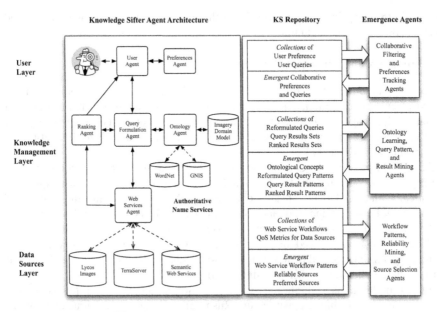

Fig. 5. Knowledge Sifter Emergence Framework

the restaurant and Sound-and-Light Show reservations can be made, provided that first the hotel reservation has been obtained and guaranteed.

Figure 5 depicts the Knowledge Sifter Emergence Framework with the KS agent architecture on the left, the KS repository in the middle, and the Emergence Agents on the right. During the normal operation of KS, artifacts will be created in response to user requests. These artifacts are stored in the KS repository according to the KS Meta-Model shown in Figures 3 and 4. The Emergence Agents access the KS Repository and perform emergence functions suggested by their names; these new emergent concept, called data-DNA are stored in the KS Repository and can be used to evolve KS at various levels. The data-DNA can be used to: 1) improve the operation of the KS agents by adapting the algorithms that govern their behavior, 2) enhance the ontological concepts known to the Ontology Agent, 3) provide collaboratively-filtered recommendations to users in query formulation, results selection, and user preference evolution.

In the following sections, we focus on the agents involved in collaborative filtering for emergent ontological concept learning, and emergent user preferences. The other emergence agents are a focus of ongoing research within the Knowledge Sifter project.

4.4 Collaborative Filtering for KS Emergent Concepts

Recommendation systems provide the right information to the right user by using both content-based filtering and collaborative filtering. One of the best-known information recommendation systems is the search engine. Most search engines such as Yahoo and AltaVista use only content-based filtering to provide web data related to user queries, and therefore they have limitations in providing information that incorporates both the user's preferences and an assessment of the quality of the data. One reason for Google's success and popularity is that is combines content-based filtering and collaborative filtering in the PageRank algorithm [31].

In this section we present some results pertaining to the use of collaborative filtering to find emergent concepts, user preferences and recommendations. New concepts from an object retrieved by a particular user query could emerge by mining the explicit and/or implicit user feedback for that object. The user query would be analyzed for the emergent concept of the object. This would increase both the recall and precision of KS search by discovering the new concept and providing user feedback for that concept. Thus, one could combine content-based filtering and collaborative filtering in the KS search process, and then show ordered results by the overall similarity of the ranking.

Assume that we have following statistical values of similarities between user queries and query results from the KS Repository in Figure 5. Actually, KS evaluates result similarity based not only on user queries but also on user preferences. However, we ignore the user preferences for the following data set, in order to obtain new emergent concepts over the entire user community.

(Query, Result, Similarity)
$(q_1, r_1, 0.7)$
$(q_1, r_2, 0.2)$
$(q_2, r_1, 0.9)$
$(q_3, r_1, 0.1)$
$(q_3, r_2, 0.8)$

The following formula calculates collaborative similarity between a new query and result.

$$sim^{col}(q_i, r_k) = \frac{\sum_{j \neq i} sim(q_i, q_j) \times \left(sim(q_j, r_k) - \theta_s \right)}{n(j)} \quad (1)$$

For $j \in \{q_j \mid sim(q_i, q_j) > \theta_q\}$ where j is in q_js that are only related with r_k, and sim^{col} and sim stand for collaborative similarity and overall similarity, respectively. We could use the above collaborative similarity (query, result) to compensate for determining the overall similarity (query, result) with measured similarity by the KS Rating Agent. The following formula represents the overall similarity. The θ_q represent the threshold for the query similarity to determine how similar queries would be used for calculating collaborative similarity with reducing noises, e.g., one history that has high similarity between a result and a query having low similarity with the new query. The θ_s represents the threshold for determining whether the instance is a positive or negative one. The following formula represents the overall similarity.

$$sim(q_i, r_k) = (1 - \alpha) \cdot sim^{con}(q_i, r_k) + \alpha \cdot sim^{col}(q_i, r_k) \quad (2)$$

where α represents a weight for collaborative similarity to determine overall similarity and the sim^{con} represents content-based similarity, i.e., KS evaluates similarity in terms of the subject of the target object by using various ontologies such as WordNet and GNIS. Therefore, the content-based similarity between the query and result could be measured by ontology mapping between the query concept ontology and data resource ontology. The similarity between two queries could be measured in same way as the content-based similarity between query and result is measured.

One of the novel approaches in the above algorithm framework is that the initial overall similarity (sim (q, r)) is a combination of both content-based similarity and collaborative similarity, which is based on user feedback. Therefore, the final overall similarity can be considered as a *mediated similarity* accounting for the difference between the KS-measured similarity and user-rated similarity. This would compensate for implicit errors in KS measurement and user ratings for the similarities between queries and results. If user feedback does not exist in a certain association between query and result, we can regard the KS-measured similarity as the initial overall similarity.

4.5 Collaborative Filtering for Emergent User Preferences

Collaborative filtering enables us to suggest recommendations to users using statistical analysis of user patterns. Applying this concept to user profile mining would allow KS to use emergent knowledge to provide the right information to the right user, i.e., to customize knowledge for a particular user.   There are two approaches to the problem: 1) determine user preferences by analyzing user profiles and 2) determine user preferences by analyzing user ratings of query data results.

In general, collaborative filtering recommendation systems filter out items by using only the statistical analysis of human assessments (user ratings) [9, 22], i.e., the systems use implicit correlation between the user ratings and user taste for the recommendations in a given domain of discourse.   On the other hand, users could pose content-based queries to find objects they want to a content-based search engine such as Knowledge Sifter. Furthermore, KS allows users to define their preferences in terms of some features for a domain object based on the domain ontology. Therefore, we also need to be concerned about the influence between the user queries and their preferences, and to use this additional information for the recommendation process. If we only consider user relationships between preferences and results in KS, it might cause the system to determine biased, or distorted, preferences because the preferences could be different over the queries, i.e., the preferences could be dependent on the objects that the user wants. To overcome this problem, we use combinations of user preferences and queries to recommend relevant results based on user queries and given user preferences.

This approach is using the methods in mining a new concept related to a certain object by using user queries as explained in equation 1 above. Assume that we have the following statistical values of similarities between three major factors in KS such as user preferences, user queries, and query results. Unlike the examples in equation1, we need to also incorporate the preference because our goal is to recommend related results based on user queries for given user preferences. Therefore, we use a combination of user preferences and queries to evaluate the similarity between the data results.

Consider the table of preference, query result and similarity measures:
(Preference, Query, Result, Similarity)

$(p_1, q_1, r_1, 0.7)$
$(p_1, q_1, r_2, 0.2)$
$(p_2, q_2, r_1, 0.3)$
$(p_2, q_3, r_2, 0.8)$
$(p_3, q_4, r_1, 0.8)$

The collaborative similarity between a result and a query that is posed by a user having preference would be calculated from following formula:

$$sim^{col}(p_i, q_a, r_x) = \frac{\displaystyle\sum_{j \neq i, b \neq a} \left(sim(p_i, p_j) \times sim(q_a, q_b) \times \left(sim(p_j, q_b, r_x) - \theta_s \right) \right)}{n(j) \times n(b)} \tag{3}$$

For $j \in \{p_j \mid sim\ (p_i, p_j) > \theta_p\}$, $b \in \{q_b \mid sim\ (q_a, q_b) > \theta_q \}$

where j is in q_js that are only posed by a user having preference p_i and contains result r_l in their result set. The $sim(p_i, q_j, r_k)$ represents the overall similarity between the query q_j at given p_i and the result r_k. The θ_p and θ_q represent the threshold for the preference similarity and the query similarity respectively to determine the similar preferences and queries for calculating collaborative similarity. This prevents KS from doing a biased evaluation by eliminating possibility of including pointless instances, e.g., one that has high similarity between a result and query having low preference and query similarity. The θ_s represents the threshold that determines whether the instance would be positive or negative one.

The following formula represents the overall similarity.

$$sim(p_i, q_j, r_k) = (1 - \beta) \cdot sim^{con}(p_i, q_j, r_k) + \beta \cdot sim^{col}(p_i, q_j, r_k) \tag{4}$$

where β represents a weight for collaborative similarity to determine overall similarity in this situation.

In order to calculate the similarity between two preferences, we need to consider two kinds of preferences, which are weight preferences and weighted value preferences for each preference criterion because a KS user could define weight preferences for name and location queries evaluation and weighted value preferences for other criteria associated with image data. The weight preferences enable KS to determine which criteria the user considers more important between rating results data and the value preferences represent what value of certain feature user prefers.

The following formula represents the overall similarity between the two preferences.

$$sim(p_i, p_j) = (1 - \gamma) sim^{v}(p_i, p_j) + \gamma sim^{w}(p_i, p_j) \tag{5}$$

where γ represents the weight for weight preferences, and sim^v and sim^w represent the similarity between two preferences for the value preferences and the weight preferences, respectively.

The similarity between two weight preferences set could be calculated from following formula, which uses the well-known Euclidean distance function.

$$sim^w(p_i, p_j) = 1 - \frac{\sum_c \sqrt{((p_i(w_c) - p_j(w_c)))^2}}{n(c)} \tag{6}$$

where c represents the criterion of preference, and w_c represents the weight for the criterion c. Then, $P_i(w_c)$ denotes the weight value for a criterion c in a preference i and n(c) represents the number of criteria in the preferences. The similarity between two preferences has 1, if the two preferences are identical. But the distance should be 0 in the case of the two preferences being identical, therefore we inverse them. Note that the weight value is normalized one having 0 to 1.

The similarity between two value preferences could be calculated from following formula, which uses weighted Euclidean distance function for each preference criterion. This formula is derived from multipoint queries shown in Mars [33] and Falcon [40], i.e., the value preferences in KS could be treated as the multidimensional queries.

$$sim^v(p_i, p_j) = 1 - \frac{\sum_c w_c \sqrt{\left(\frac{(p_i(v_c) - p_j(v_c))}{Max(p(v_c)) - Min(p(v_c))}\right)^2}}{\sum_c w_c} \tag{7}$$

where v_c represents the value for the criterion c. The $p_i(v_c)$ represents the value of the criterion c at a preference p_i. Using Max and Min value for each criterion makes the normalization over the criterion value differences, e.g. size and time criteria in KS preferences for image domain use different measure and range, therefore, we couldn't numerate and normalize the distances not referencing the Max and Min values in collaborative user preferences. In our ongoing research we are extending the concept of the user preference and results ranking to include multiple attributes and their corresponding weights, similar to our work on WebSifter II [19-21].

5   Conclusions

Knowledge Sifter is an agent-based ontology-driven search engine based on Semantic Web services. We have motivated the need for delivery of timely, focused and accurate information to users in a just-in-time fashion. We have discussed the KS architecture and the important role the semantics plays in all aspects of KS's operation. The KS agents accept a user's initial query, consult the User Preferences Agent, reformulate the query based on user preferences and ontological concepts, decompose it into subqueries handled by the Web Services Agent, and rank the query results according to user preferences, biases and context.

In order to incorporate emergence and evolution into the KS architecture, we develop the KS Meta-Model (KSMM) that allows us to capture, store and mine the artifacts produced and consumed during normal Knowledge Sifter operation. The

KSMM is a specification of the agents, activities, and communications of the system's operation. This has been specified in both in UML and Protégé, which automatically generates an OWL specification that can be shared with other services via a namespace. The KSMM schema can be instantiated with actual user queries, their reformulations, query decomposition and processing strategies, Web Services invocations, query result sets, results rankings, and user feedback regarding the relevance of the results to the task at hand.

The Knowledge Sifter Emergence Framework has been presented for discovering, mining and compiling emergent concepts, emergent user preferences, emergent collaborative recommendations, etc. We term these emergent objects as data-DNA and discuss how these can be combined into larger data-DNA fragments.

We focus on Emergence Agents involved in collaborative filtering for emergent ontological concept learning, and emergent user preferences and discuss a novel approach to calculating emergence of content that incorporates both KS-computed similarity and user-rated similarity.

In our work on the precursor to Knowledge Sifter, called WebSifter II [20], we presented a neural network model for learning user preferences and automatically updating those preferences. We plan to incorporate underlying concepts of the neural network model into the Knowledge Sifter Emergence Framework.

Acknowledgements. This work was sponsored in part by a NURI from the National Geospatial-Intelligence Agency (NGA). This work was also sponsored in part by MIC & IITA through IT Leading R&D Support Project. The authors would like to acknowledge the work on the Knowledge Sifter prototype by M. Chowdhury, A. Damiano, S. Mitchell, J. Si, and S. Smith.

References

1. Aberer, K., Catarci, T., Cudré-Mauroux, P., Dillon, T., Grimm, S., Hacid, M.-S., Illarranmendi, A., Jarrar, M., Kashyap, V., Mecella, M., Mena, E., Neuhold, E.J., Ouksel, A.M., Risse, T., Scannapieco, M., Saltor, F., de Santis, L., Spaccapietra, S., Staab, S., Studer, R. and De Troyer, O. Emergent Semantic Systems. in Bouzeghoub, M., Goble, C., Kashyap, V. and Spaccapietra, S. eds. *Semantics for a Networked World, Semantics for the Grid Databases, LNCS 3226*, Springer, Paris, France, 2004, 14-43.

2. Aberer, K., Cudré-Mauroux, P. and Hauswirth, M., The Chatty Web: Emergent Semantics Through Gossiping. in *The Twelth International World Wid Web Conference, WWW2003*, (Budapest, Hungary, 2003).

3. Aberer, K., Cudré-Mauroux, P. and Hauswirth, M. Start making sense: The Chatty Web approach for global semantic agreements. *Journal of Web Semantics, 1* (1). 89-114.

4. Chinnici, R., Gudgin, M., Moreau, J.-J. and Weerawarana, S. Web Services Description Language (WSDL) Version 1.2 (http://www.w3.org/TR/wsdl12/), W3C, 2002.

5. Fensel, D. Ontology-Based Knowledge Management *IEEE Computer*, 2002, 56-59.

6. Finin, T., Fritzson, R., McKay, D. and McEntire, R., KQML as an Agent Communication Language. in *International Conference on Information and Knowledge Management (CIKM-94)*, (1994), ACM Press.

7. Foster, I., Kesselman, C. and Tuecke, S. The Anatomy of the Grid: Enabling Scalable Virtual Organizations. *International J. Supercomputer Applications, 15* (3).

8. Hayes, C.L. What Wal-Mart Knows About Customers' Habits, The New York Times, New York, 2004.
9. Herlocker, J.L., Konstan, J.A., Borchers, A. and Riedl, J., An algorithmic framework for performing collaborative filtering. in *Proceedings of the 1999 Conference on Research and Development in Information Retrieval*, (1999).
10. Howard, R. and Kerschberg, L. A Framework for Dynamic Semantic Web Services Management. *International Journal of Cooperative Information Systems, Special Issue on Service Oriented Modeling, 13* (4).
11. Howard, R. and Kerschberg, L., A Knowledge-based Framework for Dynamic Semantic Web Services Brokering and Management. in *International Workshop on Web Semantics - WebS 2004*, (Zaragoza, Spain, 2004).
12. Huhns, M. Agents as Web Services *IEEE Internet Computing*, July/August 2002.
13. Kerschberg, L. (ed.), *Knowledge Management in Heterogeneous Data Warehouse Environments*. Springer, Munich, Germany, 2001.
14. Kerschberg, L. The Role of Intelligent Agents in Advanced Information Systems. in Small, C., Douglas, P., Johnson, R., King, P. and Martin, N. eds. *Advances in Databases*, Springer-Verlag, London, 1997, 1-22.
15. Kerschberg, L., Chowdhury, M., Damiano, A., Jeong, H., Mitchell, S., Si, J. and Smith, S. Knowledge Sifter: Agent-Based Ontology-Driven Search over Heterogeneous Databases using Semantic Web Services. in Bouzeghoub, M., Goble, C., Kashyap, V. and Spaccapietra, S. eds. *Semantics for a Networked World, Semantics for the Grid Databases, LNCS 3226*, Springer, Paris, France, 2004, 278-295.
16. Kerschberg, L., Chowdhury, M., Damiano, A., Jeong, H., Mitchell, S., Si, J. and Smith, S., Knowledge Sifter: Ontology-Driven Search over Heterogeneous Databases. in *SSDBM 2004, International Conference on Scientific and Statistical Database Management*, (Santorini Island, Greece, 2004), IEEE.
17. Kerschberg, L. and Jeong, H., Just-in-Time Knowledge Management. in *Third Conference on Professional Knowledge Management*, (Kaiserslautern, Germany, 2005), Springer.
18. Kerschberg, L., Kim, W. and Scime, A., Intelligent Web Search via Personalizable Meta-Search Agents. in *International Conference on Ontologies, Databases and Applications of Semantics (ODBASE 2002)*, (Irvine, CA, 2002).
19. Kerschberg, L., Kim, W. and Scime, A. A Semantic Taxonomy-Based Personalizable Meta-Search Agent. in Truszkowski, W. ed. *Innovative Concepts for Agent-Based Systems*, Springer-Verlag, Heidelberg, 2003, 3-31.
20. Kim, W., Kerschberg, L. and Scime, A. Learning for Automatic Personalization in a Semantic Taxonomy-Based Meta-Search Agent. *Electronic Commerce Research and Applications (ECRA), 1* (2).
21. Kim, W., Kerschberg, L. and Scime, A., Personalization in a Semantic Taxonomy-Based Meta-Search Agent. in *International Conference on Electronic Commerce 2001 (ICEC 2001)*, (Vienna, Austria, 2001), Elsevier Science.
22. Konstan, J.A., Miller, B.N., Maltz, D., Herlocker, J.L., Gordon, L.R. and Riedl, J. GroupLens: Applying collaborative filtering to Usenet news. *Communications of the ACM, 40* (3). 77-87.
23. McIlraith, S.A., Son, T.C. and Zeng, H. Semantic Web Services *IEEE Intelligent Systems*, 2001, 46-53.
24. Menascé, D.A. QoS Issues in Web Services *IEEE Internet Computing*, Nov/Dec 2002, 72-75.
25. Miller, G.A. WordNet a Lexical Database for English. *Communications of the ACM, 38* (11). 39-41.

26. Morikawa, R. and Kerschberg, L., MAKO-PM: Just-in-Time Process Model. in *Professional Knowledge Management: Workshop on Information Just-in-Time*, (Kaiserslautern, Germany, 2005), Springer.

27. Morikawa, R. and Kerschberg, L., MAKO: Multi-Ontology Analytical Knowledge Organization based on Topic Maps. in *Fifth International Workshop on Theory and Applications of Knowledge Management*, (Zaragoza, Spain, 2004).

28. Noy, N.F., Sintek, M., Decker, S., Crubezy, M., Fergerson, R.W. and Musen, M.A. Creating Semantic Web contents with Protege-2000 *IEEE Intelligent Systems*, 2001, 60-71.

29. OASIS. ebXML, http://www.ebxml.org/, 2004.

30. ObjectManagementGroup. Meta Object Facility (MOF) Specification Version 1.3, 2000.

31. Page, L., Brin, S., Motwani, R. and Winograd, T. The PageRank Citation Ranking: Bringing Order to the Web *Tech Report Series*, Stanford University; Digital Library Technologies Project, 1998.

32. Paolucci, M. and Sycara, K. Autonomous Semantic Web Services *IEEE Internet Computing*, Sept - Oct 2003, 34-41.

33. Porkaew, K., Chakrabarti, K. and Mehrotra., S., Query refinement for content-based multimedia retrieval in MARS. in *Proceedings of ACM Multimedia Conference*, (1999).

34. Pouchard, L., Cinquini, L., Drach, B., Middleton, D., Bernholdt, D.E., Chanchio, K., Foster, I.T., Nefedova, V., Brown, D., Fox, P., Garcia, J., Strand, G., Williams, D., Chervanek, A.L., Kesselman, C., Shoshani, A. and Sim, A., An Ontology for Scientific Information in a Grid Environment: the Earth System Grid. in *CCGRID 2003*, (2003), 626-632.

35. USGS. USGS Geographic Names Information System (GNIS), http://geonames.usgs.gov/.

36. Volz, R., Oberle, D. and Studer, R., Views for light-weight web ontologies. in *ACM Symposium on Applied Computing (SAC 03)*, (Melbourne, Florida, USA, 2003), ACM.

37. W3C. OWL Web Ontology Language Overview, http://www.w3.org/TR/owl-features/. McGuinness, D.L. and van Harmelen, F. eds., W3C, 2003.

38. Wouters, C., Dillon, T., Rahayu, J. and Chang, E., A Practical Walkthrough of the Ontology Derivation Rules. in *13th International Conference on Database Expert Systems Applications (DEXA '02)*, (Aix-en-Provence, France, 2002).

39. Wouters, C., Dillon, T., Rahayu, W., Chang, E. and Meersman, R., Ontologies on the MOVE. in *9th International Conference on Database Systems for Advanced Applications (DASFAA '04)*, (Jeju Island, Korea, 2004).

40. Wu, L., Faloutsos, C., Sycara, K. and Payne, T., Falcon: Feedback adaptive loop for content-based retrieval. in *Proceedings of VLDB Conference*, (2000).

Author Index

Lecture Notes in Computer Science

For information about Vols. 1–3990

please contact your bookseller or Springer